ST/ESA/362

Department of Economic and Social Affairs

I0110203

# Leaving no one behind: the imperative of inclusive development

Report on the World Social Situation 2016

United Nations

New York, 2016

# Department of Economic and Social Affairs

The Department of Economic and Social Affairs of the United Nations Secretariat is a vital interface between global policies in the economic, social and environmental spheres and national action. The Department works in three main interlinked areas: (i) it compiles, generates and analyses a wide range of economic, social and environmental data and information on which States Members of the United Nations draw to review common problems and to take stock of policy options; (ii) it facilitates the negotiations of Member States in many intergovernmental bodies on joint courses of action to address ongoing or emerging global challenges; and (iii) it advises interested Governments on the ways and means of translating policy frameworks developed in United Nations conferences and summits into programmes at the country level and, through technical assistance, helps build national capacities.

## Note

The designations employed and the presentation of the material in the present publication do not imply the expression of any opinion whatsoever on the part of the Secretariat of the United Nations concerning the legal status of any country or territory or of its authorities, or concerning the delimitations of its frontiers.

The term "country" as used in the text of this report also refers, as appropriate, to territories or areas.

The designations of country groups in the text and the tables are intended solely for statistical or analytical convenience and do not necessarily express a judgement about the stage reached by a particular country or area in the development process.

Mention of the names of firms and commercial products does not imply the endorsement of the United Nations.

Symbols of United Nations documents are composed of capital letters combined with figures.

ST/ESA/362

United Nations publication

Sales No. E.16.IV.1

ISBN 978-92-1-130336-0

eISBN 978-92-1-057710-6

# Preface

Agreed after an unprecedented global conversation, the new 2030 Agenda for Sustainable Development adopted by Member States in September 2015 has inclusion at its core.

With its central pledge to leave no one behind, the historic and ambitious new global development agenda recognizes that development will only be sustainable if it is inclusive. The emphasis on sustainability, equity and inclusion reminds us that pursuing development grounded in social justice will be fundamental to achieving a socially, economically and environmentally sustainable future. The Agenda therefore aims to put people at the heart of the development process, reaffirming the message of the World Summit for Social Development in Copenhagen just over twenty years ago.

Underpinning the renewed focus on inclusion and social justice is the realization that the benefits of social and economic progress have not been equitably shared. Inequalities pervade not only the economic, but also the social and environmental pillars of development. Differences in religion, ethnicity, age, gender, sexual orientation, disability and economic and migrant status are used to exclude and marginalize. Furthermore, climate change and recurring global economic, political, food and energy crises can quickly weaken or reverse achievements made in poverty reduction and human development.

Since 2000, the Millennium Development Goals (MDGs) have inspired Governments and other stakeholders to take concrete actions around a set of measurable goals. Building on lessons from the implementation of the MDGs, the 2030 Agenda for Sustainable Development emphasizes that global development requires a more integrated vision, grounded in sustainability, equity and inclusion. Sustainable development, therefore, is not only a matter of making progress towards narrow poverty, employment or health targets within a short time horizon or amid growing inequalities. It calls for securing social progress and resilience for all people and ensuring that it will be sustainable in the long run. It requires identifying who is being left behind by development processes and removing those underlying structural barriers that limit their inclusion.

The *Report on the World Social Situation 2016* brings social inclusion into focus. It illustrates who is being left behind and in what ways, identifying patterns of social exclusion and considering whether development processes have been inclusive. In particular, the *Report* examines the linkages between exclusion, poverty and employment trends. It looks at processes that threaten social inclusion and suggests policy imperatives to counteract them. It notes that promoting inclusion is not easy and requires concerted political effort over time. Nonetheless, the *Report* makes clear that change is possible and recommends actions that can promote social inclusion. Crucially, these actions are necessary both to meet the moral imperative to leave no one behind as well as to avoid the potential economic and social costs of exclusion.

WU Hongbo

*Under-Secretary-General for Economic and Social Affairs*

# Acknowledgements

The *Report on the World Social Situation*, prepared biennially, is the flagship publication on major social development issues of the Department of Economic and Social Affairs (DESA) of the United Nations Secretariat.

The present issue of the report was prepared by the team managed by Wenyan Yang in the Division for Social Policy and Development (DSPD). The report's core team, led by Marta Roig, also included Lisa Ainbinder, Maren Jiménez and Jonathan Perry. Valuable inputs were provided by other colleagues, including Maxwell Haywood, Frederick Heussner, Hantamalala Rafalimanana, Meron Sherif, Amson Sibanda and Makiko Tagashira. Joshua Del Duca, Bibi Sherifa Khan and Sylvie Pailler, also from DSPD, provided valuable assistance. The report was skillfully edited by John Loftus.

The report was prepared under the overall guidance of Mr. Lenni Montiel and Ms. Daniela Bas.

The analysis contained in the report was based in part on background papers prepared by independent experts Hilary Silver and Roberto Foa. The collection and analysis of population census and household survey data conducted by Rocío Canudas González was also extremely important. Özlem Eskiocak of the United Nations Relief and Works Agency for Palestine Refugees in the Near East (UNRWA) provided material for Box V.1.

The report benefitted from feedback by colleagues in other divisions of DESA, as well as the International Labour Organization (ILO), the United Nations Development Programme (UNDP), the United Nations Research Institute for Social Development (UNRISD), UN Women, the World Bank, United Nations Regional Commissions as well as other experts from outside of the United Nations System.

The team is particularly grateful to Diana Alarcón, Maitreyi Bordia Das, Arjan de Haan and Eva Jespersen for their guidance throughout the preparation of the report. Comments from Barry Herman at a later stage are also acknowledged.

# Contents

## Figures

## Tables

# Explanatory notes

The following symbols have been used in tables throughout the *Report*:

Two dots (..) indicate that data are not available or are not separately reported.

A dash (—) indicates that the item is nil or negligible.

A hyphen (-) indicates that the item is not applicable.

A hyphen (-) between years, for example, 1990-1991, signifies the full period involved, including the beginning and end years.

A minus sign (-) indicates a deficit or decrease, except as indicated.

A full stop (.) is used to indicate decimals.

A slash (/) between years indicates a statistical year, for example, 1990/91.

A dollars sign ($) indicates United States dollars, unless otherwise stated.

Annual rates of growth or change refer to annual compound rates, unless otherwise stated.

Details and percentages in tables do not necessarily add to totals, because of rounding.

When a print edition of a source exists, the print version is the authoritative one. United Nations documents reproduced online are deemed official only as they appear in the United Nations Official Document System. United Nations documentation obtained from other United Nations and non-United Nations sources are for informational purposes only. The Organization does not make any warranties or representations as to the accuracy or completeness of such materials.

The following abbreviations have been used:

| | |
|---|---|
| AIDS | Acquired Immune Deficiency Syndrome |
| DHS | Demographic and Health Survey |
| ECA | Economic Commission for Africa |
| ECE | Early childhood education |
| ECLAC | Economic Commission for Latin America and the Caribbean |
| EU | European Union |
| GDP | Gross domestic product |
| GIS | Geographic Information System |
| GNI | Gross national income |
| HALE | Health-adjusted life expectancy |
| HIV | Human immunodeficiency virus |
| ICT | Information and communication technology |

| | |
|---|---|
| ILO | International Labour Organization |
| IMF | International Monetary Fund |
| INSEE | Institut national de la statistique et des études économiques |
| IADB | Inter-American Development Bank |
| IOM | International Organization for Migration |
| LAC | Latin America and the Caribbean |
| MPI | Multidimensional poverty index |
| NEET | Neither in employment nor in education or training |
| ODA | Official development assistance |
| ODI | Overseas Development Institute |
| OECD | Organization for Economic Co-operation and Development |
| OPHI | Oxford Poverty and Human Development Initiative |
| PISA | Programme for International Student Assessment |
| PPP | Purchasing power parity |
| PROBE | Public Report on Basic Education |
| RIPESS | International Network for the Promotion of the Social Solidarity Economy |
| SSE | Social and Solidarity Economy |
| UN | United Nations |
| UNDP | United Nations Development Programme |
| UNESCO | United Nations Educational, Scientific and Cultural Organization |
| UN-HABITAT | United Nations Human Settlements Programme |
| UNICEF | United Nations Children's Fund |
| UNRISD | United Nations Research Institute for Social Development |
| UNRWA | United Nations Relief and Works Agency |
| UN Women | United Nations Entity for Gender Equality and the Empowerment of Women |
| US | United States |
| WHO | World Health Organization |
| WVS | World Values Surveys |

For analytical purposes, countries are classified as belonging to either of two categories: more developed or less developed. The *less developed regions (*also referred to as *developing countries* in the *Report)* include all countries in Africa, Asia (excluding Japan), and Latin America and the Caribbean, as well as Oceania, excluding Australia and New Zealand. The *more developed regions* (also referred to as *developed countries* in the *Report*) comprise Europe and Northern America, plus Australia, Japan and New Zealand.

The group of *least developed countries* comprises 49 countries: Afghanistan, Angola, Bangladesh, Benin, Bhutan, Burkina Faso, Burundi, Cambodia, Central African Republic, Chad, Comoros, Democratic Republic of the Congo, Djibouti, Equatorial Guinea, Eritrea, Ethiopia, Gambia, Guinea, Guinea-Bissau, Haiti, Kiribati, Lao People's Democratic Republic, Lesotho, Liberia, Madagascar, Malawi, Mali, Mauritania, Mozambique, Myanmar, Nepal, Niger, Rwanda, Sao Tome and Principe, Senegal, Sierra Leone, Solomon Islands, Somalia, South Sudan, Sudan, Timor-Leste, Togo, Tuvalu, Uganda, United Republic of Tanzania, Vanuatu, Yemen and Zambia. These countries are also included in the less developed regions.

*This report uses the following country groupings or sub groupings:*

*Sub-Saharan Africa,* which comprises the following countries: Angola, Benin, Botswana, Burkina Faso, Burundi, Cabo Verde, Cameroon, Central African Republic, Chad, Comoros, Congo, Côte d'Ivoire, Democratic Republic of the Congo, Djibouti, Equatorial Guinea, Eritrea, Ethiopia, Gabon, Gambia, Ghana, Guinea, Guinea-Bissau, Kenya, Lesotho, Liberia, Madagascar, Malawi, Mali, Mauritania, Mauritius, Comronian Island of Mayotte, Mozambique, Namibia, Niger, Nigeria, Réunion, Rwanda, Saint Helena, Sao Tome and Principe, Senegal, Seychelles, Sierra Leone, Somalia, South Africa, South Sudan, Sudan, Swaziland, Togo, Uganda, United Republic of Tanzania, Zambia and Zimbabwe.

*North Africa,* which comprises the following countries and areas: Algeria, Egypt, Libya, Morocco, Sudan, Tunisia, Western Sahara.

*Central Asia,* which comprises the following countries: Kazakhstan, Kyrgyzstan, Tajikistan, Turkmenistan, Uzbekistan.

*Eastern Asia,* which comprises the following countries and areas: China, Hong Kong Special Administrative Region, China, Macao Special Administrative Region, China, Democratic People's Republic of Korea, Japan, Mongolia, Republic of Korea.

*South-Eastern Asia,* which comprises the following countries: Brunei Darussalam, Cambodia, Indonesia, Lao People's Democratic Republic, Malaysia, Myanmar, Philippines, Singapore, Thailand, Timor-Leste, Viet Nam.

*Western Asia,* which comprises the following countries and areas: Armenia, Azerbaijan, Bahrain, Cyprus, Georgia, Iraq, Israel, Jordan, Kuwait, Lebanon, Oman, Qatar, Saudi Arabia, State of Palestine, Syrian Arab Republic, Turkey, United Arab Emirates, Yemen.

*Eastern Europe,* which comprises the following countries and areas: Belarus, Bulgaria, Czechia, Hungary, Poland, Republic of Moldova, Romania, Russian Federation, Slovakia, Ukraine.

*Northern Europe,* which comprises the following countries and areas: Åland Islands, Channel Islands, Denmark, Estonia, Faeroe Islands, Finland, Guernsey, Iceland, Ireland, Isle of Man, Jersey, Latvia, Lithuania, Norway, Sark, Svalbard and Jan Mayen Islands, Sweden, United Kingdom of Great Britain and Northern Ireland.

*Southern Europe,* which comprises the following countries and areas: Albania, Andorra, Bosnia and Herzegovina, Croatia, Gibraltar, Greece, Holy See, Italy, Malta, Montenegro, Portugal, San Marino, Serbia, Slovenia, Spain, The former Yugoslav Republic of Macedonia.

*North America,* which comprises the following countries and areas: Bermuda, Canada, Greenland, Saint Pierre and Miquelon, United States.

*In addition, the following World Bank regional groupings are also used:*

*East Asia and the Pacific,* which comprises the following countries and areas: American Samoa, Cambodia, China, Fiji, Indonesia, Kiribati, Democratic People's Republic of Korea, Lao People's Democratic Republic, Malaysia, Marshall Islands, Micronesia (Federated States of), Mongolia, Myanmar, Palau, Papua New Guinea, Philippines, Samoa, Solomon Islands, Thailand, Timor-Leste, Tonga, Vanuatu and Viet Nam.

*South Asia,* which comprises the following countries and areas: Afghanistan, Bangladesh, Bhutan, India, Maldives, Nepal, Pakistan and Sri Lanka.

*Middle East and Northern Africa,* which includes the following countries and areas: Algeria, Djibouti, Egypt, Iran (Islamic Republic of), Iraq, Jordan, Lebanon, Libya, Morocco, Syrian Arab Republic, Tunisia, Occupied Palestinian Territory and Yemen.

For the current 2017 fiscal year, low-income economies are defined as those with a GNI per capita, calculated using the World Bank Atlas method, of $1,025 or less in 2015; lower middle-income economies are those with a GNI per capita between $1,026 and $4,035; upper middle-income economies are those with a GNI per capita between $4,036 and $12,475; high-income economies are those with a GNI per capita of $12,476 or more:

*Low-income economies:* Afghanistan, Benin, Burkina Faso, Burundi, Central African Republic, Chad, Comoros, Democratic Republic of the Congo, Eritrea, Ethiopia, Gambia, Guinea, Guinea-Bissau, Haiti, Democratic People's Republic of Korea, Liberia, Madagascar, Malawi, Mali, Mozambique, Nepal, Niger, Rwanda Senegal, Sierra Leone, Somalia, South Sudan, Tanzania, Togo, Uganda, Zimbabwe.

*Lower-middle-income economies:* Armenia, Bangladesh, Bhutan, Bolivia (Plurinational State of), Cabo Verde, Cambodia, Cameroon, Congo, Côte d'Ivoire, Djibouti, Egypt, El Salvador, Ghana, Guatemala, Honduras, India, Indonesia, Kenya, Kiribati, Kosovo, Kyrgyzstan, Lao People's Democratic Republic, Lesotho, Mauritania, Micronesia (Federated States of), Moldova, Mongolia, Morocco, Myanmar, Nicaragua, Nigeria, Pakistan, Papua New Guinea, Philippines, Samoa, São Tomé and Principe, Solomon Islands, Sri Lanka, State of Palestine, Sudan, Swaziland, Syrian Arab Republic, Tajikistan, Timor-Leste, Tonga, Tunisia, Ukraine, Uzbekistan, Vanuatu, Viet Nam, Yemen, Zambia.

*Upper-middle-income economies:* Albania, Algeria, American Samoa, Angola, Argentina, Azerbaijan, Belarus, Belize, Bosnia and Herzegovina, Botswana, Brazil, Bulgaria, China, Colombia, Costa Rica, Cuba, Dominica, Dominican Republic, Equatorial Guinea, Ecuador, Fiji, Gabon, Georgia, Grenada, Guyana, Iran (Islamic Republic of), Iraq, Jamaica, Jordan, Kazakhstan, Lebanon, Libya, Malaysia, Maldives, Marshall Islands, Mauritius, Mexico, Montenegro, Namibia, Palau, Panama, Paraguay, Peru, Romania, Russian Federation, Serbia, South Africa, St. Lucia, St. Vincent and the Grenadines, Suriname, Thailand, The former Yugoslav Republic of Macedonia, Turkey, Turkmenistan, Tuvalu, Venezuela (Bolivarian Republic of).

*High-income economies:* Andorra, Antigua and Barbuda, Aruba, Australia, Austria, Bahamas, Bahrain, Barbados, Belgium, Bermuda, British Virgin Islands, Brunei Darussalam, Canada, Cayman Islands, Channel Islands, Chile, Croatia, Curaçao, Cyprus, Czech Republic, Denmark, Estonia, Faroe Islands, Finland, France, French Polynesia, Germany, Gibraltar, Greenland, Greece, Guam, Hong Kong, SAR of China, Hungary, Iceland, Ireland, Isle of Man, Israel, Italy, Japan, Kuwait, Latvia, Liechtenstein, Lithuania, Luxembourg, Macao, SAR of China, Malta, Monaco, Nauru, Netherlands, New Caledonia, New Zealand, Northern Mariana Islands, Norway, Oman, Poland, Portugal, Puerto Rico, Qatar, Republic of Korea, San Marino, Saudi Arabia, Seychelles, Singapore, Sint Maarten (Dutch part), Slovak Republic, Slovenia, Spain, St. Kitts and Nevis, St. Martin (French part), Sweden, Switzerland, Taiwan, Province of China, Trinidad and Tobago, Turks and Caicos Islands, United Arab Emirates, United Kingdom, United States, Uruguay, Virgin Islands (U.S.).

# Executive summary

Humankind has achieved unprecedented social progress over the past several decades. Poverty has declined dramatically around the world and people are healthier, more educated and better connected than ever before. However, this progress has been uneven. Social and economic inequalities persist and, in many cases, have worsened. Virtually everywhere, some individuals and groups confront barriers that prevent them from fully participating in economic, social and political life.

Against this backdrop, inclusiveness and shared prosperity have emerged as core aspirations of the 2030 Agenda for Sustainable Development. A central pledge contained in the 2030 Agenda is to ensure that no one will be left behind and to see all goals and targets met for all nations, peoples and for all parts of society, endeavouring to reach the furthest behind first.[1]

The focus of the 2030 Agenda on inclusiveness underscores the need to identify who is being left behind and in what ways. This is what the *Report on the World Social Situation 2016* sets out to do. Specifically, the report contains an examination of the patterns of social exclusion and consideration of whether development processes have been inclusive, with particular attention paid to the links between exclusion, poverty and employment trends. Key challenges to social inclusion are highlighted along with policy imperatives to promote it. It is recognized in the report that promoting inclusion will take time and political determination. Raising awareness about the consequences of leaving some people behind and recommending actions that Governments can take to avoid doing so can help generate political will.

## Identifying social inclusion and exclusion

In aspiring to empower and promote the social, economic and political inclusion of all members of society, target 10.2 of the 2030 Agenda highlights attributes that have considerable influence on the risk of exclusion when it emphasizes that all should be included "irrespective of age, sex, disability, race, ethnicity, origin, religion or economic or other status".[2] As such, social inclusion is presented as the process of improving the terms of participation in society for people who are disadvantaged on the basis of age, sex, disability, race, ethnicity, and economic and migration status. It is contended in the report that promoting social inclusion requires both removing barriers to people's participation, including certain laws, policies and institutions as well

---

[1]    General Assembly resolution 70/1, para. 4.

[2]    Ibid., target 10.2.

as discriminatory attitudes and behaviours, and taking active steps to make such participation easier.

Identifying a set of criteria to determine who is excluded and how is key to tracking progress and assessing the impact of measures undertaken to promote inclusion. However, measuring social exclusion is not easy for several reasons. First and foremost, people can be excluded from many domains of life, be they social, economic, political, civic or spatial spheres. The relative importance of each domain depends on where people live and on their age. That is to say, the concepts of social inclusion and exclusion are multidimensional and context-dependent. Translating them into a limited set of measurable indicators applicable across countries constitutes an imposing challenge. Furthermore, a proper assessment of exclusion requires indicators of people's socioeconomic status – including their income, their employment situation and whether they have access to land, housing or education and health care – but it must also take into account their subjective judgements and perceptions.

In taking into account these challenges, the report contains an analysis of three sets of indicators: those that measure access to opportunities, namely education, health and other basic services; those that measure access to employment and income; and those that measure participation in political, civic and cultural life. A relative approach is taken to exclusion: instead of defining a threshold under which individuals or groups would be considered excluded, disparities in these indicators across selected social groups are construed as symptoms or outcomes of the exclusion of those who are being left behind.

It is clear that the extent of social exclusion, the groups affected by it and the social problems it encompasses vary by context and also over time. In many ways, the world has become less tolerant of exclusion. The spread of democratic ideals and the demand for equal rights have led some Governments to loosen policies that sustain unfair treatment and have created opportunities for political participation. Meanwhile, the expansion of education and improvements in information and communications technologies (ICTs) are enabling more people to make more informed choices and exercise voice. However, these advances have not been enough to eliminate disadvantage and promote inclusive societies. Recent political events, including responses to the large movements of people seeking to escape war and destitution in their own countries, as well as the effects of climate change, pose major challenges to the continued promotion of inclusive development.

## Key dimensions of exclusion

### *Poverty, income inequality and exclusion: a vicious cycle*

To the extent that poverty is a major hindrance to social inclusion, the global progress made in reducing extreme income poverty bodes well for inclusive development. While 37 per cent of the world's population lived under the international poverty line of $1.90 a day in 1990, the proportion had declined to 10.7 per cent by 2013.[3] However, the situation of those living in deep poverty has not improved significantly and many people who have escaped poverty remain vulnerable to it.

Trends in inequality also suggest that prosperity has not been equitably shared, with income inequality having risen within many countries in the last 20 years. In general, income inequality across social groups constitutes a significant share of total income inequality, although its weight varies strongly by country.

### *Decent work deficits and exclusion*

Over the last two decades, employment has helped millions of people to escape poverty and has economically empowered women and other disadvantaged groups. In some cases, it has promoted the social inclusion of these groups, while in others it has reinforced existing divides. However, economic growth and, more broadly, development have not been sufficiently inclusive, as they have failed to reduce deficits in decent work. Many people cannot rely on stable decent jobs as means to cope with risks or secure livelihoods. The risk of holding a poorly paid, precarious or insecure job is higher today than it was in 1995. Despite rapid progress made in reducing poverty, 13.5 per cent of workers in developing countries are living in extreme poverty (on less than $1.90 a day) and 34.3 per cent are living on less than $3.10 a day (ILO, 2016a). These figures call into question the notion that jobs – any jobs – are the main solution to poverty. A large share of workers are outside the realm of regulation and are not properly represented in social dialogue and consensus-building processes in the workplace. While some informal jobs become stepping stones into formal work and empower those who hold them, particularly women, most trap individuals and groups into a spiral of low productivity and exclusion. Deficits in decent work, in particular among young people, raise fears of social instability and put the social contract under threat.

---

[3]     In October 2015, the World Bank released revised income poverty estimates based on a new set of purchasing power parity (PPPs) conversion factors and an ensuing new income poverty line of $1.90 per day. In 1990, the poverty line had been $1.00 per day and in 2008 $1.25 per day.

## Who is being left behind?

While lagging behind in education or in access to health services, or facing barriers to political participation, alone, cannot be equated with social exclusion, the report shows that disadvantages in all of these domains generally reinforce one another. Lower levels of health and education go hand in hand with higher levels of poverty and unemployment, as well as less voice in political and civic life. In the report, it is the accumulation of disadvantage among certain social groups that is taken as a symptom of their exclusion.

The inequalities observed have historical roots but tend to persist even after the structural conditions that created them change. Some ethnic groups, for instance, continue to experience significant disadvantages in countries which no longer impose formal barriers to their participation. However, discrimination continues to play a key role in holding back some groups.

It is also important to note that, while the report's analysis is based on statistically visible groups, those groups that are omitted from household surveys and censuses are frequently at the highest risk of being left behind. It is often when groups gain political recognition and social movements promote the enforcement of their rights that countries begin to identify them in censuses and surveys.

### *Denial of opportunities*

There is clear consensus across countries on the need for education and health care to benefit all people – that is, for these services to be universally accessible. Yet in both developed and developing countries, there are enduring disparities in school enrolment, educational attainment and learning outcomes based on factors beyond a student's inherent capacity to learn. For example, in 19 countries with data, the percentage of youth (aged 15-24 years) who have completed lower secondary education is on average twice as high among youth in the main ethnic group as among youth in the most disadvantaged ethnic minority.[4] Similarly, not all individuals and groups have benefited equally from improvements in health. There are wide gaps in child health and life expectancy at birth based on ethnicity, socioeconomic status and place of birth. Moreover, measures that take into account illness and functioning, such as health-adjusted life expectancy (HALE), tend to show wider gaps than life expectancy at birth.

The report's analysis suggests that progress in different dimensions of social inclusion should be monitored separately. Progress in closing gaps in child health among ethnic groups, for example, has not necessarily been

---

[4]    For details, see United Nations Educational, Scientific and Cultural Organization, World Inequality Database on Education. Available from www.education-inequalities.org. Accessed on 22 July 2016.

matched by equitable improvements in access to infrastructure and vice versa. Child mortality has generally declined faster in rural than in urban households in recent years while stronger reductions in malnutrition have been experienced in urban areas.

## Unequal income-generating prospects

There are also significant disparities in access to the labour market, employment opportunities, wages and overall income across social groups. Disadvantaged groups are not only more likely to live in poverty, but they also experience deeper poverty and are more likely to remain in poverty over the long term than the rest of the population. In the labour market, indigenous peoples, members of other ethnic minorities and international migrants receive lower wages than the rest of the population, as do women, who on average earn between 10 and 30 per cent less than men when working full time (Hall and Patrinos, 2012; OECD, 2015a; United Nations, 2015a). The exclusion of youth from the labour market is of particular concern because of its long-term effect on their well-being as well as its impact on social cohesion and stability. More than 40 per cent of the world's active youth are either unemployed or working but still living in poverty (ILO, 2015a). In countries of the Organisation for Economic Co-operation and Development (OECD), almost 39 million young people (15.5 per cent of all youth) were not working or in education or training (NEET) in 2014. [5]

Labour market disadvantages, however, are not just due to differences among workers in education, skills or place of residence. The analysis contained in the report shows that most of the occupational differences observed among ethnic groups persist, for instance, once the effects of educational attainment and other sociodemographic characteristics are accounted for. The labour market continues to reflect socially-driven distinctions based on ethnicity, race, age, gender and other personal attributes that should have no bearing on job opportunities or workers' competencies.

## Unequal participation in political, civic and cultural life

Participation in political, civic and cultural activities is a major part of social life and crucial to promoting inclusion. Individuals and groups who are excluded from these processes have limited voice or power to affect the attitudes, norms, institutions and policies that drive social exclusion in the first place. Some forms of political and civic participation also reveal subjective aspects of social inclusion that are not captured by looking at the socioeconomic status of individuals and groups.

---

[5]   See OECD Data. Available from https://data.oecd.org/youthinac/youth-not-in-education-or-employment-neet.htm. Accessed on 22 July 2016.

In many countries, racial and ethnic minorities, migrants, women and young people vote less frequently and are less likely to be represented in Government by individuals of the same social group than are other people. Here, too, education and income lead to higher political engagement as measured by voting behaviour. Lower voter turnout is, in some cases, the result of institutional barriers to registering and voting. One reason for this situation is that the right to vote in a country is generally granted to citizens only. However, differences in voting patterns often remain even when formal restrictions to voting are not present, suggesting that there are other barriers at play as well.

Lack of engagement in political activities among some individuals and groups is concerning and undermines democratic foundations – representation, rule of law and protection of freedom and rights. Data show, for instance, that levels of trust and confidence in the police and the courts in some countries are lower among racial and ethnic minorities than among other groups, thus challenging the legitimacy of these institutions in protecting the rule of law for all and promoting good and democratic governance.

Regarding participation in social life, social networks are an important source of support, power and agency for individuals, groups and communities that face multiple forms of social exclusion. Frequent contact with family, friends and neighbours provides social support that positively affects health and well-being. In many cases, members of vulnerable and marginalized groups enjoy dense networks of community group relations; what they lack is power and capital to achieve their ends.

## Prejudice and discrimination: barriers to social inclusion

The prejudicial treatment of people on the basis of their identity or their characteristics is a common cause of exclusion. Across countries, there are still laws and policies that discriminate against individuals and groups in all spheres of life, despite the considerable progress that has been achieved in recent decades to end such practices. Even where discriminatory laws have been eliminated, discriminatory practices continue to underpin group-based differences.

Publicly registered incidents of discrimination, such as legal cases brought against employers or public authorities or reported incidents of hate crimes, have limited value for cross-country comparisons or even to assess trends over time. The willingness and opportunities to report discrimination depend on efficacy, real or perceived, of the police and the justice system in addressing this ill. Instead, some surveys have gathered information on perceived instances of discrimination. Results of the European Union Minorities and Discrimination Survey in 2008 showed, for instance, that one in four respondents felt discriminated against due to ethnic or immigrant origin, sex, age, disability, sexual orientation, religion or beliefs (European Union Agency for Fundamental Rights, 2009). Perceived discrimination on the basis of ethnicity or immigrant origin was the most significant of these areas. Experimental research also shows large differential treatment based on race, ethnicity and migrant status in various domains, including job interview call-backs, apartment rentals and examination results.

Constant exposure to discrimination can lead individuals to internalize prejudice or stigma in the form of shame, low self-esteem, fear, stress and poor mental and physical health. It may further affect achievement and diminish a person's sense of agency – that is, the capacity to make decisions and act on them – leading individuals to behave in ways that conform to how others perceive them.

While discrimination is decried around the globe and there are legal obligations and guidelines to fight it, much work remains to be done to achieve a world free of discrimination and prejudice. Continued efforts to capture the extent, manifestations and effects of discrimination are a necessary step towards realizing this goal.

## Policy imperatives for leaving no one behind

No single set of policies or strategies is applicable across all countries and in all contexts to tackle exclusion and promote inclusion. Instead, successful examples point to several imperatives to address the structural causes of exclusion and social injustice.

The first imperative is to establish a universal approach to social policy, complemented by special or targeted measures to address the distinct obstacles faced by disadvantaged, marginalized or otherwise excluded social groups. Special efforts are needed, even if temporarily, to overcome the barriers which some groups face and make the universal provision of goods and services more effective in promoting social inclusion. Governments should design these measures in ways that minimize stigma and capture by local elites; they must integrate them fully into broader social protection systems. Policies aimed at tackling discrimination, as well as those that provide preferential access to some services, enable the participation of excluded persons and communities in decision-making processes.

Identifying groups that are left behind and in need of special measures may require better household and individual-level data and increased data disaggregation. Strengthened statistical offices as well as more openness to innovative social research directions could help improve the ability to meet data needs. However, improved data are not sufficient on their own. Ultimately, ensuring that all individuals are afforded the same rights and opportunities requires political will and commitment.

The second imperative is to promote inclusive institutions. The report highlights the role that institutions play in either perpetuating exclusion or promoting inclusion. Empowering workers, entrepreneurs and small producers, for instance, or pursuing inclusive land ownership schemes, new forms of collective action, or greater State capacity to engage in participatory budgeting could make economic institutions more inclusive and equitable. Similarly, promoting civil registration and legal identity, engaging more with civil society, supporting local associations and enabling the creation of social movements could help political institutions become more transparent and inclusive. Finally, promoting equal recognition through anti-discrimination laws and their effective enforcement, encouraging tolerance and challenging exclusionary attitudes and behaviours are all avenues for creating more inclusive cultural and social institutions.

Reversing entrenched prejudice and reforming institutions that perpetuate exclusion are often slow processes. Institutions are shaped by national and local circumstances, norms and behaviours that have deep historical and cultural roots. They therefore require considerable shifts in how people relate to each other and what is considered acceptable. However, concerted effort and long-term political commitment at the highest level would make such change possible.

## Conclusions

The report describes many positive trends, ranging from more representation of disadvantaged groups in political processes to a reduction of inequality in access to education. However, group-based disparities vary significantly across countries. Whether development is leaving some people behind – and, consequently, whether or not it is promoting social inclusion – depends on context as well as on the indicators used to measure progress.

Beyond the foundational role of inclusion and the moral imperative to correct imbalances in power, voice and influence, there are also practical reasons to ensure that no one is left behind. Inclusion strengthens not only the social, but also the economic and environmental dimensions of sustainable development. Awareness of the importance of inclusion, however, has not yet been translated into political commitment or the necessary normative shifts that are imperative for inclusive development, as argued in the report. Instead, over-reliance on market mechanisms, a retrenchment of the redistributive role of the State and growing economic inequalities have contributed to social exclusion and have even put the social contract under threat in many countries in the last few decades.

The commitment to leave no one behind and thus ensure that every individual can participate in social, economic, political and cultural life with equal rights and enjoy the full range of opportunities expressed in the 2030

Agenda is an important step in the right direction. Framing goals in universal terms alone, however, does not ensure universality. For example, despite aiming for universal primary education, the Millennium Development Goals left some children behind, as this report shows. The extent to which the 2030 Agenda will help to promote inclusion will depend on the strength and form of its implementation.

# Introduction

## Why social inclusion?

In September 2015, world leaders adopted an ambitious global development agenda, envisioning a just, equitable, tolerant, open and socially inclusive world in which the needs of the most vulnerable would be met.[1] The central pledge of the 2030 Agenda for Sustainable Development is to ensure "that no one will be left behind". That means, in particular, that all Sustainable Development "Goals and targets [should be] met for all nations and peoples and for all segments of society".[2] Implicit in these commitments is a broad recognition that the extraordinary economic growth observed in some parts of the world and the widespread improvement in social indicators in the last few decades have failed to reach many people and to close the deep divides within and across countries.

Humankind has indeed achieved unprecedented social progress over the past several decades. Poverty has declined dramatically around the world, and people are healthier, more educated and better connected than ever before. Important political changes, most notably the end of the cold war and the spread of democratic ideals, have created opportunities for political participation and, with improvements in information and communications technologies (ICTs) and the expansion of education, for enabling more people to make more informed choices and exercise voice.

Yet progress has been uneven. Oftentimes, rising income levels have gone hand in hand with growing inequality. In the majority of countries, the wealthy have grown wealthier while the relative situation of those who are living in poverty has improved only little. Unemployment is widespread and many workers struggle to earn sufficient income in vulnerable jobs amid inadequate opportunities for decent work. Having just emerged from the latest financial and economic crisis, many countries are faced with persistent economic uncertainty and volatility in the real economy and in the labour market. Inequalities pervade not only the economic, but also the social, political, cultural and environmental spheres, thus constituting systematic disadvantage for some social groups, that is to say, their social exclusion.

Virtually everywhere, some individuals and groups confront barriers that prevent them from fully participating in economic, social and political life. Democratization and the demand for equal rights have led some Governments to loosen legally imposed discriminatory measures as well as policies that

---

[1] General Assembly resolution 70/1, para. 8.

[2] Ibid., para. 4.

sustain unfair treatment, but these formal measures have not been sufficient to eliminate disadvantage or achieve inclusive societies. Overall, there is a growing realization that development and growth have done little to promote equality and inclusion.

In the process leading up to the new 2030 Agenda, civil society networks and organizations joined forces with the United Nations to have a voice in shaping "the world we want".[3] Unfortunately, mankind is very far from realizing the vision that emerged from those global conversations and, ultimately, from the 2030 Agenda. Moreover, there are worrying signals of more difficulties in the future. Growing nativist political movements have emerged in some countries, partly in reaction to large movements of people seeking to escape unceasing war and destitution in their own countries. Distrust is evolving into anger among neighbours, based on differences in religion, ethnicity, gender and sexual orientation, and disability.

It is against this backdrop of sharp inequalities that the commitment of the 2030 Agenda to leave no one behind must be understood. The Agenda's core message of inclusion echoes the commitment made by representatives of Governments participating in the World Summit for Social Development, held in Copenhagen 20 years earlier, to foster social justice, equality and inclusion, and is founded on the recognition that, unless development is inclusive, it will not be sustainable.

Indeed, leaving no one behind is not just a fundamental moral imperative; social exclusion also has significant economic and social costs associated with foregoing the contribution of individuals and groups that cannot access educational systems, land or the labour market. Exclusion has political costs as well, as it reflects and feeds social tensions and is at the root of many violent conflicts. Exclusion further interacts with environmental risks: excluded individuals and groups, especially those living in poverty, frequently inhabit areas that are more vulnerable to natural hazards and disasters and are disproportionately harmed by such disasters as a result. Exclusion makes societies not only less cohesive, but also less safe and productive.

The United Nations Secretariat cannot by itself change these political and social realities. What it can do, however, is describe the situation, try to raise the world's consciousness about worrying failings and recommend concerted actions that Governments might wish to take to overcome them. That is precisely what the present issue of the *Report on the World Social Situation* is designed to do.

---

[3]   General Assembly resolution 66/288, annex. The global conversations referred to and the web platform supporting them were named "The World We Want 2015". For more information about these, see www.beyond2015.org/world-we-want-2015-web-platform.

## Social inclusion in the international development agenda

The Sustainable Development Goals contained within the 2030 Agenda carry forward commitments agreed at several United Nations summits, including the World Summit for Social Development, held in Copenhagen in 1995. At a time of significant political change, including the end of the cold war, and renewed hope in the potential offered by international cooperation, that Summit gave rise to a far-reaching people-centred agenda aimed at promoting inclusive societies, social progress, justice and a higher quality of life for all. While advocating a broad vision of social development, Governments called for particular attention to be paid to eradicating poverty, promoting full and productive employment and fostering social integration – a concept that is closely linked to social inclusion.

Agreement on the need to pursue social integration as one of the goals of social development arose from the dramatic events that took place during the preparations for the Summit. The so-called ethnic cleansing and war in Bosnia and Herzegovina (1992-1995), the war in Croatia (1991-1995) and the genocide in Rwanda (1994) loomed large in the Summit's outcome. These horrors of conflict and genocide added to the rising concerns about the social polarization and fragmentation that existed in some of the newly independent countries of the former Union of Soviet Socialist Republics as well as in post-apartheid South Africa. The Summit thus posited social integration as a goal, namely that the world should endeavour to create a "society for all" based on respect for all human rights and fundamental freedoms, cultural and religious diversity, social justice and the special needs of vulnerable and disadvantaged groups.[4] Fostering social integration thus called for the active pursuit of social inclusion of the most disadvantaged groups.[5]

International efforts to advance social integration since the Copenhagen Summit led to the subsequent adoption of new international instruments aimed at realizing the rights of particular social groups. Some of the major instruments are the Beijing Declaration and Platform for Action for women in 1995,[6] the World Programme of Action for Youth and the Supplement to the World Programme of Action for Youth to the Year 2000 and Beyond,[7] the Political Declaration and Madrid International Plan of Action on Ageing,[8] the

---

[4]    Report of the World Summit for Social Development, Copenhagen, 6-12 March 1995 (United Nations publication, Sales No. E.96.IV.8), chap. I, resolution I, annex I, para. 66.

[5]    The concepts of social inclusion and social integration are nonetheless distinct; see chap.1 and box I.1 of the present publication.

[6]    Report of the Fourth World Conference on Women, Beijing, 4-15 September 1995 (United Nations publication, Sales No. E.96.IV.13), chap. I, resolution 1, annexes I and II.

[7]    General Assembly resolution 50/81, annex, and resolution 62/126, annex.

[8]    Report of the Second World Assembly on Ageing, Madrid, 8–12 April 2002 (United Nations publication, Sales No. E.02.IV.4), chap. I, resolution 1, annexes I and II.

Convention on the Rights of Persons with Disabilities[9] and the United Nations Declaration on the Rights of Indigenous Peoples.[10]

The Copenhagen Summit also influenced the outcomes of several subsequent global intergovernmental conferences. Notably, in September 2000, the Millennium Declaration[11] reaffirmed the centrality of many of the values and principles that had been advocated at the Summit, including equality, solidarity and tolerance. Concerns related to the challenge of exclusion, however, were not absorbed into the Millennium Development Goals. Despite a prominent commitment to gender equality and women's empowerment, the Goals have been criticized for insufficiently integrating the principles of social justice and equality. That is, since the Goals were largely monitored by measures of average progress towards each indicator, they could be reached – and in some cases were reached – amid large and even growing inequalities in human development, entirely bypassing some vulnerable and disadvantaged social groups.

Thus, renewed determination to promote inclusion has become visible in the 2030 Agenda. In order to hold Governments accountable for their pledge to leave no one behind, several targets of the Sustainable Development Goals include specific reference to vulnerable and disadvantaged groups, and indicators have been proposed to measure progress achieved by these groups, including through data disaggregated by age, sex and other criteria. In particular, one target under Sustainable Development Goal 10 on reducing inequality within and among countries is specifically aimed at empowering and promoting by 2030 "the social, economic and political inclusion of all, irrespective of age, sex, disability, race, ethnicity, origin, religion or economic or other status" (target 10.2). Moreover, the term "inclusive" is used repeatedly, as in relation to education (Goal 4), economic growth (Goal 8), industrialization (Goal 9), cities and human settlements (Goal 11) and, more broadly, societies and institutions (Goal 16).

## Aim of the report

The focus of the 2030 Agenda on inclusion underscores the need to clarify what constitutes social inclusion and to identify who is being left behind and in what ways so as to inform policy action. In the present issue of the report, patterns of social exclusion are examined, and the question of whether or when development processes are inclusive is considered, with particular attention being paid to the links among exclusion, poverty and employment trends. It is recognized that the promotion of inclusive societies and inclusive

---

[9]    United Nations, Treaty Series, vol. 2515, No. 44910.

[10]    General Assembly resolution 61/295, annex.

[11]    General Assembly resolution 55/2.

development processes requires the eradication of poverty, the reduction of inequalities and the creation of decent jobs for all workers. The importance of promoting economic and social policies and public institutions that are inclusive is underscored in the report.

The report comprises five chapters. Chapter I contains a conceptual overview of social inclusion and exclusion and illustrates the challenges of identifying indicators to measure these broad concepts across countries. The chapter's discussion underscores the need to maintain close links between indicators of exclusion and the problems that they are intended to address, as few measures serve as all-purpose indicators or are applicable in all contexts (United Nations, 2010). In chapter II, there is an assessment of the progress being made towards the eradication of poverty, the reduction of income inequality and the attainment of full employment and decent work as essential elements of inclusive development processes. In doing so, findings from previous editions of the *Report on the World Social Situation* are consolidated in this chapter and complemented with new analysis as well as a discussion on the links between these key social indicators and social inclusion.[12] Chapter III illustrates patterns of social exclusion across several dimensions, with the focus being primarily on an assessment of the disadvantages faced by particular social groups in gaining access to opportunities, resources and participation in political and cultural life. The chapter brings out the diversity of trends and patterns of exclusion around the world. Chapter IV explores the role of discrimination as a key driver of exclusion. In reviewing the empirical literature on discrimination, the challenges involved in capturing its presence and measuring its impact are highlighted. In chapter V, consideration is given to policy implications of the analysis, including for implementation of the 2030 Agenda. Attention is drawn to the need for addressing the structural causes of exclusion, including exclusionary institutions, policies and norms, and ways are proposed for promoting inclusion through the empowerment and active participation of vulnerable and disadvantaged groups in social, economic and political life. More and improved methods for monitoring and analysing social inclusion are called for, as well as additional research and an exploration of practical strategies to advance social inclusion.

---

[12]    The *Report on the World Social Situation 2010* sought to rethink poverty and ways to eradicate it (United Nations, 2009). The *Report on the World Social Situation 2007* addressed the employment imperative (United Nations, 2007), while the reports published in 2005 and 2013 assessed the inequality predicament and reasons why inequality matters, respectively (United Nations, 2005 and 2013a).

Chapter I

# Identifying social inclusion and exclusion

## Key messages

- *Social exclusion is a multidimensional phenomenon not limited to material deprivation; poverty is an important dimension of exclusion, albeit only one dimension. Accordingly, social inclusion processes involve more than improving access to economic resources.*

- *Social inclusion is defined as the process of improving the terms of participation in society, particularly for people who are disadvantaged, through enhancing opportunities, access to resources, voice and respect for rights.*

- *Measuring social exclusion is challenging due to its multidimensional nature and the lack of standard data sources across countries and for all social groups at highest risk of being left behind. Despite limitations, the existing data allow for a meaningful analysis of key aspects of exclusion. The report presents these data while illustrating data gaps.*

- *While inclusion is a core aspiration of the 2030 Agenda, conceptual and analytical work on what constitutes inclusion, as well as efforts to improve data availability, are needed.*

## A. The concept of social inclusion

Enshrined in the 2030 Agenda is the principle that every person should reap the benefits of prosperity and enjoy minimum standards of well-being. This is captured in the 17 Sustainable Development Goals that are aimed at freeing all nations and people and all segments of society from poverty and hunger and to ensure, among other things, healthy lives and access to education, modern energy and information. Recognizing that these goals are difficult to achieve without making institutions work for those who are deepest in poverty and most vulnerable, the Agenda embraces broad targets aimed at promoting the rule of law, ensuring equal access to justice and broadly fostering inclusive and participatory decision-making.

These goals and targets, when effectively translated into action and properly benchmarked, represent essential elements of social inclusion processes. However, social inclusion encompasses a broader set of concerns than those reflected in the Sustainable Development Goals. No single global, goal-setting agenda can adequately address the multiple dimensions of exclusion or comprehensively promote inclusion, particularly given the diversity of circumstances around the globe.

This chapter presents working definitions of social exclusion and social inclusion and discusses concepts as well as measurement issues. Different places have different histories, cultures and institutions, which shape norms, values and therefore different approaches to social inclusion. It is contended, however, that the goal of achieving a society for all must conform to some general principles, even if the country-specific and evolving nature of social exclusion concerns and approaches to inclusion is recognized.[13]

## 1. Social exclusion

Although there is no universally agreed definition or benchmark for social exclusion, lack of participation in society is at the heart of nearly all definitions put forth by scholars, government bodies, non-governmental organizations and others (see box I.1). Overall, **social exclusion describes a state in which individuals are unable to participate fully in economic, social, political and cultural life, as well as the process leading to and sustaining such a state**. [14]

Participation may be hindered when people lack access to material resources, including income, employment, land and housing, or to such services as education and health care — essential foundations of well-being that are captured in Agenda 2030. Yet participation is also limited when people cannot exercise their voice or interact with each other, and when their rights and dignity are not accorded equal respect and protection. Thus social exclusion entails not only material deprivation but also lack of agency or control over important decisions as well as feelings of alienation and inferiority. In nearly all countries, to varying degrees, age, sex, disability, race, ethnicity, religion, migration status, socioeconomic status, place of residence, and sexual orientation and gender identity have been grounds for social exclusion over time.

The term social exclusion was used for the first time by former French Secretary of State for Social Action, René Lenoir (1974), to refer to the situation of certain groups of people – "the mentally and the physically handicapped, suicidal people, aged invalids, abused children, drug addicts, delinquents, single parents, multi-problem households, marginal, asocial persons, and other 'social misfits'" – whom he estimated to comprise one tenth of the population

---

[13]   The Programme of Action of the World Summit for Social Development noted that the aim of social integration was to create a "society for all" in which every individual, each with rights and responsibilities, has an active role to play. See footnote 2.

[14]   Accordingly, the concept of social exclusion is used throughout the report as a general term to describe lack of participation in or exclusion from economic, political, cultural, civic and/or social life. Lack of participation in political processes, in civic life or in the labour market are construed as aspects of overall social exclusion.

---

## Box I.1

### Illustrative definitions

#### Social exclusion

"**Exclusion** consists of dynamic, multi-dimensional processes driven by unequal power relationships interacting across four main dimensions—economic, political, social and cultural—and at different levels including individual, household, group, community, country and global levels. It results in a continuum of inclusion/exclusion characterized by unequal access to resources, capabilities and rights which leads to health inequalities", (Popay and others, 2008, p. 2).

"**Social exclusion** is a complex and multi-dimensional process. It involves the lack or denial of resources, rights, goods and services, and the inability to participate in the normal relationships and activities, available to the majority of people in a society, whether in economic, social, cultural or political arenas. It affects both the quality of life of individuals and the equity and cohesion of society as a whole" (Levitas and others, 2007, p. 9).

"**Social exclusion** is what can happen when people or areas suffer from a combination of linked problems such as unemployment, poor skills, low incomes, poor housing, high crime, poor health and family breakdown"(United Kingdom Office of the Deputy Prime Minister, 2004, p. 2).

#### Social inclusion

" The process of improving the terms for individuals and groups to take part in society" and "The process of improving the ability, opportunity, and dignity of people, disadvantaged on the basis of their identity, to take part in society" (World Bank, 2013, pp. 3-4).

"**Social inclusion** is a process which ensures that those at risk of poverty and social exclusion gain the opportunities and resources necessary to participate fully in economic, social, political and cultural life and to enjoy a standard of living that is considered normal in the society in which they live. It ensures that they have greater participation in decision making which affects their lives and access to their fundamental rights"(Commission of the European Communities, 2003, p. 9).

---

of France and who were considered vulnerable yet outside the realm of social insurance systems of the welfare state. The concept soon took hold in other developed countries; more recently, the European Union dedicated 2010 as the European Year for Combating Poverty and Social Exclusion.

Experts have questioned the utility of the social exclusion framework to lower-income, developing countries (Saith, 2001). Where the majority of a population work in informal and insecure employment, lack social protection coverage or do not complete secondary education, standards of normality as benchmarks of inclusion or exclusion are not what are aspired to. Yet, in Sen's (2000) view, the concept and its focus on relational features has led to richer analysis of processes that result in poverty and capability deprivation, many aspects of which are common across regions even at different levels of development. Issues related to the status, segregation and disempowerment of migrants, for instance, affect a growing number of countries − developed and developing.

While intertwined, the concepts of poverty and social exclusion are nonetheless distinct. Poverty is an outcome, while social exclusion is both an outcome and a process. Poverty and exclusion need not go hand in hand; not all socially excluded groups are economically disadvantaged. People are often excluded due to a disability or because of their sexual orientation, for instance, without necessarily living in poverty. Levitas and others (2007) observed: "Many of the attempts to define social exclusion distinguish it from poverty... on the basis of its multi-dimensional, relational and dynamic character". Indeed, whereas poverty is most commonly defined in monetary terms, social exclusion takes a more holistic view of human development.

## 2. Social inclusion

In the policy discourse, efforts to promote social inclusion have arisen from concerns over social exclusion. For the purpose of the present report, social inclusion is defined as **the process of improving the terms of participation in society for people who are disadvantaged on the basis of age, sex, disability, race, ethnicity, origin, religion, or economic or other status, through enhanced opportunities, access to resources, voice and respect for rights**. Thus, social inclusion is both a process and a goal. In the present report, it is contended that promoting social inclusion requires tackling social exclusion by removing barriers to people's participation in society, as well as by taking active inclusionary steps to facilitate such participation. As a political response to the exclusion challenge, social inclusion is thus a more deliberate process of encompassing and welcoming all persons and embracing greater equality and tolerance.

It should be noted that fostering social inclusion may or may not increase the capacity of people to live together in harmony. Societies that are otherwise cohesive may exclude some sectors of the population (United Nations, 2010). Similarly, social inclusion is not the same as social integration, even though the two terms are at times used interchangeably. Social integration and social inclusion should, however, contribute to making societies more cohesive (see figure I.1). Although the present report touches on some aspects of social cohesion and social integration and examines indicators that are relevant to both concepts, its focus is on the elimination of social exclusion and the promotion of social inclusion.

## 3. Elements of exclusion and inclusion

The report's definition of social inclusion explicitly refers to *people who are disadvantaged on the basis of age, sex, disability, race, ethnicity, origin, or economic or other status* for two reasons. First, although anyone may be potentially at risk of social exclusion, certain attributes or characteristics increase such risk. These are often linked to identity or group ascription. Kabeer (2006) described

Figure I.1

## Social inclusion, integration and cohesion

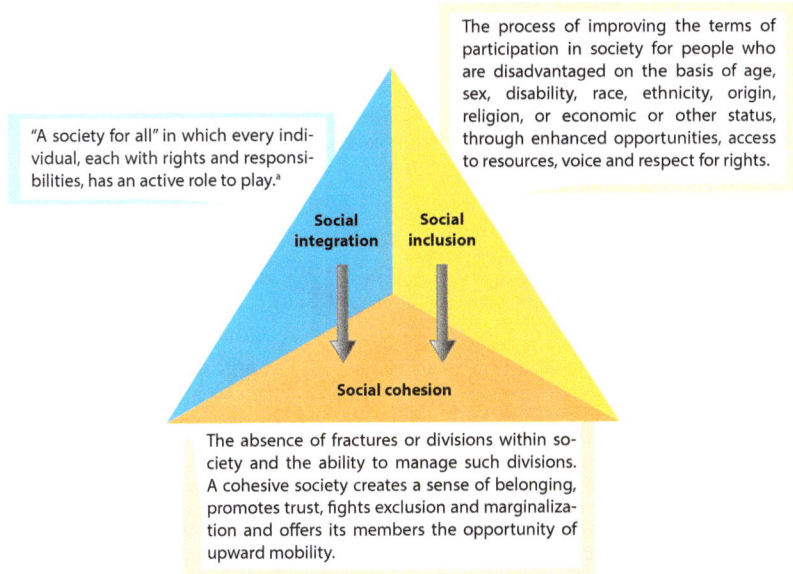

The process of improving the terms of participation in society for people who are disadvantaged on the basis of age, sex, disability, race, ethnicity, origin, religion, or economic or other status, through enhanced opportunities, access to resources, voice and respect for rights.

"A society for all" in which every individual, each with rights and responsibilities, has an active role to play.[a]

**Social integration**

**Social inclusion**

**Social cohesion**

The absence of fractures or divisions within society and the ability to manage such divisions. A cohesive society creates a sense of belonging, promotes trust, fights exclusion and marginalization and offers its members the opportunity of upward mobility.

*Source:* Based on Easterly (2006), Hulse and Stone (2007), OECD (2011a), United Nations (2010).
[a] Report of the World Summit for Social Development, Copenhagen, 6-12 March 1995, para. 66.

two types of identity. One relates to "groups of people who acknowledge their common membership, have shared beliefs and values and act in collective ways. Caste, ethnicity and religion are examples of such group identities". The other refers to categories of people defined on the basis of some shared characteristic rather than shared values and way of life. Members of these categories do not necessarily know each other and share very little in common, aside from the nature of the discrimination they face. Street children, people with leprosy or AIDS and undocumented migrants are examples of such socially excluded categories. In the present report, the term "group" refers to both types of identity and is recognized as a social construct used to facilitate the analysis.

Second, in aspiring to empower and promote the social, economic and political inclusion of all members of society, target 10.2 of the 2030 Agenda draws attention to these attributes; under that target, it is emphasized that all should be included "irrespective of age, sex, disability, race, ethnicity, origin, religion or economic or other status". The bases of disadvantage included in the report's definition are therefore those explicitly included by Governments in the Sustainable Development Goals. While not comprehensive, the list highlights many of the attributes that have historically put individuals most at risk of exclusion.

The present report's definition of social inclusion also refers to the process of improving the terms of participation in society. Social inclusion processes require both addressing the drivers of exclusion, including certain policies and institutions as well as discriminatory attitudes and behaviours, and actively "bringing people in". To the extent that policies and institutions define the "rules of the game" for social interactions and the distribution of power, status and control over resources, they can drive social exclusion or, alternatively, mitigate its impacts. As discussed in chapter V of the present report, some institutions systematically deny particular groups of people the recognition which would enable them to participate fully in society. Discriminatory attitudes and behaviours further drive exclusion, although they are not its only cause. People living in remote areas may not be able to fully participate in social, cultural or political life, for instance, without being discriminated against by law or by the rest of society. As described in chapter IV, discrimination can hinder access to and enjoyment of goods, services, justice, opportunities and culture, discourage the efforts of social groups to advance their interests, all of which results in spatial segregation. Norms, policies and institutions can also result in participation in society but on adverse terms (Hickey and Du Toit, 2007). For instance, participation in the labour market may be imposed or engaged in voluntarily but under precarious conditions.

## B. The challenge of measuring social exclusion

Identifying a set of criteria to determine who is excluded and in what ways is key to track progress, assess the impact of measures undertaken to promote inclusion and ultimately ensure that no one is left behind. Yet quantifying social exclusion presents considerable challenges. People are excluded from many domains of life – social, economic, political, civic and spatial – and the salience of each domain depends strongly on the country and local contexts as well as on the stage of a person's life course. That is to say, the concepts of social inclusion and social exclusion are multidimensional and context-dependent. Consequently, translating them into a limited set of indicators constitutes a considerable challenge. National definitions and measurement are thus the starting point for monitoring and analysis, although a limited set of measurable attributes applicable across countries is also necessary for global monitoring and analysis.

Furthermore, adequately assessing who is being left behind and how not only requires "objective" indicators of the status of individuals and social groups, but also must take into account their subjective judgments and perceptions. Exclusion is, after all, a personal experience, and the views of those affected by it or at risk of being left behind cannot be disregarded (United Nations, 2010). Relational issues, such as the presence of discrimination, the level of personal safety or the extent of participation in political processes or social life, must also be factored into key dimensions of inclusion and exclusion processes. Measuring exclusion therefore involves some compromise between the theoretical considerations discussed in section A of this chapter and what is possible empirically. Data availability and quality have improved significantly in the last 10 years, but considerable efforts are still needed to fill knowledge gaps and foster access as well as appropriate use of data, as discussed in box I.2.

Given the multiple dimensions of social exclusion, data to measure it generally come from a variety of sources that are different in scope and purpose. National population censuses and some internationally standardized surveys, including labour force surveys, demographic and health surveys, multiple indicator cluster surveys and living standard measurement

---

**Box I.2**

## A data revolution for all?

In 2013, the High-level Panel of Eminent Persons on the Post-2015 Development Agenda called for a "data revolution" for sustainable development, with initiatives to improve the quality of statistics and information available to people and Governments (United Nations, 2013b). In their report to the Secretary-General, a year later, the Independent Expert Advisory Group on a Data Revolution for Sustainable Development noted that the massive increase in the volume and types of data available brought about by digital technologies opened unprecedented opportunities for transformation and development, but also brought risks (Independent Expert Advisory Group on a Data Revolution for Sustainable Development, 2014). In particular, the Group stated that the data revolution poses challenges regarding access to data and their use, and threatens to open up new divides between the data "haves" and the "have-nots".

Much more is indeed known about poverty and human development now than 20 years ago, partly as a result of data investments made to monitor the Millennium Development Goals. However, considerable efforts are still needed to ensure that everyone is counted—many people and entire groups of the population are statistically invisible, as this chapter explains—and that important events are registered. Civil society organizations, academics and companies, which increasingly collect and analyze their own data, are helping fill some of these gaps. Yet assessing whether and how growing data availability is benefitting those left behind is a challenging task. Data generation itself often responds to society's demand for information and is helping improve policymaking and increase participation, although it can also be used to discriminate and harm.

Growing data openness is making information available to more and more people but much data, including so-called big data, are in private hands, and owners are reluctant to share them. New technologies are helping bring data within people's reach, but there, too, a large divide exists in access and use across communities and social groups, as described in chapter III. Beyond data access, potential beneficiaries often do not have the skills needed to use existing data, or else data are not provided in user-friendly formats or at appropriate levels of disaggregation. In addition, the quality of data produced is often unreliable, and standards are harder to apply as the range of data producers grows. Leaving no one behind in the data revolution will entail closing key gaps in access and use, including by improving data and statistical literacy. Doing so may also require a more democratic approach, not only to transparency and openness in data dissemination, but also with regard to what is measured.

surveys, as well as selected opinion polls, are available for a large number of countries and are fairly comparable across countries. However, each of these sources is designed for a specific purpose and none of them alone allows for comprehensive international assessments of social exclusion. Only limited attempts have been made to link microdata from different sources, although it is increasingly possible to do so.[15] Thus indicators of social exclusion have rarely been combined at the individual level into one composite index.[16] Assessing changes in indicators of exclusion over time results in additional challenges, as some data sources are available for one point in time only and comparability issues arise even between censuses or surveys of the same type. Even though cross-country assessments can hardly gauge the multiple dimensions of exclusion, in-depth, quantitative indicators should, whenever possible, be accompanied by qualitative evidence, including participatory assessments and in-depth interviews. There are important elements of the exclusion experience that cannot be reduced to statistical analyses.

Ideally, empirical studies should determine which individual characteristics or combinations thereof increase the risk of disadvantage and exclusion. However, lacking the information necessary for individual-level analysis, most studies of social exclusion, including the present one, pre-select some criteria that have been proven empirically to increase the risk of exclusion – most often age, sex, ethnic background, income, nationality or place of birth.[17] While grouping is a fundamental tool of social analysis, aggregate-level approaches based on traditional criteria run the risk of missing new forms of exclusion and are limited in their capacity to examine intersecting inequalities. As Brubaker (2002, p. 165) noted, the tendency to partition the social world into deeply constituted, quasi-natural groups "is a key part of what we want to explain, not what we want to explain things *with*; it belongs to our empirical data, not our analytical toolkit". While statistical groups are useful analytical categories, it is important to note that they are not necessarily factual entities with common agency or even common purposes.

---

[15]   Mapping information using geographic information system (GIS) technologies is enabling experts to combine and map multiple indicators in order to better understand the geography of deprivation, although their use in assessing the role of individual characteristics or social identity, beyond ethnic identity, as estimated by geographical location, has so far been limited.

[16]   The Social Exclusion Survey 2009, carried out in six countries in Eastern Europe and Central Asia and co-sponsored by the United Nations Development Programme (UNDP) and the United Nations Children's Fund (UNICEF), constitutes a notable exception. Designed for the purpose of measuring exclusion, the survey allowed for the construction of a multidimensional exclusion index. The survey was not used to sample pre-defined population groups at high risk of exclusion only; instead it was assumed that all individuals face some risk. Survey results are presented in a UNDP publication covering countries in transition (UNDP, 2011).

[17]   The African Social Development Index, introduced by the United Nations Economic Commission for Africa in 2015 and in its initial phase of implementation at the time of writing, illustrates disparities by sex and by place of residence (ECA, 2015). It combines indicators of neonatal mortality, child malnutrition, youth literacy, youth unemployment, income poverty and life expectancy after age 60.

The objective and subjective indicators of exclusion that can be obtained from existing sources should be disaggregated at least by age, sex, ethnic group, race, income level, place of residence, place of birth or nationality and level of disability. Data should allow for assessments of the combined effect of these factors, taking into account that the risk of exclusion faced by each individual depends on the combination of his or her characteristics and that many people belong to more than one disadvantaged group. Yet household surveys designed to be nationally representative frequently include few respondents from numerically small groups, including ethnic minorities, thereby often impeding essential decomposition analyses.

An additional challenge to measuring social exclusion is that the definitions used to classify a population by nationality and by migrant, ethnic or disability status vary across countries (box I.3 highlights the challenges and efforts to standardize data on disabilities in this regard). In addition, household surveys inevitably omit some groups at high risk of exclusion and poverty, such as homeless persons, people in institutions – including prisons, hospitals and refugee camps, among other such places – and mobile, nomadic and pastoralist populations. Many surveys are targeted at specific

---

**Box I.3**

### Challenges and efforts to standardize data on disability across countries

The number of developed and developing countries collecting data on disability has continuously increased over recent decades thanks in part to the increased attention being paid to addressing the rights of persons with disabilities and to ensuring their equal participation in society and their access to services. In spite of this increase in data availability, data on disability are still largely not comparable across countries for a variety of reasons. For one, there is a general lack of agreement among countries about what constitutes "disability" for measurement purposes in different cultural and environmental contexts. For another, the underlying classifications and methodologies applied in data-collection processes still vary greatly among countries, thereby hampering the comparability of international data. A review by the United Nations Statistics Division of disability questions in censuses of the 2010 round showed that, even among countries that had used the recommended guidelines, there were marked differences that have implications for data comparability (United Nations, 2013c). Another challenge regarding international comparability of data is that countries rely on different sources to generate data. While many countries use censuses, others rely on household surveys and still others on administrative sources, each with its own advantages and disadvantages for generating good-quality data on disability.

The 2030 Agenda for Sustainable Development provides an opportunity to galvanize the international community to work towards the compilation of high-quality fit-for-purpose statistics on disability. Under the Agenda, persons with disabilities are recognized as a vulnerable group and a commitment is made to enhance the capacity-building support extended to developing countries by 2030 in order to increase significantly the availability of high-quality, timely and reliable data on disability. Capacity-building activities include more concerted efforts to assist countries to scale up their activities to generate and utilize high-quality statistics on disability.

age groups and cannot be used to analyse the situation of persons outside the age groups. In practice, also, household surveys typically underrepresent urban slum populations, those in insecure or isolated areas and atypical households – single-parent households, those headed by older persons with young children, large households with foster children or unrelated orphaned children, child-headed households and children cared for by neighbours as well as those in exploitative fostering relationships or in groups and gangs (Carr-Hill, 2013). While population censuses do not omit homeless persons or any of these groups by design, they often underenumerate them, mainly because such people are difficult to reach. Global estimates of the number of homeless people are therefore highly unreliable, but national estimates suggest that homelessness is highly prevalent even in developed countries: in the United States of America, for example, close to 600,000 people were homeless on a given night in January 2014 (United States Department of Housing and Urban Development, 2014). In France, 141,000 people were homeless in 2012 (INSEE, 2013). Overall, Carr-Hill (2013) estimated that, as a result of omissions and underenumeration, an estimated 300 million to 350 million of the people at highest risk of exclusion and extreme poverty may not be represented in household surveys in developing countries.

In taking into account these challenges and based on a review of the empirical literature, the present report contains an examination of three sets of indicators: those that measure access to opportunity, namely education, health services and infrastructure; those that measure access to employment and income; and those that measure participation in political, civic and cultural life. A relative approach is taken to exclusion: instead of defining thresholds under which individuals would be considered excluded or left behind, the report construes disparities in these indicators across selected social groups as symptoms or outcomes of the exclusion of those who are lagging behind or participating less (see figure I.2). While the main focus is therefore on the outcomes of exclusion, the report contains an exploration of the dynamic links among different indicators. Specifically, it examines how education and health affect access to resources across groups, as well as participation in political life. Also considered in the report are some of the key drivers of exclusion in all these dimensions, with a particular focus on discrimination.

As is often the case in studies on social exclusion, data availability determines the choice of indicators. In addition to being widely used in empirical analyses (Labonté, Haddi and Kauffmann, 2011), the indicators used in the present report have been selected because the underlying data are available and comparable across countries. They are therefore presented as a minimum set of indicators for a global analysis on the topic. Cross-country comparisons are often based on data for a limited number of countries and are meant to illustrate concrete aspects of exclusion, although the report aims at ensuring regional balance when possible.

The analysis relies on data from national population censuses when

Figure I.2
**Symptoms of exclusion**

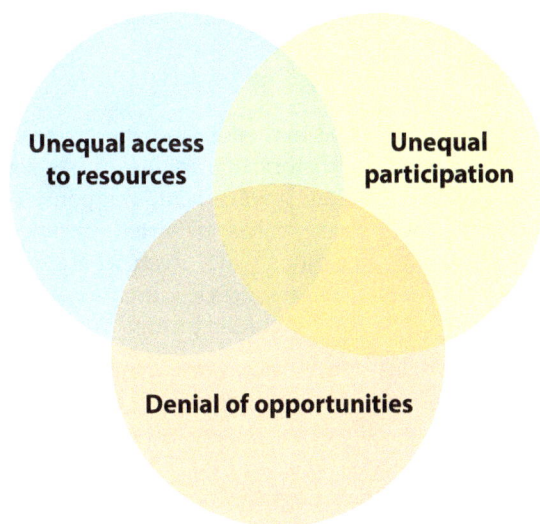

possible and complements such data with information from household surveys, mainly those under the Demographic and Health Surveys (DHS) supported by the United States Agency for International Development, and public opinion surveys, mainly the World Values Surveys (WVS) supported by the World Values Survey Association (Stockholm). Despite their focus on reproductive and other health issues, DHS surveys contain a wealth of socioeconomic information and can therefore produce a comprehensive picture of populations of reproductive age. In view of their coverage, consistency and comparability across countries, they are an exceptional source of information for cross-country analyses. WVS contain nationally representative samples from more than 90 countries. As such, they comprise the largest non-commercial, cross-national source of information on human beliefs and values. Opinion polls and values surveys are critical in assessing the role of some of the relational features and perceptions that bring about exclusion.

The evidence presented in this present report suggests that, while inclusiveness underpins the 2030 Agenda, conceptual and analytical work on what constitutes inclusion, as well as efforts to improve data availability to assess who is being left behind and how, are still needed. Measuring exclusion from a global perspective is challenging due to the multidimensional and context-specific nature of exclusion as well as the lack of comprehensive, standard data sources across countries and over time. Despite these limitations, the existing data allow for a meaningful analysis of key aspects of exclusion.

The report presents these data while illustrating data gaps. When possible, it also relies on country-specific research and case studies, which provide greater insight into the experience of exclusion in concrete country settings.

## C. Social exclusion and major global trends

It is clear that the extent of social exclusion and the groups affected by it vary by context and over time. Historically, exclusion has sometimes been condoned and institutionalized by government, religious, community or other authorities. At other times, it has persisted unsanctioned among members of society in subtle, insidious ways. Even where racism and other forms of prejudice have been formally redressed, their legacies may continue to adversely affect the well-being of excluded groups.

While extreme examples of exclusion are too numerous to mention in this chapter, certain cases stand out in the context of the report. For example, multiple forms of slavery date from ancient history. In many cases, the exclusion of its victims has been so severe that individuals were viewed as property, while in other cases some degree of personal freedom may have been permitted in certain respects, such as family life. Slavery has often occurred in the context of plunder by victors of war and has largely affected religious, racial and ethnic minorities, indigenous peoples, women and migrants. The legacy of the transatlantic slave trade, in particular, continues to be deeply felt in numerous countries, including in the form of racism. Among contemporary forms of slavery are labour and sex trafficking and domestic servitude, which particularly affect women, children, migrants and persons with disabilities.

Colonization has also created various forms of exclusion. In Africa, the arbitrary delineation of national borders by Western powers served to both separate individual ethnic groups and join different groups together (Michalopoulos and Papaioannou, 2011). Colonial powers further tied legal status to a hierarchy of ethnic and racial groups, privileging some over others (Mamdani, 2001). The legal system of apartheid in South Africa was also, in part, an outgrowth of colonization. Colonization additionally had devastating effects on the world's indigenous peoples, against whom mass atrocities had been committed. Many indigenous peoples continue to live amid long-standing conflicts or hostility with governments, dominant population groups and industries. They have been subject to displacement and dispossession of their lands and resources, marginalization, denial of their cultural rights and of their voice in political processes.

In many ways, the world has become less and less tolerant of social exclusion. However, major trends in climate change, demographic change and globalization have affected exclusion and continue to affect it. Globally, the number of climate hazards caused by droughts, extreme temperatures, floods and storms has increased (World Meteorological Organization, 2014).

Social exclusion increases vulnerability to environmental shocks, which, in turn, render affected individuals and groups more susceptible to exclusion, as described in box I.4 (United Nations, 2016a).

---

**Box I.4**

## Social exclusion, climate change and natural disasters

Social exclusion increases exposure and vulnerability to natural hazards and disasters in several ways. Certain groups, such as indigenous peoples, are more likely to live in rural areas and to be reliant on natural assets, such as forests, bodies of water, or fish or livestock, to sustain their livelihoods and meet their basic needs; all such assets are heavily affected by climate and weather events (Olsson and others, 2014; World Bank, 2010). Other groups often inhabit areas and housing structures that are highly exposed and susceptible to natural disasters, such as urban slums and other informal settlements, marginal areas prone to floods, landslides and mudslides, and areas where the infrastructure is lacking or weak (Arnold and de Cosmo, 2015; Ghesquiere and others, 2012). At the same time, excluded groups often lack the means to access insurance, credit and other productive resources that could help them to buffer against (as well as recover from) shocks and invest in adaptation (Ribot, 2010; World Bank, 2010). Exclusion also frequently entails limited political participation and clout, such that excluded groups may lack influence over resource allocation and representation in policies and strategies related to environmental protection and disaster prevention and management (Ribot, 2010). For persons with disabilities and older persons, gaps in accessibility can be a significant challenge, for example in obtaining information about risk and in evacuating in the event of a disaster.

The effects of natural hazards and disasters similarly tend to cause disproportionate harm to vulnerable and disadvantaged individuals and groups (Ghesquiere and others, 2012). They are more likely to be affected by injury, illness or death, damage to homes, workplaces and essential infrastructure, and by limited or absent public services and the availability or affordability of water, food and other consumption items. Socioeconomic factors and geographic location may increase risk for climate-sensitive health outcomes (Balbus and Malina, 2009). In four cities in the United States of America, for example, between 1986 and 1993 blacks were found to have a higher prevalence of heat-related mortality than whites (O'Neill, Zanobetti and Schwartz, 2005). Worldwide, women are more likely than men to be killed by natural disasters (World Health Organization, 2014).

Insecurity and destruction following disasters affect livelihoods and prevent children from attending school, thereby reducing productivity and income and creating irreparable learning gaps among young people. In parts of Bolivia with a high incidence of disasters, gender disparities in primary education achievement widened following a natural disaster, while other education indicators also deteriorated, as they did, too, in similar areas of Nepal and Viet Nam (United Nations Office for Disaster Risk Reduction, 2011). Following a disaster, some children and youth are typically kept home from school to help their families cope. Human capital is further weakened by injury and illness and the separation or displacement of families and communities. By deepening inequalities, disasters also risk contributing to civil unrest and conflict (Ghesquiere and others, 2012).

Although all countries are susceptible to natural disasters and climate change, developing countries have less financial and institutional capacity to manage natural catastrophes and adapt to climate change (Intergovernmental Panel on Climate Change, 2012; World Bank, 2010). Between 1970 and 2008, more than 95 per cent of lives lost due to natural disasters were in developing countries, which also suffered greater economic losses as a proportion of GDP than did developed countries (Intergovernmental Panel on Climate Change, 2012). Indeed, climate change is expected to intensify social exclusion and threaten development gains in both developing and developed countries (Olsson and others, 2014).

One aspect of the evolving global society that is changing the nature of social exclusion is urbanization. Cities are focal points of economic growth, paid employment and social mobility. On average, urban residents have better access to education, health care and other basic services than rural residents, as illustrated in chapter III.[18] Cities also offer a more diverse and open social milieu than do villages. Nevertheless, they also create new axes of exclusion (World Bank, 2013). For one thing, income and wealth in urban areas are more unequal than in rural areas. High levels of wealth and modern infrastructure coexist with areas characterized by severe deprivation and lack of services, creating a strong divide between the "haves" and the "have-nots" and intensifying the social exclusion of the latter.

In parallel with urbanization, declining fertility rates combined with increasing life expectancy have led to population ageing across countries. The process of population ageing is projected to accelerate rapidly in the coming decades, especially in developing countries.[19] Where employment creation and gains in productivity, growth and public investment and savings have not preceded population ageing, and where social protection systems are not in place and robust, greater numbers of older persons are being put at risk of social and economic exclusion. Not only do they face the prospect of lower incomes and poorer health, but they are also at risk of losing their independence and becoming limited in their ability to make decisions that affect their well-being.

Although international migration is not a new phenomenon, a growing number of people choose or are forced to migrate. Likewise, an increasing number of countries receive international migrants. In recent years, the dangerous journeys of large numbers of refugees and migrants and the harsh conditions they endure once they reach their destination have made headlines around the world. While the settlement and social inclusion of migrants has long polarized politics across countries and in international forums, the issue is now at the forefront of public debate. Migration itself separates families and fractures social networks, even though improvements in ICTs and in transportation are increasingly enabling migrants to keep in contact with their communities of origin. International migrants are vulnerable to coercion, exploitation and substandard labour conditions and benefits. They often suffer from discrimination and are confined to the margins of the societies in which they live.

Countries that receive migrants differ significantly in the ease with which they allow migrants to obtain employment, qualify for public benefits, become citizens and vote in national and local elections. Provisions for the

---

[18]     See also United Nations (2013a).

[19]     Data from the United Nations Population Division. Available from: https://esa.un.org/unpd/wpp/ (accessed in April 2016).

acquisition of citizenship, for instance, tend to be more restrictive where migration is conceived of as a temporary phenomenon than in countries where long-term or permanent migration has traditionally been the norm. In most countries, however, a common response to the recent large flows of refugees and migrants has been to tighten immigration policies, criminalize irregular migration and erect barriers to prevent migrants' entry. Experience shows that these measures, however, do not fully deter migration; rather, they lead to the marginalization and social exclusion of migrants, reinforce hostility and discrimination against them and ultimately undermine socioeconomic stability.

Finally, technological change and ICTs in particular can serve as critical channels for social inclusion. They connect people with information sources and opportunities that may otherwise be inaccessible or poorly accessible, such as public services, legal rights, skills training, jobs and markets. The internet and mobile phone texting, for instance, enable individuals, including members of marginalized groups, to consult with medical professionals and receive reminders to take essential medication (World Bank, 2016). Further, digital ICTs foster connection among family and friends as well as social networks that enable people to organize. They also foster public transparency and accountability. Yet vast inequality in access to such technologies, referred to as the "digital divide", also perpetuates exclusion and widens disparities in many respects, as illustrated in chapter III. In addition to creating new divides, ICTs can worsen exclusion through, for example, the spread of misinformation, as well as digital crime and censorship.

In sum, some global trends have been favourable to social inclusion while others have served to foster social exclusion. Under the status quo, there is no evidence that the world will overcome exclusion. Rather, this social ill must be addressed directly if mankind is to actually leave no one behind. Success in doing so will require that people of good will support the efforts of excluded communities and people to be included. It also will require personal bravery and persistence as the process typically involves deep social change. But it is the right thing to do.

Chapter II

# Poverty, inequality and decent work: key dimensions of exclusion

## Key messages

- *Societies cannot be considered inclusive if poverty remains widespread, inequalities are high or growing and decent work opportunities are lacking.*

- *While the world has made great progress in reducing income poverty, many people remain vulnerable to it and those living in the most extreme forms of poverty are being left behind.*

- *Although closely linked, the reduction in income inequality and progress in social inclusion do not always evolve at the same pace or respond to the same forces.*

- *Labour market participation has helped millions of people escape poverty and has economically empowered women and other disadvantaged groups. However, employment trends have not been sufficiently inclusive, a situation that could threaten social stability.*

The critical linkages among poverty, income inequality, deficits in decent work and exclusion have been well acknowledged in the international policy arena. At the World Summit for Social Development in 1995, Governments recognized that the common pursuit of social development aimed at creating social justice and building societies for all not only calls for fostering social integration, but also demands the eradication of poverty and the promotion of full employment. In adopting the 2030 Agenda for Sustainable Development, Governments and the international community at large reaffirmed with renewed urgency that striving for an inclusive world means addressing several interdependent goals, including the eradication of poverty, the reduction of inequalities, the pursuit of inclusive and sustainable economic growth and decent work for all, among other goals. At the same time, attempts to define and quantify the inclusiveness of growth and of wider development processes by analysing trends in poverty, inequality and employment have gained space in national and international policy and academic debates.[20]

---

[20] See, for instance, Ramos, Ranieri and Lammens (2013), Rauniyar and Kanbur (2010), OECD (2014) and McKinley (2010). In Ramos, Ranieri and Lammens (2013, p. 1), the following was pointed out: "The still limited number of studies seeking to measure inclusive growth...replicate the understanding that even though inclusive growth involves dimensions other than income, poverty and inequality are central to the meaning of inclusiveness".

In recognizing that no society can be considered genuinely inclusive if poverty remains widespread, economic inequalities are high or growing, or decent work opportunities are lacking. This chapter describes recent trends in these key areas. Disparities across social groups in these and other dimensions of exclusion will be examined in chapter III.

## A. Poverty, economic inequality and exclusion: a vicious cycle

More than two centuries ago, Adam Smith noted that being able to afford certain commodities was a necessity for engaging in public life without shame and disgrace. Despite the great progress achieved in reducing the prevalence and depth of poverty since then, deprivation continues to limit the participation of people in today's society. Social barriers to participation, in turn, still keep people in poverty and make it harder for them to sustain their escape from poverty.

Poverty is inextricably linked to social exclusion, both as a cause and as one of its consequences. Moreover, poverty is increasingly framed in ways which overlap with social exclusion, namely the capacity of an individual or a household to participate fully in society (Sen, 2000). As scholars have proposed measuring poverty using several indicators beyond income or consumption, the linkages between social exclusion and poverty have become more explicit. In his pioneering study of poverty in the United Kingdom, Townsend (1979) defined relative deprivation as covering several aspects of living standards and participation in social life. Since then, different analytical approaches have highlighted the social, political and environmental aspects of poverty, together with its economic aspects. The publication of the first Human Development Index (UNDP, 1990) along with Amartya Sen's capabilities approach to poverty (Sen, 1999), as well as the more recent emphasis on the multiple dimensions of poverty, have been notable landmarks in this conceptual shift.[21] At the regional level, the European Union's 10-year growth and jobs strategy, Europe 2020, combines the fight against poverty and social exclusion into a single priority area and provides a joint set of measures and targets.[22] These broader approaches to poverty address important relational issues which affect material deprivation and further hinder the ability of those living in poverty to participate fully in society and live the lives they wish to lead. Poverty in India or Nepal, for example, could not be fully understood

---

[21] One well-known measurement that considers several dimensions of poverty is the global multidimensional poverty index (MPI) adapted for UNDP, which is aimed at capturing severe deprivations that each person faces at the same time with respect to education, health and living standards. Available from www.ophi.org.uk/multidimensional-poverty-index, the index is an adaptation based on the methodology of Alkire and Foster (2011).

[22] The strategy has set the target of "lifting at least 20 million people out of the risk of poverty and social exclusion" by 2020 (European Commission, 2014).

without focusing attention on the caste system of socioeconomic stratification.

There is also a close relationship between levels of income inequality and the exclusion of some sectors of society. Not only does high or growing income inequality hamper poverty reduction and economic growth but, without appropriate institutions to prevent it, inequality also leads to a concentration of political influence among those who are already better off and therefore tends to create or preserve unequal economic and social opportunities through uneven access to public services (United Nations, 2013a). The denial of political voice or influence among those at the lower end of the inequality spectrum can reinforce social tensions and cause political instability and conflict (see box II.1). Yet trends in income inequality between individuals or households – also termed "vertical inequalities" (Stewart, 2004) – do not always go hand in hand with inequalities across social groups, as is illustrated in this section.

This section presents a number of positive trends, including rapid declines in income poverty. However, it also sounds a note of caution as some trends, including those based on a higher poverty line or on different dimensions of poverty, continue to raise concern, as does persistently high and in some cases growing income inequality. Such trends suggest that prosperity has not been adequately shared.

## 1. Poverty trends: implications for inclusive development

To the extent that material deprivation is a major barrier to social inclusion, the progress made globally in reducing extreme poverty in the 21 years since the World Summit for Social Development bodes well for inclusive development. While 37 per cent of the world's population lived under the current international poverty line of $1.90 a day in 1990, only 10.7 per cent did by 2013.[23] However, the world is far from meeting the Sustainable Development Goal target of eradicating poverty: close to 800 million people were still living under the same poverty line in 2013.

The overall headline improvements have been driven in significant part by countries in East Asia and the Pacific, particularly by China, where the percentage of its population living in extreme poverty fell from 66.6 per cent

---

[23] In October 2015, the World Bank released revised income poverty estimates based on a new set of purchasing power parity (PPPs) conversion factors and an ensuing new income poverty line of $1.90 a day. Because the line was designed to preserve real purchasing power in poor countries, the revisions led to relatively small changes in the incidence of global poverty: from 14.5 per cent for 2011 according to the previous estimates (based on a $1.25 a day poverty line) to 14.1 percent using the new poverty line. Changes in the regional composition of poverty are also relatively small. The revised estimates are available in the PovcalNet database, available from http://iresearch.worldbank.org/PovcalNet/ (accessed in October 2016).

Box II.1

## Social exclusion, inequalities and conflict

Social exclusion leads to discontent that is often a prelude to violent forms of conflict, including civil wars. Exclusion and the disparities associated with it can be particularly threatening to peace when there is a perception that they are the result of deliberately discriminatory political processes.

There are numerous examples of this phenomenon. In Uganda in the 1970s and 1980s, there were conflicts between the relatively well-off Bantu majority and the deprived non-Bantu groups. In Sri Lanka in the 1980s, there was a civil war between the minority Tamil community and the Sinhalese majority. In Mexico and various Latin American countries in the 1990s, there were the Chiapas rebellion and revolts by indigenous peoples respectively. All these conflicts were linked to development processes that had left behind certain regions and groups (Stewart, 2002; Kanbur, 2007; Kanbur and Venables, 2005). In India, civil unrest has also been linked to disparities in the distribution of employment opportunities, access to land and other productive assets and use of and access to social services and public institutions (Justino, 2015; Hardgrave, 1993; Brass, 2003; Wilkinson, 2004 and 2005). Research also suggests that exclusion affects the economic incentives to fight, thus lowering the opportunity cost of civil disobedience and violence among those who are left behind (Stewart, 2002).

Conflict is also often a driver of social exclusion and inequality, exacerbating existing cleavages between groups and creating new ones. For example, in conflict and post-conflict countries, women and girls are subject to increased gendered – including sexual – violence, higher rates of maternal mortality and child marriage, and lower primary school enrolment (United Nations, 2015a; Strachan and Haider, 2015). Social stigmatization of women and girls as a result of their rape, injury or HIV infection during wartime is common in post-conflict settings. Conflict is also a major cause of displacement. Refugees and internally displaced persons often suffer from extreme exclusion and marginalization, in many instances being kept apart from the population of the place or country to which they have moved.

Conflict results in deterioration in living standards and employment opportunities. It disrupts and destroys lives, livelihoods, homes and essential infrastructure, such as roads and hospitals, has adverse impacts on public services, such as health care and education, and the delivery channels for food and other consumption items. Insecurity may further prevent adults and children from accessing jobs and schools, reducing productivity and income and creating learning gaps among young people, a situation which may be irreparable. With increased stress on livelihoods, the competition for fewer resources becomes more intense, undermining social cohesion and inclusion (Ncube and Anyanwu, 2012; Alvaredo and Piketty, 2014). Conflict can also erode transparency, accountability and trust in government as normal instructional functions are suspended or circumvented, and illicit financial flows increase.

in 1990 to only 1.8 per cent in 2013.[24] Poverty reductions in South Asia and sub-Saharan Africa, particularly the least developed countries within these areas, have been slower. The proportion of people living in poverty in sub-Saharan Africa dropped from 54.3 per cent in 1990 to 41.0 per cent in 2013. However, the absolute number actually increased from 276 million to 389 million. It is

---

[24]  World Bank, PovcalNet database. Available from http://iresearch.worldbank.org/PovcalNet/ (accessed in October 2016).

important to note also that people living in poverty remain further below the poverty line in sub-Saharan Africa than in any other region – that is, poverty is deeper in sub-Saharan Africa than elsewhere in the world. Meanwhile, there have also been differences in rates of poverty reduction within regions – for example Botswana and Ethiopia have experienced poverty decline faster than many other sub-Saharan African countries.

Additional data, however, suggest caution in interpreting these overall positive trends as early indications of success in eradicating poverty. Ravallion (2014), for instance, argued that people living in the most extreme forms of poverty are being left behind. Specifically, there has been little success in raising the standard of living of those in the lowest bound of the consumption distribution – defined here as a "consumption floor" of less than half of the $1.25-a-day line. Most of the progress against poverty has instead come from improvements in living standards of people whose income is above this floor. In fact, Ravallion estimated that the overall consumption floor of the developing world increased by just 0.4 per cent per annum in the past 30 years, less than half the rate seen in the developed world between 1850 and 1950. Thus the modest rise in the mean consumption of people living in poverty observed over the last 30 years has been accompanied by rising inequality, leaving room for almost no gains in the level of living of the poorest people. Milanovic (2012) also found no evidence of an increase in the real incomes of the poorest 5 per cent of the population worldwide between 1998 and 2008.

Furthermore, trends based on relative measures of poverty are less positive than those based on absolute measures. Relative measures, which classify individuals as being poor if they have less than a certain proportion of the income enjoyed by other members of society, reflect the fact that relative deprivation affects welfare. That is, well-being depends not only on an individual's income but also on the income of the individual's reference group, be that his or her neighbours, co-workers or fellow citizens of the country in which the person lives. Such measures, used in many developed countries, support the notion that what matters for well-being is the cost of social inclusion – that is, the cost of goods that are deemed to have a role in assuring that a person can participate with dignity in customary social and economic activities – and that such a cost increases with the mean income of a person's country of residence. Based on a "weakly relative measure" of poverty proposed by Ravallion and Chen (2011), the percentage of people living in poverty fell from 63 per cent in 1981 to 47 per cent in 2008, a percentage more than twice as high as the estimated share of people living in absolute poverty in the same year (Chen and Ravallion, 2012, table 5, p. 30).[25] They also found that this speed of decline was not sufficient to reduce the total number

---

[25]   The weakly relative poverty measure maintains the international poverty line at a constant level up to a certain income and raises it for countries with per capita incomes above that level (Ravallion and Chen, 2011).

of people living in weakly relative poverty, which rose from 2.3 billion in 1981 to 2.7 billion in 1999 and remained at 2.7 billion in 2008. Another study in Vanuatu comparing current poverty levels according to different measures suggested that, while 5 per cent of all children in Vanuatu currently live in absolute poverty as defined by the international $1.00-a-day measure, 23 per cent live in households with income below 50 per cent of the median and 30 per cent with income below 60 per cent of the median (Deeming and Gubhaju, 2015).

Evidence concerning the dynamics of poverty, however, indicates that poverty is less a state that applies to a fixed group of individuals than a condition which people are at risk of experiencing at some point in time, and one which they have the potential to move out of as well as face the risk of falling back into it.[26] Certain circumstances, including periods of ill health, unemployment, natural disasters, drought, violence and conflict or a combination of these shocks, may put an individual or a household particularly at risk of impoverishment (ODI, 2014). Globally, more than 2.6 billion people – 37 per cent of the global population – are living on less than $3.80 a day and could easily fall back into extreme poverty with a sudden change in their circumstances.[27] In South Asia alone, 41 per cent of that area's population – about 720 million people – live just above the international extreme poverty line, earning between $1.90 and $3.80 a day.[28] In Latin America and the Caribbean, more than half of the region's population (50.9 per cent) can be considered vulnerable to poverty, according to estimates by the Economic Commission for Latin America and the Caribbean (ECLAC, 2015).[29] Additional research drawing on the experience of those living just above the poverty line in Latin America shows that, even as people move up the income ladder, they remain at high risk of impoverishment. For instance, 23 per cent of households living above the $4-a-day line in Mexico and 19 per cent of those living above that threshold in Peru in 2002 were living on less than $4 a day by 2005 (Birdsall, Lustig and Meyer, 2013). The same researchers found that, for these households, higher household income was not accompanied by equivalent improvements in risk protection measures, such as unemployment insurance or affordable health care, and the households remained highly vulnerable to falling back into poverty. The eradication of poverty therefore requires not only lifting people out of poverty but also protecting vulnerable people against major risks.

---

[26]  For example, see Addison, Hulme and Kanbur (2009), Birdsall, Lustig and Meyer (2013), ODI (2014) and UNDP (2014).

[27]  Data are from http://iresearch.worldbank.org/PovcalNet/ (accessed in October 2016). Total population figures are from the United Nations Population Division. Available from www.un.org/en/development/desa/population/ (accessed in October 2016).

[28]  Ibid.

[29]  An individual is defined as vulnerable to poverty if he or she has an income 1.8 times the poverty line or less.

Non-monetary measures of poverty also show that important barriers to inclusive development remain, even where income levels have improved. According to the multidimensional poverty index (MPI) adapted for UNDP, which considers overlapping deprivations in health, education and living standards, 1.6 billion people lived in multidimensional poverty in 2015 as compared with close to 900 million living in income poverty in 2012 (Alkire and others, 2016). Indeed, in the vast majority of countries, the incidence of poverty estimated using multiple indicators is higher than the incidence of income poverty. Among countries with necessary data there appears to be no clear relationship between the reduction in income poverty and the reduction in multidimensional poverty. The incidence of MPI poverty is higher than that of income poverty in more than 60 per cent of the countries covered. Differences are significantly large in South Asian countries, where MPI is generally high due to malnutrition (Alkire, Roche and Vaz, 2014). Thus, even though income poverty, hunger, poor health and low educational outcomes are strongly linked, it is also the case that deprivations in education and health can persist even in the context of rising incomes, and that such deprivations make it difficult for individuals and groups to break the cycle of poverty and exclusion.

Overall, a growing body of evidence on poverty suggests that the impressive reductions in income poverty observed at the global level do not adequately capture the diversity of experiences of those living in poverty. In particular, these reductions have not resulted in major improvements in the situation of those that are left furthest behind, that is, those living in the most extreme forms of poverty or in the poorest countries. This situation is part of the unfinished business that the 2030 Agenda for Sustainable Development is aimed at addressing.

In-depth poverty assessments suggest that a number of key barriers to participation can persist, even if income levels rise above the extreme poverty line. A review of whether development processes have been genuinely inclusive based on reductions in poverty must take into account the dramatic variations in poverty rates between and within countries and depending on the indicators used, as well as the fact that many of those who have escaped poverty remain vulnerable to it. Promoting inclusion calls for lifting people out of poverty, but it also requires creating resilience – that is, protecting people against major risks.

## 2. Trends in income inequality

While poverty trends have long been a focus of the international debate on development, there have been rising concerns about the distribution of development outcomes. Concerns about inequality in income, in particular, have become prominent in discussions about growth or development trajectories during the last decade.

Income inequality across countries increased sharply from 1980 to 2000 but has declined somewhat since 2000 (United Nations, 2013a). This decline has been driven by stronger income growth in poorer than in richer countries. Despite this recent improvement, international inequality remains high. Excluding China, the Gini coefficients of international inequality were actually higher in 2010 than they had been in 1980.[30]

Over the same period, income distribution has become increasingly unequal within a significant number of developed countries and in some large developing countries, as wealthier segments of society have seen their incomes rise at a faster rate than the rest. Between 1990 and 2012, inequality in disposable income (after taxes and transfers) increased in 65 of the 130 countries for which data trends were available (United Nations, 2013a). These countries are home to two thirds of the global population. In general, income inequality has increased in countries and regions that enjoyed relatively low levels of inequality in 1990, namely some large, emerging economies and the majority of developed countries, particularly countries in Eastern Europe. However, there are also countries where inequality has decreased, noticeably in Latin America and the Caribbean where the Gini coefficient declined between 1990 and 2012 in 14 of the 20 Latin American countries with available data (United Nations, 2013a). Among these countries is Brazil, where the incomes of its historically poorest northern and north-eastern regions converge with those of the southern regions, while the share of income going to the top population quintile declined since 2000 – particularly since 2008 (ECLAC, 2014). In Africa, available data suggest that inequality fell in more countries than it rose, that is, in 19 countries compared with 13 respectively.

As described in box II.2, total income inequality comprises inequality across social groups – examined in this report as a symptom of social exclusion – and inequality between individuals within these groups. In general, income inequality across groups constitutes a significant share of total income inequality, although its relative weight varies strongly by country (World Bank, 2005). For instance, inequality between racial groups accounted for an estimated 50 to 55 per cent of total inequality in South Africa in the mid-2000s,[31] 30 to 50 per cent of the total in Guatemala, Panama and Paraguay, but less than 15 per cent of the total in many developed countries (Liebbrandt and others, 2010; Elbers and others, 2005). Inequality between rural and urban populations explained more than 50 per cent of total inequality in Senegal but less than 10 per cent in Côte d'Ivoire, Ethiopia or Niger (Elbers and others, 2005).

---

[30]    International income inequality can be assessed through the Gini coefficient of the per capita income of each country, weighted by each country's population, or just unweighted. Declines in international income inequality are observed regardless of the measure used, even if China is excluded from the calculation (United Nations, 2013a).

[31]    Liebbrandt and others (2010) estimated the weight for South Africa at 50 per cent in 2000 and 48 per cent in 2008, while Elbers and others (2005) estimated it at about 55 per cent in the mid-2000s.

---

Box II.2

## Components of inequality

The extensive use of the concept of inequality throughout the present report calls for some conceptual clarification. Income inequality, described in this section, as well as inequalities in consumption, wealth and other indicators of economic welfare are often used to measure disparities in "outcomes". Some of the outcome inequalities observed may be explained by differences in personal effort and ability, but a significant proportion stems from inequalities in circumstances or, more broadly, in opportunities. Differences in access to education – and in the quality of education received – or to health and other basic services, for instance, influence access to employment and income and therefore affect the opportunities people have in life. Opportunities are also influenced by other circumstances that are out of an individual's control, namely the socioeconomic situation of the person's family, the place where the person was born and such attributes as race, ethnicity, gender or having a disability. In chapter 3, an examination is made of the influence of these personal attributes on both opportunities and outcomes.

In order to measure total inequality, individuals or households are ranked according to their income or any other variable of interest. Total inequality can be "decomposed" into inequality across groups – with populations most often being grouped by age, sex, ethnic background, income, nationality or place of birth, as described in chapter 1– and inequalities within these groups. Disparities across groups, also known as "horizontal" inequalities (Stewart, Brown and Mancini, 2005), are construed in this report as symptoms or consequences of the exclusion of those groups that are lagging behind, that is, inequalities across groups are intrinsic to the measurement of social exclusion. Given that they reflect mostly the impact of attributes over which individuals have little control, persistent inequalities across groups constitute an important challenge to inclusive development and stand against the principle of social justice.

---

Trends in these two key components of income inequality – across groups and within groups – are not always in harmony. In South Africa, for instance, the total Gini coefficient increased relatively rapidly during the post-apartheid period, from 66 in 1993 to 70 in 2008, despite continued economic growth, significant poverty reduction and the expansion of social assistance programmes (Narayan and Mahajan, 2013). While between-race inequality remains very high by international standards, it has fallen since the end of apartheid: on average, per capita incomes of black Africans increased from 8.5 per cent of the per capita incomes of whites in 1987 to 15.9 per cent in 2000, declining slightly to 13 per cent in 2008 (Liebbrandt and others, 2010, table 1.1, p.13). Yet inequality within racial groups has risen, particularly in urban areas. The estimated Gini coefficient of the African population increased from 54 in 1993 to 62 in 2008, while that of the white population grew from 43 to 50 during the same period (Liebbrandt and others, 2010, table 2.6). The rise in intraracial inequality is due mostly to increasingly unequal wage incomes and joblessness, with capital incomes and remittances playing a very small part in the observed trends. Similarly, in the United States, while total income inequality as measured by the Gini coefficient increased steadily from the early 1980s to the start of the 2008 recession, the poverty gap between whites and racial and ethnic minorities declined (Mather and Jarosz, 2014). However, the gap has increased since the 2008 recession, partly because the job prospects of racial and ethnic minorities were disproportionately affected by the downturn (Mather and Jarosz, 2014). In contrast, research from Mexico suggests that, despite declining income inequality at the national level since 2000, income growth has been slower for indigenous than for non-indigenous populations and differences in the incidence of poverty have increased (Solt, 2014; Servan-Mori and others, 2014). The percentage of indigenous peoples living on less than $50 a month was twice as high as that of the non-indigenous population in 2002, but three times as high in 2010 (Servan-Mori and others, 2014).

These examples illustrate that reducing income inequality and promoting social inclusion are related yet separate processes that can become delinked. Even in cases where Governments have made conscious efforts to bring different people, in particular historically marginalized groups, into the development and growth processes, overall income inequality can remain unaffected, as is the case in South Africa. Conversely, declining income inequality does not automatically translate into improved welfare outcomes for all marginalized individuals or groups. Measures to reduce income inequality and those aimed at promoting social inclusion are both important components of inclusive development processes that need to be pursued in conjunction with each other.

## B. Deficits in decent work and exclusion

### 1. Does employment promote inclusion?

Jobs shape the opportunities people have in life as well as their children's future. They are most likely to be a foundation of social inclusion and well-being when they provide sufficient earnings to maintain adequate living standards, and particularly when they come with access to social protection, decent working conditions and prospects for career development. Beyond being an important source of income, employment often confers social identity and brings social acceptance to people's lives, particularly when the workplace enables them to create social and economic ties and build networks. Where they promote social dialogue, employment gives workers a voice and therefore enables them to play an active role in making decisions that affect their well-being. Jobs that offer few opportunities for social mobility or voice, in contrast, can lead to the marginalization and exclusion of workers.

With regard to overall life satisfaction, the negative impact of not having a job is well-established; the impact remains significant even after controlling for the effects of unemployment on income and on access to social protection.[32] That is, financial hardship is only one among many negative outcomes of unemployment, a situation which also results in isolation and psychological

---

[32]  See, for instance, Kunze and Suppa (2014), Blanchflower and Oswald (2004) and Deaton (2008).

stress. Indeed, existing research indicates that a person's employment situation affects his or her social networks, levels of civic engagement and overall trust in other people as well as in institutions.[33] Workers who are able to use their skills productively, who perceive that they are treated fairly and are not disadvantaged in their search for jobs are less likely to disengage from social life and political institutions (Wietzke and McLeod, 2013). Even a single period of unemployment can have long-lasting effects on individuals, families and communities through its negative impact on health, social ties and participation in social life (Kunze and Suppa, 2014; Brand and Bugard, 2008; Narayan and Petesch, 2002). Using survey data for 69 countries, Altindag and Mocan (2010) found that joblessness translated into negative opinions about the effectiveness of democracy, particularly if unemployment lasts longer than one year, both in developed and in developing countries. The effects of vulnerable employment – own-account work and work in family businesses, often in the informal sector – and those of insecure, temporary contracts are similar to those of unemployment in that they curtail access to social protection and sever links with social and political organizations, including unions. While workers can therefore be "included" in the labour market, it really may be on terms that are unfavourable (de Haan, 2015; Nathan and Xaxa, 2012).

The way in which employment affects inclusion, however, does not depend only on a worker's labour market situation or on the type of job, but it is also influenced by the economic, institutional and political context as well as the specific needs and aspirations of each worker. Cross-country analysis of values surveys indicates that, in general, levels of self-reported well-being and life satisfaction are lower among unskilled manual workers and among farmers in high-income countries than in low-income countries (Wietzke and McLeod, 2013). In contexts of generalized poverty, widespread institutional failure or where social institutions restrict the autonomy of certain social groups, even an informal job can bestow skills, autonomy and agency – the capacity to act individually or collectively to further one's own interests or those of a group. In particular, jobs can positively transform the role of women and disadvantaged groups, both in their communities and in societies at large. Kabeer and Kabir (2009) documented, for instance, how jobs in retail garment factories of Bangladesh, generally characterized by poor working conditions, have expanded women's scope for decision-making, their social networks and their opportunities to participate in the public domain. Women's greater independence has, in turn, benefited other disadvantaged groups as well. Similar case studies in Morocco and Pakistan, among other developing countries, have documented the generally positive impact on the empowerment of women when they participate in the labour market, even in the informal sector (Dudwick, 2012).

---

[33] For examples from the empirical literature, see Norton and de Haan (2012), Dudwick (2012) and Wietzke and McLeod (2013).

Values surveys also indicate that, overall, perceived levels of exclusion are less among workers in the informal sector or among jobless persons when levels of vulnerable employment or unemployment are higher (Kunze and Suppa, 2014; Clark, 2003). These findings do not imply that informal work should be acceptable in some settings and not in others. The rights to just and favourable conditions of work, protection against unemployment, equal pay for equal work, access to trade unions and to social security are universal and unalienable. Informal work carries fiscal losses and has potentially negative consequences for competitiveness and growth as well as social cohesion. Recognition that informal work has given opportunities to groups that were formerly excluded from the labour market helps to highlight the positive contribution of informal employment and the need to support informal workers. However, it does not justify the absence of decent work or security safeguards.

It has also been argued that informal jobs and self-employment can serve as a stepping stone to formal, more secure employment for youth and other new entrants into the labour market (Perry and others, 2007). However, the transition from informal to formal jobs is far from assured and is not automatic. According to data for four developing countries, namely South Africa, Turkey and urban areas in China and Colombia, between 30 per cent and 80 per cent of workers in informal jobs annually transition to other informal jobs while only 8 to 35 per cent transition to formal jobs, mostly under fixed-term contracts in both urban China and Colombia (OECD, 2015b). The probability of transitioning to unemployment or inactivity is higher among workers in informal employment than among those in formal employment (OECD, 2015b). In many developing countries, the labour force is, as a matter of fact, growing significantly faster than the formal economy. Labour force projections for sub-Saharan Africa, for instance, suggest that only one in four youth will find wage employment in that region between 2005 and 2020, and only a small fraction of such employment will be formal employment in modern enterprises (Fox and others, 2013).

In fact, low mobility and persistent wage gaps between informal and formal jobs suggest the presence of a divide between workers in each sector who are, in practice, part of different labour submarkets (IADB, 2008; Duryea and others, 2006). A similar divide exists in developed countries between adequately protected workers under open-ended labour contracts and many of those under temporary, as well as other non-standard, labour contracts, among whom young workers, women, migrants and members of other disadvantaged groups are overrepresented.

Such a divide is reinforced by processes of discrimination and by an absence of social ties between different types of workers, both within and outside the workplace. Both occupational and residential segregation contribute to the breakdown of interactions across social groups and to the subsequent loss of employment opportunities for disadvantaged groups

(Wilson, 1997; Grusky and Kanbur, 2006; Bertaux and Thompson, 1997). As the example in box II.3 illustrates, residential segregation has been shown to cause persistent disadvantage in the labour market in the long term, in addition to creating social rifts between minorities and the rest of the population (Portes and Rumbaut, 2006; Iceland, 2014).

While a profession or trade has traditionally been an important source of social identity, some workers under temporary contracts or those who are outside of an employment relationship altogether may develop little identity through their jobs. In view of their vulnerable situation, such workers also face particular challenges in mobilizing and organizing collectively (King and Rueda, 2008; Rueda, 2005). Unions that are organized around the traditional

---

### Box II.3

## Impact of residential segregation on the employment of migrants

Migration is most often linked, directly or indirectly, to the quest for decent work. In 2014, the Migration Policy Institute and the International Labour Office conducted a project to examine the movement of immigrants into skilled employment in the years following their arrival in Czechia, France, Germany, Sweden and the United Kingdom. It was found that generally unemployment rates tended to be higher for immigrants from outside the European Union than for natives of those countries (Benton and others, 2014).

Income differentials determine in which neighbourhoods native and immigrant groups will live. Immigrants are more likely to settle in neighbourhoods where there are communities or groups of the same ethnicity or from the same country of origin (Scarpa, 2015). In France, for instance, 42 per cent of immigrants from North Africa, sub-Saharan Africa and Turkey lived in the 10 per cent of neighbourhoods with the highest unemployment levels in 2008, and they represented 28 per cent of the population of disadvantaged neighbourhoods (Pan Ké Shon, 2011).

These communities play various supportive roles, including the provision of information on jobs and other opportunities (Scarpa, 2015). In the long term however, clustering in ethnically homogenous, often poor, neighbourhoods has had negative labour market impacts for immigrants. Social networks often steer immigrants into a few specific areas of work that create an ethnic division of labour and contribute to the segregation of immigrants from other workers in the labour market (Parks, 2005). A low level of interaction with the majority population results in difficulties learning the language, lack of country-specific knowledge and lack of valuable social capital (Klinthäll and Urban, 2016), all important factors that hamper access to the broader labour market. Employers in turn often have negative perceptions of candidates from poor or ethnically segregated neighbourhoods (Dickerson, 2007).

It should be noted, however, that immigrants turn to neighbourhood social networks as a result of ethnic discrimination in the labour market. Lack of opportunities in the formal labour market also contribute to high self-employment among immigrants, who use this approach as an alternative route to economic mobility by starting small businesses in their ethnic neighbourhoods (Van Tubergen, 2006).

Overall, in residentially segregated communities, neighbourhoods are the incubators of ethnic social capital. Such social capital can be useful to migrants initially, but in the long term it has been found to restrict their opportunities in the labour market and their socioeconomic mobility overall.

employer-employee relationship are not well-suited to give voice to those who do not work for a wage, or who do so outside the formal sector and run the risk of deepening the divide between workers under standard contracts and those under non-standard contract arrangements (World Bank, 2012; ODI, 2013). In addition, political parties which had historically represented the most disadvantaged have increasingly advanced the interests of workers in standard employment as well in industrialized countries (Kitschelt and others, 1999; Rueda, 2005 and 2006). It is in this context that attributes other than socioeconomic background or occupation, including ethnicity, race and gender, are gaining salience as a basis for worker mobilization. Organizations representing workers structured along ethnic group and geographical community lines, rather than through the workplace, have emerged in some countries as effective pressure groups on local governments concerning a range of issues, including working conditions, but also housing, health and education (Fine, 2005; King and Rueda, 2008).

Beyond its importance for the social inclusion of individuals and groups, employment has society-wide impacts, including on social cohesion and stability. While empirical evidence on the impact of employment trends on overall social cohesion is limited, an analysis of the determinants of social unrest following the 2008 financial and economic crisis put unemployment and economic growth at the heart of protests and other forms of unrest (ILO, 2013a). Individuals who do not have access to good jobs often see their interests diverge from those of the rest of society, particularly when exclusion from the labour market affects some social groups disproportionately, especially youth (Urdal, 2012; Azeng and Yogo, 2015). However, the risk of unrest is mediated by institutional factors and particularly the availability of democratic institutions to channel concerns and frustration – civil society, unions and the rule of law.

## 2. Trends in the world of work: prospects for inclusive development

Over the last two decades, the world has witnessed important changes in the way in which work is performed and managed. The evidence presented in this section indicates that labour market trends have generally not been conducive to social inclusion or, more broadly, to inclusive development, with important exceptions. Growing job instability and the rise of poorly paid, precarious work have fuelled inequality and income insecurity among workers in the developed world. The standard employment contract, usually entailing access to social security and other statutory employment rights and protection against termination, has ceased to be the norm. Workers are increasingly employed under non-standard contracts, often in the informal sector, as described in this section. However, greater labour market flexibility has not been accompanied by more employment opportunities for all workers.

In developing countries, labour market participation has enabled many people to escape poverty. Participation in the manufacturing sector, in particular, has economically empowered women and other disadvantaged groups and often transformed their role in society. However, while higher growth and the increases in labour productivity observed in many countries have been translated into higher incomes and better working conditions for some workers, this is not the case for all. Thus the divide has grown between a well-protected group of workers in the formal sector of the labour market – especially better educated adults – and unskilled young people, women and migrants who work more often in informal jobs (as illustrated in chapter III). The 2008 financial and economic crisis has exacerbated these trends, as employment has become more unstable or precarious for a growing number of workers since the crisis, and those unemployed are at growing risk of long-term exclusion from the labour market (ILO, 2014a and 2015b).

## a. Persistent joblessness

The employment statistics available are not encouraging. Even during the period of expansion that preceded the financial and economic crisis of 2008, employment growth was not sufficient to absorb the growing labour force: the global unemployment rate hovered between 6.0 and 6.5 per cent from 1995 to 2005, while the number of jobless persons grew from 156 million in 1995 to close to 186 million in 2005.[34] The crisis led to sharp falls in employment. Globally, the number of jobless persons reached 197 million in 2015 and is projected to continue growing at least until 2017, while the unemployment rate is expected to stabilize at 5.8 per cent (ILO, 2016a). Countries in North Africa and West Asia are projected to continue suffering from the highest unemployment rates worldwide, while there will be some relief for developed countries, including countries in Southern Europe, although joblessness will remain well above pre-crisis levels.

In addition, in the majority of countries, the average duration of unemployment has increased since the crisis. In OECD countries, 15.2 million people – more than one in three of the unemployed – had been out of work for 12 months or more in the fourth quarter of 2014, almost twice the number unemployed in 2007 (OECD, 2015b). Longer periods of unemployment result in substantial financial hardship, a loss of valuable skills and deeper impacts on social participation and other aspects of exclusion described in the previous subsection. In some countries, the increase in long-term unemployment can be explained by persistently sluggish economic growth. However, in the majority of developing countries, the employment intensity of growth declined from the 1990s to the post-crisis period (2007-2014), a trend that has led to a jobless recovery and continues to raise fears over long-term, structural joblessness.

Many more people find themselves excluded from the labour force

---

[34]    ILO Statistics and Databases, Key Indicators of the Labour Market, 9th ed. Available from www.ilo.org/ilostat/faces/home/statisticaldata/technical_page?_afrLoop=224207380903115#%40%3F_afrLoop%3D224207380903115%26_adf.ctrl-state%3D12qwcwaka6_433 (accessed on 13 July 2016).

altogether, particularly women and youth. Globally in 2014, 2 billion people of working age were not participating in the labour force, and the number is projected to continue growing (ILO, 2016b). Part of the increase is explained by a rise in the number of years spent in education and by the phenomenon of population ageing. Since 2008, however, many rich countries and some middle-income countries have witnessed an increase in the number of discouraged workers, who are not counted among the unemployed as they are no longer actively seeking employment. In particular, the crisis reinforced the long-term downward trend in youth participation rates. Crisis-led rises in youth unemployment would have been stronger had many young workers not dropped out of the labour market. While some youth may have returned to the education system, the share of those who are NEET increased in 30 of the 40 countries with data from 2007 to 2014.[35] This severe waste of human potential can have drastic repercussions in terms of marginalization and exclusion both for the young people affected and for societies at large.

### b. Decent work deficits

Trends in unemployment do not fully reflect lack of decent work opportunities, given that not all existing jobs take people out of poverty or promote social inclusion. In countries with high levels of poverty and lacking formal social protection systems, most workers cannot afford to stay unemployed. In developing countries, which are home to 82 per cent of the world's working-age population, the majority of people work but they struggle to earn income through what is commonly defined as vulnerable employment (own-account work and work in family businesses), often in the informal sector where salaries are lower than in formal employment, social protection is largely absent and working conditions are poorer. For the majority of workers, informal jobs are not a choice but reflect the limited availability of formal, more desirable jobs, as well as workers' limited bargaining power in the businesses that employ them.

There are few reliable estimates of informality or of the total extent of underemployment – the shortfall in the income that can be earned from work or in the number of hours of work – which makes difficult the monitoring of the global employment situation. One series of comparable estimates puts the share of informal employment outside of agriculture at 82 per cent of total employment in South Asia, 65 per cent in East Asia (excluding China) and South-East Asia, 51 per cent in Latin America and the Caribbean and 66 per cent in sub-Saharan Africa (ILO, 2013a and 2014b).[36] Adding data on the agricultural sector would raise these averages, as much of agricultural employment in developing regions is informal as well. Alternative estimates

---

[35]   Ibid.

[36]   Data for sub-Saharan Africa are available for a limited number of countries. Data and metadata on women and men in the informal economy are also available online through the ILO labour statistics database Laborsta (http://laborsta.ilo.org).

put the share of informal employment at even higher levels. In one study, two thirds of workers in the Middle East and North Africa were found not to have access to social security, a deficit often used to estimate informal employment (Gatti and others, 2014).

Vulnerability in the world of work has also risen in developed countries, especially through the increase in the incidence of involuntary temporary and part-time employment as well as own-account work, often in the informal sector.[37] From 1995 to 2005, a period of job growth in the European Union, most low-skilled, low-paying jobs created were part-time or fixed-term jobs, while permanent low-paying employment was destroyed or remained stagnant (European Foundation for the Improvement of Living and Working Conditions, 2007). This was also a period of labour market deregulation in many European countries. In those countries suffering from high unemployment, such as Spain and other Southern European countries, strongly regulated labour markets which imposed high hiring and firing costs had been found to discourage job creation. However, deregulation and greater flexibility were not applied equally across all sectors. Thus greater labour market flexibility has generally resulted in greater insecurity for some workers and increased inequalities in wages and working conditions, given that some jobs have remained protected while others have been made highly flexible.

Workers employed on non-standard contracts, among whom young people, women, migrants and other disadvantaged groups are overrepresented, earn less than workers on standard contracts, are not afforded the same protection as employees working full-time and long-term wage workers and bear the brunt of employment losses during recessions, while little adjustment is made through wages in the more protected segment of the labour market. A similar segmentation exists in developing countries, where workers in the formal sector benefiting from some degree of social protection coexist with a large informal economy, and mobility across the two segments is very limited (Gatti and others, 2014).

The trend towards greater job insecurity stands in contrast to the progress observed in reducing income poverty, but is not incompatible with such progress. In developing countries, the proportion of workers who live on less than $1.90 a day declined from 33.4 per cent in 2000 to 12 per cent in 2015 and so did the share of those living on between $1.90 and $3.10 a day (ILO, 2016a; Kapsos and Bourmpoula, 2013). Working poverty remains a deep-seated problem in South Asia and sub-Saharan Africa, where the proportion of working poor remains above 60 per cent, but it has declined quickly in other regions. At the same time, the number and proportion of workers living on between $5 and $13 a day has increased. These trends reflect long-term rises in average labour productivity in all developing regions and suggest some

---

[37]  Informality was estimated in 2013 at 18.8 per cent of GDP in the European Union and at 8.6 per cent on average in Australia, Canada, Japan, New Zealand and the United States (Schneider, 2015).

improvement in average returns to labour, even though wage growth has lagged behind productivity growth. An economic slowdown can, however, reverse these positive trends, particularly since, as shown in section A, workers living near the poverty line and even those living on more than $5 a day, remain at significant risk of falling back into poverty.

In the current context of economic insecurity and increasing job instability, social protection measures should play a key role in reducing vulnerability and preventing a deterioration of living conditions. However, while social protection coverage has expanded significantly during the last decade, only 27 per cent of the working-age population and their families had access to comprehensive social security systems in 2012,[38] according to ILO estimates (ILO, 2014c).

Many developing countries have made efforts to expand the coverage of contributory social insurance schemes, but their reach is still limited. Where they exist, unemployment benefits, old-age pensions and other benefits cover only certain categories of workers in the formal sector, leaving those in the informal economy with no protection at all. Only some 5 per cent of workers in vulnerable employment have access to contributory social protection schemes (ILO, 2016a). Non-contributory schemes or those involving voluntary affiliation have gained in importance and some benefit workers in non-standard forms of employment. Effective coverage gaps, however, continue to limit their reach as well. In 2013, only 53 per cent of legal coverage based on voluntary contributions was effectively implemented (ILO, 2015b).

Growing vulnerability in the world of work has taken place alongside declines in union membership. Even recently, data on bargaining coverage rates from 2008 to 2013 show an average drop of 4.6 per cent in coverage in 48 countries with data (ILO, 2015c). Where coverage has declined, the erosion of bargaining power began well before 2008. In the United States, for instance, private sector union membership declined from 23 per cent of all workers in 1973 to 15 per cent in 1995 and further to about 11 per cent in 2014 (OECD, 2011b, figure I.18; and Visser, 2015). In Germany, the erosion of collective bargaining began after reunification in 1990 and continues today (ILO, 2015c).

In addition, collective bargaining has become decentralized, with the process of negotiation increasingly taking place at the firm level. On average, union members and workers covered by collective bargaining arrangements earn higher wages than their non-unionized counterparts, with the union wage effect being generally greater among less skilled workers than among skilled workers (Blunch and Verner, 2004; Menezes-Filho and others, 2005; Freeman, 2009). However, unions organized around the traditional employer-

---

[38] Comprehensive social security systems cover by law eight areas (sickness, unemployment, old age, employment injury, family responsibilities, maternity, invalidity and survivorship) in line with ILO Convention No. 102 – Social Security (Minimum Standards) Convention, 1952. Health care (the ninth and final area of the Convention) is not included in the estimate for methodological reasons.

employee relationship are not well-suited to give voice to those who do not work for a wage, or who do so outside the formal sector.[39]

The growing incidence of informal and non-standard forms of employment has created momentum for innovative organizations. Associations of self-employed workers or cooperatives – two different types of representative, membership-based organizations – for instance, have improved the terms on which workers in vulnerable employment engage in the labour market and have strengthened their capacity to take collective action (ODI, 2013). Some of these associations often represent members' interests with a particular municipal authority or local government and so more closely resemble social movements than conventional trade unions (World Bank, 2012). Rather than being organized around employment demands, analysis of women's workers organizations shows that they are organized around local priorities (Kabeer, Milward and Sudarshan, 2013). In box II.4, the role that cooperatives and other organizations belonging to the broader and "social and solidarity economy" can play in promoting the rights and interests of traditionally excluded groups is illustrated.

### c. Wages and productivity

Employment growth has taken place alongside a redistribution of income towards capital and away from labour. The share of wages in total gross domestic product (GDP) declined sharply in more than 65 per cent of high-income countries as well as in the majority of middle- and lower-income countries with data, although less steeply from 2000 to 2008 (ILO, 2014a). Thus there is a growing divergence between productivity growth and wage growth. Wage stagnation is likely to harm disproportionately workers in the middle and at the bottom of the income distribution, since they rely mostly on labour income. Furthermore, the wage gap between top and bottom earners has also increased in most countries, mainly owing to an increase in top salaries that is not fully explained by a growing demand for highly skilled workers (United Nations, 2013a). While technological change and, to a certain extent, globalization have contributed to wage inequality, declines in real minimum wages and other changes in labour market policies and institutions account for much of the increase in wage disparities in recent decades (OECD, 2011b).

In many of the developing countries that have experienced growth in labour productivity since the 1990s, such growth has come primarily with a shift away from agriculture to the services sector. The experience of such countries contrasts with that of developed countries and even emerging countries in East and South-East Asia, where structural transformation

---

[39]    There are exceptions. The Uganda Public Employees Union, for instance, expanded its definition of "public employees" so as to widen its membership beyond workers employed in the public sector to anybody working to serve the public (Chen, Vanek and Carr, 2004).

Box II.4

## Social and solidarity economy and its promotion of social inclusion

Included under the concept of the social and solidarity economy (SSE) are cooperatives, self-help groups, service-delivery non-governmental organizations, income-generating activities, consumer groups, fair trade networks, mutual associations, community-based saving schemes, informal workers organizations, community forestry groups, microfinance or solidarity finance institutions and food networks (Utting, 2013). SSE is characterized by diverse forms of cooperative, associative and solidarity relations involving workers, producers and consumers. Solidarity-based economic units rest upon a model of democratic decision-making and a participatory and transparent management system, which is aimed at ensuring collective ownership and responsibility for the outcomes of economic activities.

The cooperative model is a major component within SSE, and it is known globally for its inclusive practices, including voluntary and open membership, democratic member control, member economic participation and concern for community. Globally, cooperatives have more than 1 billion members, employ 12.6 million people and generate $3 trillion in annual revenue.

In Europe, social and solidarity economy enterprises and organizations employ more than 14.5 million people, which is equivalent to about 6.5 per cent of total European paid employment (Ryder, 2013). In India, more than 30 million people (mainly women) participate in self-help groups. The global Fairtrade[a] market employs some 1.2 million workers and farmers producing certified products. Globally, 170 million people are provided with health and social protection services by mutual benefit societies (ILO, 2011a).

SSE has contributed to empowering women and it shows great potential as a way to promote their inclusion. While women hold only 2.6 per cent of leadership positions in the world's top 500 companies, they control 13.6 per cent of those positions in cooperatives and the mutual insurance sector. The Spanish Confederation of Worker Cooperatives noted that 49 per cent of worker cooperative members in Spain are women and 39 per cent have directorial positions compared with 6 per cent in other enterprise models. Similarly, women make up 60 per cent of the cooperative members in South Africa, and 95 per cent of members in consumer cooperatives are women and are in important leadership positions, according to the Intercontinental Network for the Promotion of the Social Solidarity Economy, which is best known by its acronym RIPESS.

In promoting food security and empowering small-scale farm holders, agricultural cooperatives contribute to social inclusion. Smallholders are mostly poor and lack access to finance and markets. Poor farmers or smallholders who are members of cooperatives stand a better chance of getting better prices for their products. Empowerment of smallholders via cooperatives enables them to increase productivity.

The financial sector within SSE is essential in the strategy to promote social inclusion. Globally, financial cooperatives and mutual societies have more than 700 million members and more than 2 million employees, according to RIPESS. These financial enterprises of SSE provide access to affordable services, especially for the poorest segments of the population.

---

[a] "Fairtrade" is an alternative approach to conventional trade and is based on a partnership between producers and consumers. Fairtrade offers consumers a powerful way to reduce poverty through their everyday shopping. When a product carries the Fairtrade Mark it means the producers and traders have met Fairtrade standards. For further information, see www.fairtrade.net/about-fairtrade/what-is-fairtrade.html.

to higher productivity took place with an initial transfer of labour from agriculture to labour-intensive manufacturing. Enabled by the spread of information and communications technology and declining transportation costs, some developing countries have achieved high productivity growth in modern services, such as banking, business services and tourism, as well as in services linked to manufacturing. Several studies indicate that aggregate labour productivity in developing countries has been driven as much by industry as by services since 2000 – or the mid-2000s in the least developed countries – despite strong variations across countries (Roncolato and Kucera, 2014; ILO, 2014d, figure III.7).

It is uncertain whether services-led economic development can be a viable alternative to structural transformation and growth in decent work through manufacturing. Currently, higher shares of manufacturing remain associated with higher income levels in developing countries, although the employment intensity of growth in the manufacturing sector has been affected by the nature of technological progress and the growth of global production systems. Owing to competitive pressures in the global economy, developing countries have imported capital-intensive and skill-intensive forms of technology. However, the services sector remains highly polarized, especially in low-income countries. Low-productivity, informal service jobs continue to expand alongside highly skilled occupations, with the disappearance of medium-skilled jobs further raising the barriers preventing unskilled workers from moving up the social and economic ladder (UNRISD, 2010).

## C. Conclusions

Millions of people have transitioned above the extreme income poverty line of $1.90 per day over the past few decades, alleviating an important dimension of deprivation for those at the low end of the global income distribution. However, the situation of those living in deep poverty has improved little, and many people that previously escaped poverty still remain vulnerable to it. Trends in inequality also suggest that prosperity has not been equitably shared, with inequality within countries often rising. Inequality across social groups constitutes an important component of total inequality, and it does not always evolve at the same pace or respond to the same forces as inequality within groups.

Labour market participation has helped millions of people to escape poverty and has economically empowered women and other disadvantaged groups. In some cases it has promoted the social inclusion of these groups while in others it has reinforced existing divides. Overall, however, economic growth and, more broadly, development have not been sufficiently inclusive, as they have failed to reduce deficits in decent work. Many individuals and families therefore are not able to rely on stable decent jobs as means to cope with risks or to secure their livelihoods. The risk of holding a poorly paid, precarious, insecure job is actually higher today than it was in 1995. Rapid progress in reducing poverty notwithstanding, more than half of the developing world's workers are either poor (living on less than $2 a day) or near poor (living on between $2 and $4 a day). They comprise an enormous proportion of the population in developing countries, a situation which calls into question the notion that jobs – any jobs – are the main solution to poverty. A significant and persistent share of workers remains outside the realm of regulation and has not been adequately represented in social dialogue and consensus-building processes in the world of work. While some informal jobs become stepping stones to formal work and empower those who hold them, particularly women, most trap individuals and groups within a spiral of low productivity and exclusion. Deficits in decent work, in particular among young people, are so significant and large that they raise fears of social instability and put the social contract under threat.

Promoting a more inclusive development path will require reducing such deficits and addressing the current disconnect between labour market regulations and the reality of the world of work. Given the social significance of work as a foundation of social inclusion and personal dignity and as a source of stability and development, political inaction is not a sustainable option.

In recent decades, many countries have undertaken reforms intended to reduce labour protection and lower labour costs. The unbalanced implementation of such reforms, however, has generally resulted in increased inequalities, as some jobs have remained highly protected while others have been made highly flexible. Therefore, an initial step towards creating more and better work for all is to address this segmentation and ensure a more equitable distribution of labour market risks and benefits. Facilitating transitions from informal to formal jobs should be part of this effort. However, given that the world of work is shifting away from the standard employment model of stable, full-time jobs, the main challenge is to ensure adequate protection for workers in all types of employment.

Despite their importance, labour market policies and institutions alone will not bring about the structural transformations that are necessary to promote inclusive development. The main obstacles to the creation of decent work and the reduction of poverty and inequalities lie outside the labour market. In chapter V, the essential elements of a comprehensive policy framework aimed at promoting inclusion will be discussed.

Chapter III

# Who is being left behind? Patterns of social exclusion

## Key messages

- *Factors beyond an individual's skill and effort, such as ethnicity, age, disability status, place of residence or gender, affect access to opportunities, resources and participation in political, civil and cultural life. However, the effect of these characteristics is not uniform across countries. Much depends on the norms, institutions and policies in place.*

- *The disadvantages some groups experience reinforce one another; lower levels of health and education go hand in hand with higher levels of poverty and unemployment, as well as less voice in political and civic life.*

- *The inequalities observed are often rooted in historical circumstances but tend to persist after the structural conditions that created them change.*

- *The degree to which development is leaving some people behind and, consequently, whether development is promoting social inclusion, depends on context as well as on the indicators used to assess progress.*

As is recognized in the 2030 Agenda, attributes such as age, gender, ethnicity, race, and migration and disability status continue to affect the risk of being left behind in both rich and poor countries and preclude the full participation of some groups in society. Yet the risks each of these groups faces does not result in uniform disadvantages across countries: the extent of exclusion and its outcomes depend on the economic, social, political and environmental context, including national and local institutions, norms and attitudes as well as laws and policies in place.

In this chapter, the outcomes of exclusion across countries are examined in respect of the three domains described in chapter I: (a) denial of opportunities, with a focus on disparities in access to education, health care and other basic services; (b) limited access to employment and income; and (c) uneven participation in political and civic life. Owing to data availability issues, cross-country comparisons are often based on data for a limited number of countries and are meant to illustrate concrete aspects of exclusion, as explained in chapter I. Where possible, the analysis highlights examples from both developed and developing countries. It should be noted that lagging behind in education or in access to health services or facing barriers to political participation, alone, cannot be equated with social exclusion. Disadvantages in each of these domains, however, generally reinforce one another: lower levels of health and education go hand in hand with higher levels of poverty and unemployment, as well as less voice in political and civic life. In this report, it is the accumulation of disadvantage across multiple domains among certain social groups that is taken as a symptom of their exclusion.

While the analysis is centred mainly on the disadvantages – or advantages – experienced by youth, older persons, indigenous peoples, ethnic and racial minorities, persons with disabilities and migrants, it is important to recognize that these groups are not homogeneous. In this chapter, it is considered how gender, place of residence and wealth intersect with other group attributes as a way to illustrate heterogeneity. It is also important to note that many other social groups are at risk of exclusion. Those groups that are statistically invisible – that is, omitted from the sample design of household surveys and population censuses – are frequently those at the highest risk of being left behind. It is often when groups gain political recognition and social movements promote the fulfilment of their rights that countries begin to identify them in censuses and surveys.

Based on the data available, the analysis in this chapter shows that, overall, development is not giving all individuals and groups equal opportunities to participate meaningfully in economic, social or political life. Development is leaving some people behind. Unequal access to health, education and other markers of opportunity feeds the vicious cycle of disadvantage and exclusion in which some groups find themselves. The analysis suggests, however, that not all observed disparities in income or participation in the labour market and in political processes can be explained by differences in access to good-quality education or other markers of opportunity across social groups. The chapter concludes with a discussion of the dynamics of disadvantage.

## A.  Denial of opportunities

Education, health care and access to other basic services give people, particularly children, the opportunity to reach their human potential and realize their life goals. Whereas many aspects of high and persistent inequalities polarize political debates across countries, there is clear consensus on the need for education and health care to benefit all people, regardless of their circumstances, that is, for these services to be universally accessible. Health care and education are protected as fundamental human rights and have been reflected in Sustainable Development Goals 3 and 4, which stress the need for universal health coverage and equitable access to good-quality education. Notable improvements in access to these key dimensions of inclusion over the past 20 years have opened avenues for addressing new challenges, such as the quality of education and the transition to secondary school, the increased incidence of years lived with a disability and gaps in access to ICT, particularly broadband Internet. In this section, disparities are described in these key dimensions of opportunity – education, health and access to other basic services – and some of the factors are discussed that have contributed to the exclusion of vulnerable groups from the general improvements seen over the last few decades. Exclusion is reflected both in lack of access to these markers of opportunity as well as in the quality of services received.

## 1. Education

Access to good-quality education provides individuals with opportunities to learn and to realize their potential, building capacity to participate in social, economic, political and cultural life. The adult skills survey of the Organisation for Economic Co-operation and Development (OECD) found that adults with high proficiency in literacy are more likely than those with low proficiency to report being in good health, to believe that they can influence the political process, to participate in volunteer or associative activities and to have high levels of trust in others (OECD, 2013a). The educational system as an institution that imparts norms, values and accepted behaviours to the next generation, however, can also act to reinforce discrimination and perpetuate social exclusion. Even where there are no formal barriers to access or where special measures are in place to foster learning outcomes among disadvantaged groups, educational curricula, school policies and the overall school environment, including interactions among students, teachers, parents and school management staff, can subtly exclude some learners and reproduce existing power structures.

Worldwide, progress in improving school attendance has been notable. The primary school net enrolment ratio is estimated to have reached 93 per cent in 2015, up from 84 per cent in 1999, while the gross secondary school enrolment ratio increased from 71 per cent to 85 per cent between 1995 and 2012, with the vast majority of the gains occurring in developing countries (UNESCO, 2015a).

Despite such progress, 124 million children and young adolescents were estimated to have been out of school worldwide in 2013, including more than 59 million children of primary school age (UNESCO, 2015b). More than half of all out-of-school children live in 19 developing countries, including several countries affected by conflict, according to UNESCO. In addition, there are enduring disparities within both developed and developing countries in school enrolment, completion and learning outcomes based on factors external to a student's inherent capacity to learn. Children with disabilities and those belonging to ethnic or linguistic minorities face unique barriers to accessing opportunities through the educational system. In Europe, for example, at least 10 per cent of Roma children aged 7-15 were not in school in Bulgaria, France, Greece, Italy and Romania in 2011, as compared with less than 5 per cent of non-Roma children (European Union Agency for Fundamental Rights,

2012). Gaps across groups are observed also in early childhood education (see box III.1). Poor-quality education contributes to higher drop-out rates among poor children and those in other disadvantaged minority groups. Even where school fees have been withdrawn and enrolment has increased, drop-out rates have often risen, partly because of increases in average class sizes and pressure on limited school resources (Sabates and others, 2010).

With notable success achieved at the global level in the provision of universal primary education, gaps in school enrolment and completion in secondary school have received increased attention, including in the Sustainable Development Goals. Lower secondary education is part of basic education, widely acknowledged as a minimum requirement for personal and professional development. Upper secondary education is becoming increasingly important for the development of job skills and other attributes necessary to function productively in today's global economy. Yet the barriers to accessing primary education are magnified at secondary school levels. In most countries, disparities in secondary school attendance based on household income and other characteristics are larger than those observed in primary school (United Nations, 2013a), with lower rates of transitioning from primary school to secondary school among certain groups and individuals, as well as higher rates of dropping out and repeating grades at older ages.

Data from eight countries show, for instance, that attendance rates of children with disabilities dropped from primary education to secondary

---

**Box III.1**

**Early childhood education**

The provision of early childhood education (ECE) is widely recognized to contribute substantially to better educational and wider societal outcomes, especially among the most disadvantaged children and communities (OECD, 2013b). Since 2000, considerable progress has been made in increasing the number of children enrolled in pre-primary schools worldwide. However, children living in poverty and in rural areas – who could benefit most from ECE – are systematically less likely to participate in ECE programmes, even in countries where most children attend an early learning programme (UNICEF, 2016; UNESCO, 2015a).

Important disparities in ECE access by ethnicity, race, indigenous status and immigrant status are also present in both developed and developing regions. In Europe, the proportions of children aged 3-4 years who attended ECE programmes were 6-8 times higher nationally than among Roma groups in Bosnia and Herzegovina, Serbia and the former Yugoslav Republic of Macedonia (UNICEF, 2014). Similarly, in the late 2000s in Ecuador, the enrolment rate in pre-primary schools was only 50 per cent for indigenous children compared with close to 70 per cent for children of African descent and close to 80 per cent for children who were not of indigenous or of African descent (Vegas and Santibáñez, 2010).

A key factor driving these disparities is that many countries have not yet incorporated early childhood education into public school systems. As a result, nearly a third of all children enrolled at the pre-primary level attended private institutions; thus, the expansion of ECE has been driven in part by those families and households that can afford it (UNESCO, 2015a).

education by 8-10 percentage points (Filmer, 2008).[40] Similarly, children and youth from indigenous and other ethnic minority groups are less likely than their non-indigenous and ethnic majority peers to complete lower secondary school. Children from linguistic minorities frequently face the challenge of instruction in a language that is not their own. It is estimated that as much as 40 per cent of the world's population does not have access to education in a language they speak or understand (UNESCO, 2016).

Children in these groups also often suffer from multiple disadvantages that are mutually reinforcing: for instance, living in rural areas continues to have a negative impact on school enrolment and educational achievement, and indigenous peoples as well as other ethnic minorities in many developing countries live predominantly in rural areas (Hall and Patrinos, 2012; UNESCO, 2015a). According to figure III.1, not only do children in rural areas fare worse than those in urban areas in terms of school completion, but the educational disadvantage suffered by indigenous children and children in ethnic minority groups is also at times larger in rural than in urban areas. In Belize, for instance, the percentage of *mestizo* children completing lower secondary school is two-thirds that of Creole children in rural areas, as compared with nearly 90 per cent in urban areas. In the former Yugoslav Republic of Macedonia, the percentage of Albanian children completing this level of schooling is less than 75 per cent that of Macedonian children in rural areas but close to 90 per cent in rural areas. Thus, the interaction of ethnicity and rural residence can produce a stronger effect on lower secondary school completion than each factor separately. In contrast, in Guatemala disparities between non-indigenous and the most disadvantaged indigenous children are larger in urban than in rural areas.

Research in Latin America indicates that the leading reasons for lower participation of indigenous peoples in secondary and post-secondary education include high rates of poverty, child and adolescent labour, distance to schools, particularly in rural areas, the low quality of educational facilities to which they have access, and discrimination (ECLAC, 2015). However, a study of eight countries in the same region suggests significant progress in increasing the school attendance of indigenous children between 2000 and 2010, particularly among children of secondary school age (ECLAC, 2015, figure I.9).

Likewise, gender gaps in enrolment are wide and girls' dropout rates are high in secondary school despite the significant progress made in increasing girls' primary school education. In countries where gender disparities in educational attainment still exist, they usually intersect with other disparities in education, such as those based on wealth, place of residence and race or ethnicity. Data from the World Inequality Database on Education show that gender gaps in attainment are generally found among the poorest families, in

---

[40]    The eight countries included in the study are Colombia, India, Indonesia, Jamaica, Mongolia, Mozambique, Romania and South Africa.

Figure III.1

**Percentage of youth who completed lower secondary education, by ethnicity and area of residence in selected countries, latest available data since 2011**

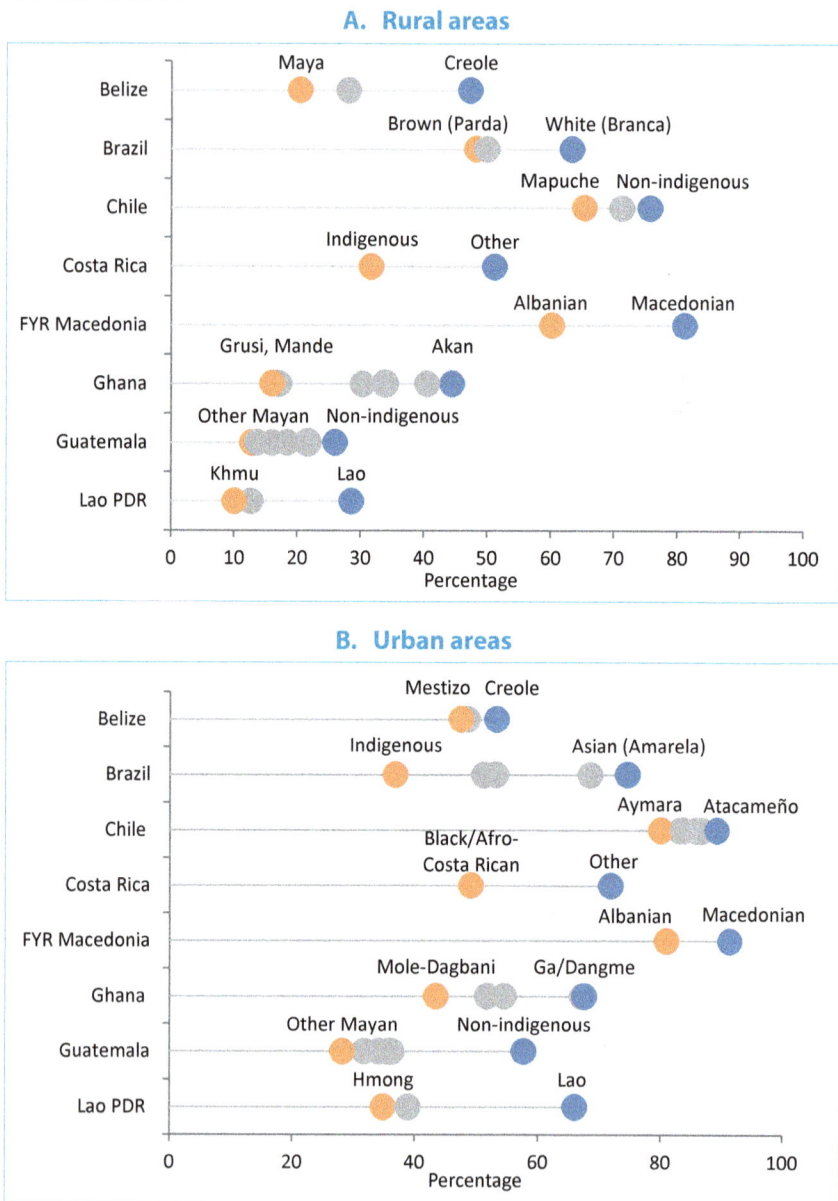

### A. Rural areas

### B. Urban areas

*Source:* World Inequality Database on Education, UNESCO. Available from www.education-inequalities.org (accessed on 21 September 2016)
**Note:** Data are displayed for countries with information from 2011 and later, and where samples of each racial and ethnic group numbered 100 or larger.

rural areas and among indigenous or ethnic minority groups.[41] In Pakistan in 2012 for instance, the proportion of youth (15-24 years of age) who completed lower secondary school was slightly more than 80 per cent for both females and males in the richest families, but much lower among the poorest families, where just 4 per cent of females and 19 per cent of males completed lower secondary education. Similarly, based on data from DHS, the interaction between ethnicity and place of residence explains from 12 per cent (Zimbabwe) to 40 per cent (Plurinational State of Bolivia) of the total inequality in women's educational attainment (Lenhardt and Samman, 2015).

Beyond school enrolment and completion, the effective acquisition of relevant knowledge and skills – that is, the quality of education – is a key determinant of future opportunities. Research on OECD countries indicates that improvements in learning outcomes, as measured by the Programme for International Student Assessment (PISA) and other international tests, are associated with high economic returns (OECD, 2010). Across OECD countries, in 2012 students from an immigrant background on average scored 34 points lower in the PISA mathematics examination than students with a non-immigrant background.[42] The educational achievement gap between immigrant and non-immigrant students is still significant when controlling for their families' socioeconomic status, although it declined to 21 points (OECD, 2013c).[43] In other words, immigrant children are penalized academically by their socioeconomic background, but migrant status also has a net effect on their achievement.

Despite persisting inequalities, the evidence available suggests some progress in ensuring equitable access to good-quality education. For instance, the variation in student performance in mathematics by socioeconomic status declined slightly, from 17 per cent in 2003 to 15 per cent in 2012, in the countries covered by the PISA programme, while the immigrant-non-immigrant gap narrowed by 10 percentage points during the same period (OECD, 2013c). In Latin America, periodic assessment studies indicate that the rural-urban gap in academic proficiency declined as mean achievement increased from 2006 to 2013 in all but three countries (UNESCO, 2015a).

---

[41]    UNESCO, World Inequality Database on Education. Available from www.education-inequalities. org (accessed on 21 September 2016).

[42]    PISA is an ongoing programme and tool of OECD that helps assess 15-year-old students' acquisition of knowledge and skills in mathematics, science and reading across high- and medium-income countries. In the PISA 2012 round, 65 countries and economies participated in the examination, including 34 OECD member countries and 31 partner countries and economies in Asia, Eastern Europe and Latin America.

[43]    In the context of PISA assessments, OECD measures socioeconomic status (or social, economic and cultural status) on the basis of indicators of parental education and occupation, the number and type of home possessions that are considered proxies for wealth, and the educational resources available at home (OECD, 2013c, box II.2.1). See also https://stats.oecd.org/glossary/detail.asp?ID=5401.

Given the importance of a student's peers as well as the stigma associated with schools in disadvantaged neighbourhoods, more equitable learning opportunities may come about by reducing socioeconomic and other types of segregation in schools and neighbourhoods. Yet OECD data suggest little progress has been made from 2003 to 2012 in promoting greater integration in schools (OECD, 2013c). In box III.2, some of the research to date is discussed in terms of the effect of neighbourhood and school environments on educational outcomes.

The persistent exclusion of some children and youth from the educational system, combined with global trends in youth unemployment and changing labour markets due to technological advancement, highlight the importance of inclusive and equitable-quality education and lifelong learning opportunities for all. Such education is essential for ensuring that youth obtain not only basic skills, but also livelihood skills to support the transition from school to work. While there are limited comparable data on the role of technical and vocational education and training in supporting the transition from school to work, the existing data for low and middle-income countries show that few youth have participated in job-related skills training, and those who have are highly educated, suggesting that those who may need this type of training are least likely to participate in it (Valerio and others, 2014).[44]

## 2. Health

Health is both an input to and a desirable outcome of sustainable development. Significant progress in health outcomes has been achieved in past decades in terms of both lowering illness and mortality levels. Worldwide, life expectancy at birth increased from 47 years in the period 1950-1955 to 65 years in that of 1990-1995, and reached 70 years in the period 2010-2015.[45] Additionally, under-five mortality rates fell rapidly, declining by 44 per cent at the global level from 2000 to 2015; nevertheless, an estimated 5.9 million children under the age of 5 died in 2015 (United Nations, 2016b).

Not all individuals and groups have benefited equally from advances in health care, however; the result has been large numbers of preventable deaths and illnesses. Health inequalities between social groups have evolved differently across countries, regions and by group. By way of example, figure III.2 shows recent trends in the proportion of children stunted (having low

[44] Findings in Valerio and others (2014) are from the World Bank's STEP Skills Measurement Program (STEP), an initiative to measure skills in low- and middle-income countries. The programme currently has data from Armenia, Azerbaijan, the Plurinational State of Bolivia, Colombia, Georgia, Ghana, the Lao People's Democratic Republic, Sri Lanka, the former Yugoslav Republic of Macedonia, Ukraine, Viet Nam and Yunnan Province of China.

[45] Data from the United Nations Population Division. Available from: https://esa.un.org/unpd/wpp/ (accessed on April 2016).

---

Box III.2

## The geography of opportunities: residential segregation and educational outcomes

The social composition of the schools or neighbourhoods where children are raised has a significant impact on their development and livelihoods. Growing up in a disadvantaged neighbourhood has been shown to affect educational outcomes negatively because of social, cultural and linguistic isolation, scarce institutional resources – including poorly funded and often underperforming schools – environmental health hazards and stress as a result of violence and crime.

It has been found in a large body of literature that, while the socioeconomic characteristics of students and their families have a large impact on educational outcomes, the effect of neighbourhood and school characteristics cannot be ignored, particularly for children in poor households. Educational outcomes are often better in more well-off neighbourhoods and schools, independent of the socioeconomic status of a student's family.[a] In Montevideo, improvements in the socioeconomic status of a neighbourhood resulted in corresponding improvements in public school students' composite scores on mathematics and native language examinations, even when holding constant socioeconomic characteristics of each student's household. Nearly a third of variability in test scores could be attributed to the socioeconomic composition of the school that children attended or the neighbourhood where they resided (Kaztman and Retamoso, 2007).

In the United States, experimental groups of households with children living in poverty-stricken areas were randomly selected from five cities (Baltimore, Boston, Chicago, Los Angeles and New York) and assigned to a treatment group where families received counselling as well as public assistance to access housing in areas with less than 10 per cent of poverty. Evaluations of the programme have provided various insights into the interplay between individual characteristics and the characteristics of neighbourhoods, and how these interact to influence outcomes. Chetty, Hendren and Katz (2016) found that children younger than 13 whose families moved away from very low-income areas through participation in the experiment achieved better educational and economic outcomes in the long run than their peers who did not move. On average, these children were 16 per cent more likely to attend college or university, and as adults their incomes were 31 per cent higher than those children whose families were assigned to the control group (Chetty, Hendren and Katz, 2016). Children older than 13 actually fared slightly worse than the control group, however. Those researchers reasoned that the disruptive effects of the move among this group, such as a loss of social networks, outweighed the benefits of moving. Furthermore, the experiment not only reduced the effects of neighbourhood poverty on children in the treatment group but also led to an intergenerational reduction in the exposure to spatial concentrations of poverty. As adults, these children were more likely to live in areas with lower poverty rates, higher mean incomes, less racial segregation and a lower share of female-headed households.

While the mechanisms that create residential segregation are not entirely clear, the study of neighbourhood effects has provided evidence that the characteristics of where families live represent an important factor in the improvement or deterioration of their material conditions, in what can be referred to as the "geography of metropolitan opportunity" (Galster and Killen, 1998).

[a] See, for instance, Brännström (2008) for Sweden; Chetty, Hendren and Katz (2016) and Jencks and Mayer (1990) for the United States; Kaztman and Retamoso (2007) for Uruguay; Kauppinen (2007) for Finland; and Montgomery and Hewett (2005) for health outcomes in developing countries.

height for age) by ethnic group in three developing countries.[46] Slow growth in height in early life, a strong indicator of poor nutrition and reduced health, has long-term effects on cognitive development, educational performance and economic outcomes (Victora and others, 2008).

Ghana has made great strides in improving child health in the last two decades. The country has achieved improvements in health-care coverage and declines in socioeconomic disparities in access to key interventions along the continuum of care.[47] As shown in panel A of figure III.2, for children in the three ethnic groups that were lagging behind in terms of their stunting levels at the start of the period in 1998, their situation improved remarkably from 1998 to 2008 – stunting declined by 4.2 per cent annually among these groups but only by 0.9 per cent in total. Despite continued progress, however, those same three ethnic groups experienced little relative improvement from 2008 to 2014. In Mali (panel B), stunting declined more slowly among children in the three ethnic groups that were faring worse in the first year of observation than among the rest of the population, that is, children in these groups were relatively worse off at the end of the period – they were being left behind. In Peru, rapid progress in improving child health has masked significant variation across regions, socioeconomic groups and ethnic communities. The prevalence of stunting was more than twice as high among children in the poorest indigenous group, the Quechua people, compared with children in Spanish-speaking households in both 2000 and 2012 (panel C). However, for indigenous children their situation improved more than Spanish-speaking children on average from 2000 to 2012. The stunting rate fell by more than 20 percentage points among Quechua children during the period as well as among Aymara children from 2007/08 to 2012 alone, partly as a result of increased government and international efforts to reverse decades of marginalization of communities in remote Andean regions, particularly through increased spending on the quality and coverage of health services as well as through targeted anti-poverty initiatives (Huicho and others, 2016). Thus, on the basis of this indicator alone, development was inclusive of minority ethnic groups in Peru during this period.

As in education, persistent health disparities linked to income, ethnicity or race often intersect with exclusion based on area of residence or the sex of the persons concerned, even in countries with comprehensive health-care systems. While higher income often leads to higher life expectancy, Chetty

---

[46]   These three countries were selected because data on ethnicity are available from three successive surveys and because inequality trends in stunting and other indicators differ across them. In all three cases, sample sizes for all ethnic groups shown number at least 200. These countries are highlighted for illustrative purposes only.

[47]   See Countdown to 2030, Maternal, Newborn and Child Survival. Available from www. countdown2015mnch.org/country-profiles/ghana. In particular, see  Ghana Health Data-2015 Equity Profile (accessed on 9 March 2016).

and others (2016) found that, in the United States, longevity varies much more geographically among individuals in the lowest income quartile, even when adjusting for race and ethnicity, than among individuals at the top of the income distribution. In other words, area of residence disproportionately affects individuals at the bottom of the income distribution.

Global decreases in premature mortality have been accompanied by an increase in the number of years a person lives with illness or disease, with a disproportionate share of years lived with a disability being found among disadvantaged individuals and social groups. Measures that take into account

## Figure III.2

### Recent trends in the proportion of children stunted, by ethnic group in selected countries

#### A.  Ghana, 1998-2014

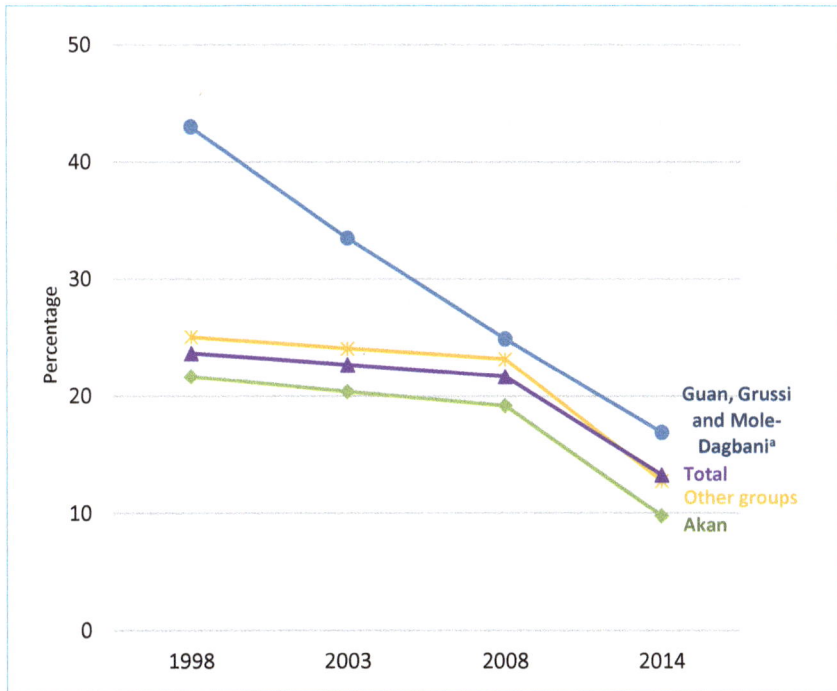

*Source:* Calculations are based on data from Demographic and Health Surveys (DHSs).

**Note:** Ethnic minorities have been grouped based exclusively on the prevalence of stunting in the starting year (1998), according to DHSs. Samples for all groupings number at least 200. A child is considered stunted if (s)he is below minus two standard deviations from the median height-for-age of the World Health Organization Child Growth Standards.

[a] Annual change (1998-2008) among Guan, Grussi and and Mole-Dagbani groups combined: -4.2 per cent. Annual change (1998-2008) among the total population: -0.9 per cent.  Annual change (2008-2014): Guan, Grussi and Mole-Dagbani: -3.2 per cent. Annual change (2008-2014) among the total population: -3.9 per cent.

## B. Mali, 2001-2012/13

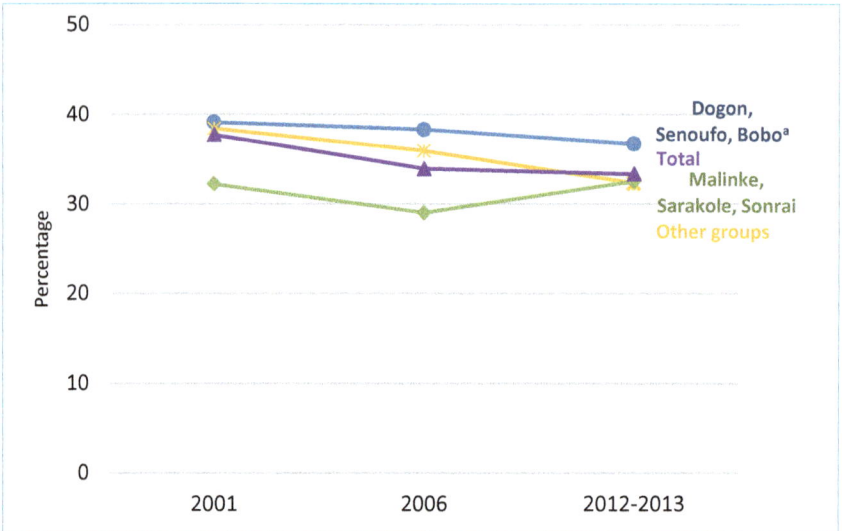

Source:_ Calculations are based on data from Demographic and Health Surveys (DHSs).
**Note:** Ethnic minorities have been grouped based exclusively on the prevalence of stunting in the starting year (2001), according to DHSs. Samples for all groupings number at least 200.
[a] Annual change (2001-2012/13) among Dogon, Senoufo and Bobo groups combined: -0.5 per cent. Annual change (2001-2012/13) among the total population: -1.0 per cent.

## C. Peru, 2000-2014

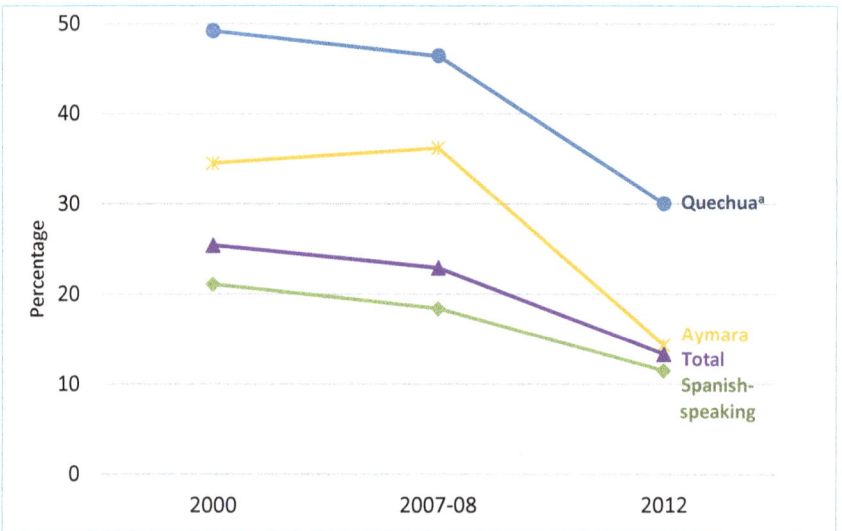

_Source:_ Calculations are based on data from Demographic and Health Surveys (DHSs).
[a] Annual change (2000-2012) among the Quechua people: -.4.0 per cent; the Aymara people: -4.9 per cent; and the Spanish-speaking population: -3.8 per cent.

mortality, illness and functioning simultaneously, such as health-adjusted life expectancy (HALE), tend to show wider gaps based on socioeconomic status, race and ethnicity than life expectancy does (Crimmins and Hagedorn, 2010). In China, for instance, men of higher socioeconomic status can expect to live 20-37 per cent longer than men of lower socioeconomic status, whereas their healthy life expectancy ranges from 30 to 77 per cent longer than that of men of lower socioeconomic status (Kaneda, Zimmer and Tang, 2005). Similar results have been found in Brazil, where a 20-year-old woman residing in a Rio de Janeiro slum may expect to live a healthy life of 37.1 years, whereas a woman of the same age residing in a wealthy neighbourhood could expect to live 56.2 years in good health (Landmann and others, 2011). These inequalities are due to many factors, including the environment in which people live, individual lifestyles and behaviours and, most prominently, disparities in access to good-quality health-care services.

### 3. Other basic services

The improvements in health and mortality over the last century came about in large part thanks to improvements in basic infrastructure and services. Basic infrastructure – roads, water and sanitation, energy, broadband and other telecommunication infrastructure – facilitates access to health and education services, as well as to jobs, and is therefore essential for reducing poverty, inequality and exclusion. Investment in improved water supply and sanitation in particular can generate high returns, as it helps prevent malnutrition and disease and ultimately promotes productivity. Indeed, inadequate infrastructure and inequalities in access to water supply and sanitation lead to poor hygiene and preventable infectious diseases, such as diarrhoea, that cause the death of millions of people, mostly children, every year.

As in child health, progress in reducing inequalities in access to infrastructure across groups varies significantly across countries. Figure III.3 shows recent trends in the proportion of rural women in households with access to electricity – one of the indicators for target 7.1 of the Sustainable Development Goals on access to modern energy services – by ethnic group in the three developing countries highlighted in the previous section. In Ghana, rural women in the most deprived ethnic groups are being left behind in terms of access of electricity (panel A of figure III.3). Access increased by 1.6 per cent annually in the period 1998-2014 among the most deprived groups, while it grew by 2.6 per cent in 1998 among those who were already better off. Success in reducing disparities in child health in Ghana is not mirrored in inclusive improvements in access to electricity. In Mali, the same ethnic groups that lagged behind in child health at the national level are being left behind in rural areas in terms of access to electricity (panel B). In Peru (panel C), where levels of electrification are higher, indigenous women have benefited more than Spanish-speaking women from its expansion in rural areas since 2000, partly an outcome of the Government's efforts to promote inclusion (Ministerio de Energía y Minas, República del Perú, 2011).

Regarding access to ICTs, in recent years rapid technological innovation has allowed for a significant expansion of broadband connections and growth in the use of mobile communications to do business, create new livelihoods, improve productivity and promote development. It is estimated that the number of mobile phone owners now surpasses the number of those who have access to electricity or clean water (World Bank, 2016). Growing access to ICTs has also been crucial in enabling participation, giving individuals and groups the ability to voice their opinions and helping them organize around common causes and across geographical boundaries. The potential of ICTs is particularly broad for youth, who are already using social media in significant numbers to connect, share and inspire others.

Figure III.3

**Recent trends in the proportion of rural women in households with access to electricity, by ethnic group in selected countries**

### A. Ghana, 1998-2014

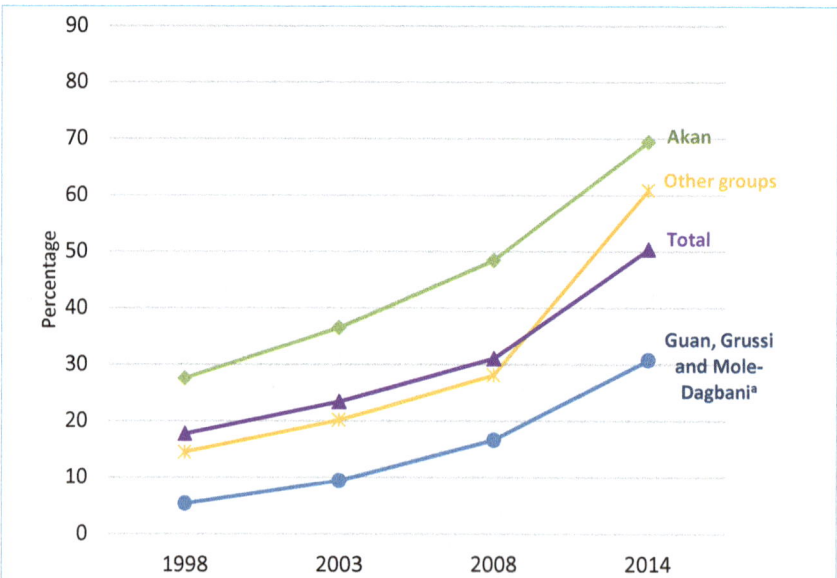

*Source:* Calculations are based on data from Demographic and Health Surveys (DHSs).
**Note:** The data cover women of reproductive age (15-49 years). Ethnic minorities have been grouped based exclusively on access to electricity in the starting year (1998), according to DHSs. Samples for all groupings number at least 200.
[a] Annual change (1998-2014) among Guan, Grussi and Mole-Dagbani groups combined: 1.6 per cent. Annual change (1998-2014) among the Akan group: 2.6 per cent. Annual change (1998-2014) among the total population: 2.0 per cent.

## B.  Mali, 2001-2012/13

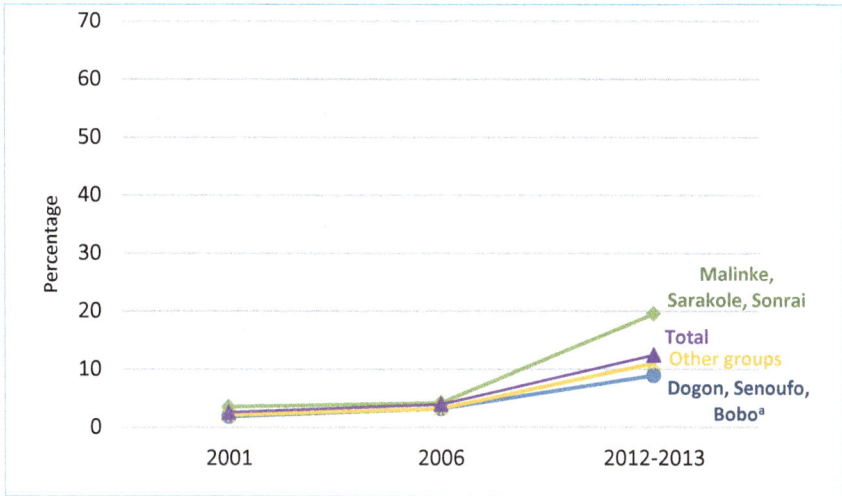

*Source:* Calculations are based on data from Demographic and Health Surveys (DHSs).
**Note:** Ethnic minorities have been grouped based exclusively on access to electricity in the starting year (2001), according to DHSs. Samples for all groupings number at least 200.
[a] Annual change (2001-2012/13) among Dogon, Senoufo and Bobo groups combined: 0.6 per cent. Annual change (2001-2012/13) among Malinke, Sarakole and Sonrai groups combined: 1.4 per cent. Annual change (2001-2012/13) among the total population: 0.9 per cent.

## C.  Peru, 2000-2012

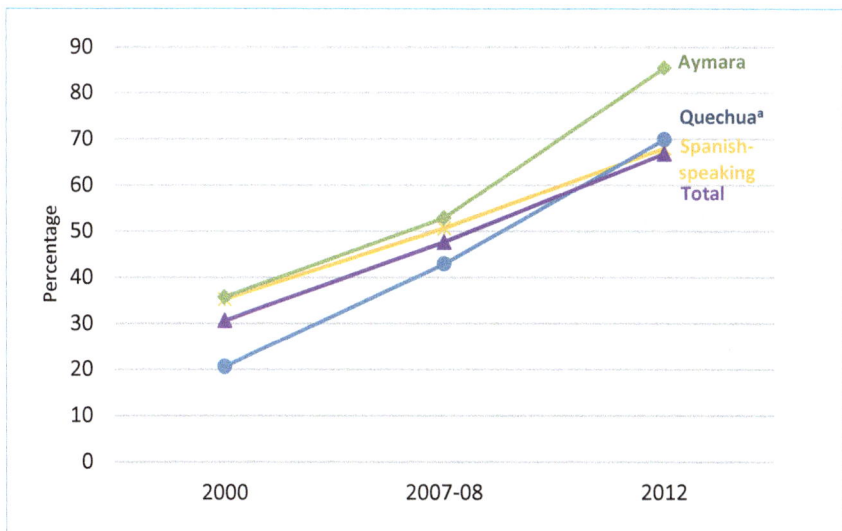

*Source:* Calculations are based on data from Demographic and Health Surveys (DHSs).
[a] Annual change (2000-2012) among the Quechua people: 4.1 per cent; the Aymara people: 4.1 per cent; and Spanish-speaking population: 2.7 per cent.

Yet significant disparities in ICT access and skills limit the benefits ICTs offer certain groups. In Africa for instance, the percentage of individuals who use the Internet differs significantly by household wealth, age, area of residence and sex (World Bank, 2016). Disparities in connectivity are associated with significant disparities in the skills and capability to use ICTs, threatening to widen inequality and reinforce exclusion of certain individuals and groups. Indeed, evidence suggests a high return to ICT skills among workers in 19 countries, yet these returns are understandably highest in jobs that rely heavily on ICT skills (Falck, Heimisch and Wiederhold, 2015). Returns to education are also higher in jobs that rely heavily on ICT skills. Thus, the continuing spread of ICTs, particularly in the workplace, threatens to exacerbate inequality if educational systems cannot impart the knowledge and skills needed in an increasingly digital world (World Bank, 2016).

## 4. Conclusions

Education, health and other basic services are key determinants of opportunity and well-being throughout the life course. Despite broad progress in school enrolment, learning outcomes, child health, a healthy life expectancy and access to electricity and ICTs, population censuses and household survey data show significant disparities across social groups in all these indicators. Often, it is individuals and groups that face multiple disadvantages who are left further behind from access. Although the evidence reviewed shows some encouraging trends, it also suggests that progress in reducing disparities in one indicator is not necessarily echoed by progress in other indicators of opportunity. In describing disparities in employment and in the prevalence of poverty, the next section illustrates how access to education and other markers of opportunity affects the labour market situation and the income of different social groups.

## B. Unequal income-generating prospects

Labour earnings, savings and other productive assets provide the means to withstand shocks and are key to people's empowerment. Unequal access to such assets is both a symptom of exclusion and is likely to generate further exclusion among current and future generations. Lack of decent work opportunities, in particular, curtails access to social protection systems, social services and social networks, and therefore increases the risk of long-term exclusion.

In this section, there is a description of barriers to full and productive employment and decent work for all, including disparities in labour market participation and employment opportunities, and of the role that human capital and other opportunity gaps play in explaining these disparities.

The section also contains an examination of the impact of these gaps on the prevalence of income poverty.

## 1. Labour market participation and employment opportunities

As discussed in chapter II, labour is the main and only productive resource at hand for many people, particularly those living in poverty. There is little point in denying the fact that access to decent and productive jobs is the most effective means of reducing poverty and is a key foundation of social inclusion. Yet labour market inequalities persist and are, in some cases, growing. Indigenous peoples, members of other ethnic minorities and international migrants, for instance, receive lower wages than the rest of the population, as do women, who on average earn between 10 and 30 per cent less than men when working full time (United Nations, 2015a; Hall and Patrinos, 2012; OECD, 2015a). Youth unemployment is almost three times as high as adult unemployment (ILO, 2016c). In the European Union, about 65 per cent of Roma aged 16 or older are currently unemployed or have been without a regular paid job during the last five years, as compared with 29 per cent of non-Roma living nearby (European Union Agency for Fundamental Rights, 2012).

This section illustrates that such inequalities are not simply due to differences in education and skills among workers. The labour market continues to make socially driven distinctions based on ethnicity, race, caste, sex, age and other personal attributes that should have no bearing on job opportunities or workers' competencies or ability.

The exclusion of youth from the labour market is of particular concern because of its long-term effect on well-being as well as its impact on social cohesion and stability. For every young person, a decent job is an important step to completing the transition to adulthood and a milestone towards achieving independence and self-reliance. According to ILO, which estimates that more than 40 per cent of the world's active youth are either unemployed or working but living in poverty, the financial and economic crisis of 2008 has led to a "lost generation" of young people who have lost all hope of being able to work for a decent living. Not only do unemployment and underemployment affect young people's material, physical and mental well-being, they also hamper their future economic opportunities. Research shows that joblessness among youth is associated with lower wages and lower labour market participation later in life (Székely and Karver, 2015; Bell and Blanchflower, 2011). It also leaves marks in the form of young people's distrust in the political, social and economic systems. Protests and other expressions of social unrest have indeed been particularly acute in countries and regions where youth unemployment is widespread or has been rising quickly in the last decade (ILO, 2013a and 2016c). Specifically, since the 2008 crisis youth unemployment has been stubbornly high in Western Asia and Northern Africa, particularly among highly educated youth, as well as in Southern Europe, reaching record-high levels in such countries as Greece, Italy and Spain; in Greece the proportion of unemployed youth stood at 52 per cent in May 2015.[48]

High and growing youth unemployment rates are coupled with longer job searches and with a surge in the number of discouraged young workers who are not counted among the unemployed because they are not actively seeking employment and are therefore at high risk of long-term labour market and overall social exclusion. While some of these discouraged youth may have returned to the education system due to poor job prospects during the crisis, the number of youth who are neither in employment nor in education or training (NEET) increased during the crisis, and remain stubbornly high. In OECD countries alone, almost 39 million young people (15.5 per cent of all youth) were neither working nor in education or training in 2013.[49] The estimated percentage was higher in Latin America (20 per cent) in 2011 (ILO, 2013c). Data for Brazil highlight the gender and racial dimensions of this predicament: 14 per cent of young men were not in education or in paid employment in 2013 as compared with one in every four young women (ECLAC, 2015). However, the percentage of NEETs went up to 30 per cent among young women of African descent (ECLAC, 2015).

Beyond the discouragement brought about by lack of youth employment opportunities, expanding educational prospects have also contributed to a long-term decline in labour force participation rates among young women and men. Thus lowering participation rates are not necessarily a cause or a symptom of growing exclusion among youth. In fact, high labour market participation among adolescents in sub-Saharan Africa and Asia strongly curtails their future economic prospects (ILO, 2015a). However, the persistent gender gap in participation rates among youth does indicate that, for young women, low participation is not only due to rising education but also to their disproportionate burden in performing unpaid tasks, such as housework and care of family members, and to other sociocultural factors that keep them excluded from completing their education and engaging in paid work (UNRISD, 2010; ILO, 2015a).

Labour market exclusion is also stark among persons with disabilities, who may be employed but unable to fully use their human capital, may not be able to find jobs due to a wide range of barriers or may have left the labour force in the face of a lack of opportunities. Census data estimates indicate that the labour force participation rate of persons with disabilities is 20 percentage points below that of the rest of the population on average in the 27 countries

---

[48]     Eurostat database. Available from http://ec.europa.eu/eurostat/data/database.

[49]     OECD Data. Available from https://data.oecd.org/youthinac/youth-not-in-education-or-employment-neet.htm.

shown in figure III.4.[50] Persons with mental health difficulties or intellectual impairments often have the lowest employment rates (WHO and World Bank, 2011).

While lower participation rates among persons with disabilities are to be expected, as their impairment may prevent them from performing certain tasks or limit the amount of work they can do, the existing evidence suggests that their potential has been largely unfulfilled. Persons with disabilities face physical barriers in accessing education as well as the workplace, especially in their daily travel. Moreover, there are misconceptions among employers and society at large about the ability of persons with disabilities to work and about their potential productivity, as well as open discrimination. Studies in developed countries show that, when employed, persons with disabilities earn less than workers without disabilities who demonstrate similar productivity, for instance (Jones, 2008; Burchardt, 2000; Statistics New Zealand, 2014). A study of the economic losses associated with the gap between the potential and actual productivity of persons with disabilities – diminished by such aspects as lack of adequate transport and physical accessibility, and lower education – puts such losses between 3 and 7 per cent of GDP in the 10 low- and middle-income countries covered (Buckup, 2009). In addition to these losses are those incurred by family members with caretaking responsibilities, particularly in countries lacking comprehensive social protection systems.

Unemployment and inactivity do not fully reflect the scope and nature of the employment challenge among youth, persons with disabilities and other disadvantaged groups. In contexts of high levels of poverty or where social protection systems are lacking, most workers cannot afford to stay unemployed. Differences in employment status as well as those in occupational level give additional insight into the disadvantages faced by youth and other social groups. Regarding employment status, youth work without pay as contributing family workers more often than adults do (figure III.5), as do individuals of all ages self-reportedly belonging to an indigenous group in the Latin American countries shown in figure III.6.[51] Unpaid workers, who are most often employed in small family-owned farms but are increasingly present in non-farm house-

---

[50]   The labour force participation rate of persons with disabilities is significantly below that of persons without disabilities in all countries shown except for Cambodia, Kenya, Liberia, Malawi and Mali, where differences in participation between the two groups are not significant. In general, participation rates of persons with disabilities are relatively higher in poorer countries – relative to participation rates of persons without disabilities – where social protection systems are lacking, as many people, including those with disabilities, cannot afford not to work.

[51]   Unpaid workers are persons who work without pay in an economic enterprise, most often operated by a related person living in the same household. Unpaid workers are therefore in the labour market and should not be confounded with individuals performing unpaid work outside the labour market in activities that, although productive, are not included in the System of National Accounts production boundary. Information on unpaid work outside the labour market is often collected in time-use surveys. For an analysis of gender aspects of unpaid work, see United Nations (2015a).

Figure III.4

**Labour force participation, by disability status in selected countries and areas, latest available data since 2000**

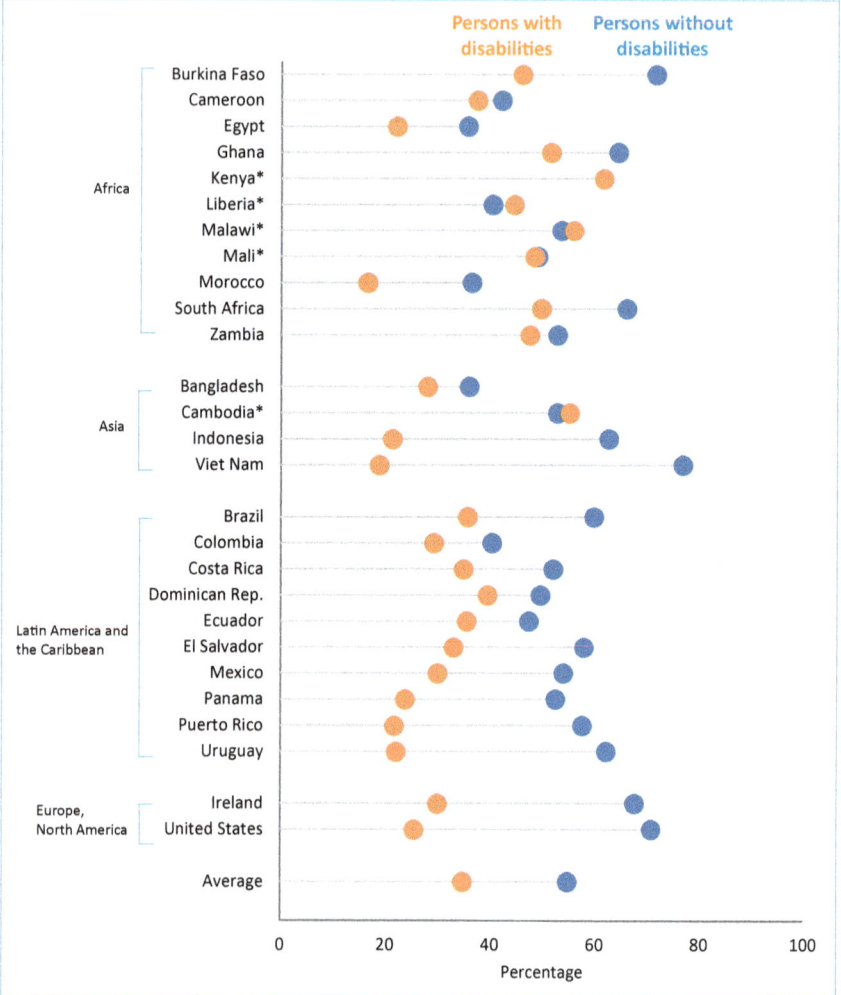

*Source:* Calculations are based on census data from the Minnesota Population Center (2015)
**Note:** The figure shows data from the most recent national population census of each country or area shown (2000 or 2010 round), as collected by national statistical offices, containing data on labour force participation and disability status, and available from the Minnesota Population Center repository. Census questions on disability differ among countries and areas, and there are likely to be cultural interpretations of disability that cause differences in response rates as well. In addition, some census questionnaires explicitly state that only permanent conditions are to be considered as disabilities. Where samples provide several degrees of difficulty in carrying on daily tasks, the Minnesota Population Center repository applies the threshold of "significant" or "severe" difficulty to define disability. While the percentage of persons reporting a disability may differ across census samples, disability data are used here mainly to compare persons with disabilities, however defined, with persons without disabilities within each country or area shown.

* Differences in the participation rate are not significant at the p<0.001 level.

Figure III.5

## Share of workers in unpaid jobs, by age and region, latest available data since 2000

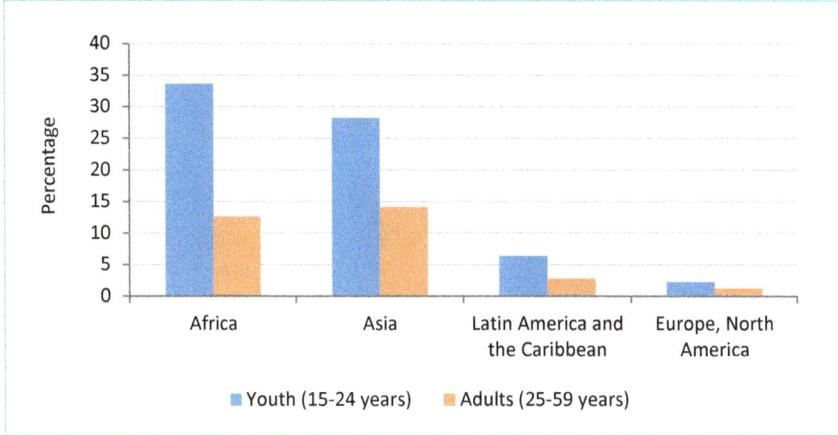

*Source:* Calculations are based on census data from the Minnesota Population Center (2015)
**Note:** Weighted regional averages are based on data from the most recent population census of 15 countries in Africa, 12 in Asia, 15 in Latin America and the Caribbean and 11 developed countries as collected by national statistical offices and available from the Minnesota Population Center repository.
Workers are classified according to the International Classification by Status in Employment (ISCE-93) system as employees, employers, own-account workers, members of cooperatives, unpaid family workers and non-classifiable workers.

hold enterprises, have scarce opportunities to organize collectively or to voice their concerns, little ability to accumulate savings and assets as well as limited access to social protection and are, therefore, at high risk of poverty.

Regarding occupation, even though the skill composition of the workforce varies greatly by country, the share of ethnic or racial minority workers in managerial, professional and technical occupations is consistently lower than that of non-indigenous workers, as is the share of persons of African descent and of mixed race, as compared with whites in the countries shown in annex figures A.III.1 and A.III.2. Many of the labour market disadvantages observed stem from the opportunity gaps described in section A, particularly in terms of access to good-quality education. For some groups, namely indigenous peoples and some ethnic minorities, employment opportunities are also curtailed by spatial disadvantages, as they live more often in rural, remote areas characterized by poor infrastructure and little access to off-farm work (Hall and Patrinos, 2012).

Most of the occupational differences observed among ethnic groups, however, persist once the effects of educational attainment and other sociodemographic characteristics are accounted for. By way of example, the results of a logistic regression model shown in table III.1 indicate that,

Figure III.6

**Share of workers in unpaid jobs, by indigenous status in selected countries in Latin America, latest available data since 2000**

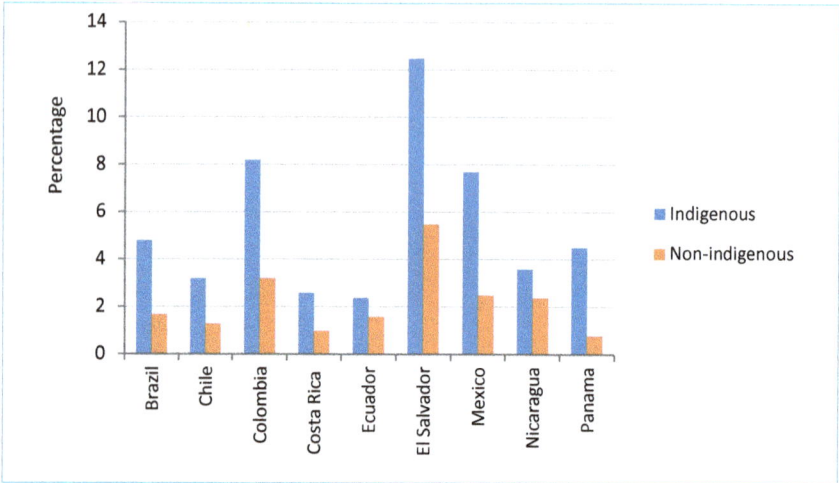

*Source:* Calculations are based on census data from the Minnesota Population Center (2015)
**Note:** Data are from the most recent population census (2000 or 2010 round) containing data by indigenous status and employment status, as collected by national statistical offices and available from the Minnesota Population Census repository.
Workers are classified according to the International Classification by Status in Employment (ISCE-93) system as employees, employers, own-account workers, members of producers' cooperatives, unpaid family workers and non-classifiable workers.

adjusting for differences in education, age and place of residence, the racial and indigenous/non-indigenous occupational gaps remain significant in seven of the eight countries included. Odds ratios below 1 indicate a lower likelihood of holding a skilled job relative to that of white, non-indigenous workers.

Race has a strong effect on occupation, particularly in South Africa, where formal discrimination and the denial of opportunities during the apartheid era has left a legacy of racially embedded inequalities, including in the labour market. The relative odds of working in skilled jobs are more than 80 per cent lower for persons of African descent as compared with persons of European descent with equivalent levels of education in that country. Racial differences in occupation are also large in some of the Latin American countries shown, namely Brazil and Ecuador, but are much smaller in Cuba and non-significant in Costa Rica, where members of the Afro-descendant minority work as often as the white majority in senior management and professional positions.[52] Data

---

[52]    As opposed to persons of African descent in many of the other countries included in this table, most Costa Ricans of African descent do not trace their lineage to slaves but are primarily the descendants of immigrants from the English-speaking Caribbean that travelled to work as labourers on railway lines and plantations in the Pacific coast (Andrews, 2004). In 1949, immigrants were granted citizenship and access to social programmes (Andrews, 2004).

Table III.1

**Logistic regression coefficients of the effect of indigenous status and race on working in a high- or semi-skilled non-manual job[a] in selected countries**

| Country | Census year | Race | Coefficient (odds ratio) | Significance[b] |
|---|---|---|---|---|
| Brazil | 2010 | | | |
| | | (White)[c] | | |
| | | Black | 0.55 | *** |
| | | Indigenous | 0.89 | |
| | | Mixed race | 0.62 | *** |
| Costa Rica | 2000 | | | |
| | | Black | 1.05 | |
| | | Indigenous | 0.47 | * |
| | | Mixed race | 0.92 | |
| Cuba | 2002 | | | |
| | | Black | 0.83 | *** |
| | | Mixed race | 0.84 | *** |
| Ecuador | 2010 | | | |
| | | Black | 0.35 | *** |
| | | Indigenous | 0.30 | *** |
| | | Mixed race | 0.73 | *** |
| El Salvador | 2007 | | | |
| | | Black | 0.35 | *** |
| | | Indigenous | 0.64 | ** |
| South Africa | 2007 | | | |
| | | Black | 0.19 | *** |
| | | Mixed race | 0.26 | *** |
| Canada | 2001 | | | |
| | | Black | 0.91 | ** |
| | | Mixed race | 0.81 | *** |
| United States | 2010 | | | |
| | | Black | 0.73 | *** |
| | | Indigenous | 0.67 | *** |
| | | Mixed race | 0.93 | *** |

*Source:* Calculations are based on census data from the Minnesota Population Center (2015).
**Note:** The logistic regression model controls for race and indigenous status (coefficients shown) and also for age group, educational level (less than primary, completed primary, secondary and tertiary) and place of residence (urban, rural), as defined by each country. The coefficients presented are odds ratios; they represent the multiplicative change in the odds of holding a skilled job for persons of African descent or mixed race and indigenous peoples with respect to white, non-indigenous persons.
[a] Defined as the share in managerial, professional, technical and clerical occupations (International Standard Classification of Occupations 2008 groups 1, 2, 3 and 4). Clerical occupations include mainly insurance and real estate agents, secretaries and other office employees, clerks, bankers and cashiers. These are non-manual jobs that require some secondary education and training and are frequently performed away from home.
[b] *p<0.05;**p<0.01;***p<0.001.
[c] White, non-indigenous persons are the reference category for all countries shown in table III.1.

show occupational disadvantages for the Afro-descendant minority in the two developed countries included in the analysis as well, that is, in Canada and, particularly, the United States.

Indigenous status has a strong negative effect on occupation in most of the countries shown, developing and developed, and particularly in Ecuador, where the odds of working in a skilled job are more than 70 per cent lower for members of indigenous communities than for the non-indigenous – the odds ratio of indigenous to non-indigenous is 0.30. In Brazil, the indigenous occupational disadvantage is not significant, suggesting that place of residence and exclusion from good-quality education are key factors in the observed indigenous/non-indigenous gap in occupational status in this case. In sum, indigenous peoples and ethnic minorities are disadvantaged in employment - or overeducated for the jobs they do – in most of the countries shown.

Research shows that immigrants also tend to be overeducated for the jobs they do. For example, across the OECD countries, more than one third of immigrants with a tertiary degree were found to be overqualified for their jobs as compared with one in four native-born persons (OECD, 2015a). The gap is even wider in Southern Europe, where as many as 50 per cent of migrants are overqualified as compared with 25 per cent of natives, as well as among immigrant women as compared with both immigrant men and native women (OECD, 2015a). Overqualification affects even those immigrants who obtained their degrees in their host country.

As discussed in section A, many individuals belong to more than one disadvantaged group and as a result experience cumulative disadvantages. In Europe, for instance, labour market participation and employment rates fell faster among immigrant youth than among adults during the 2008 crisis and have continued to fall during the post-crisis period (2011-2014), while they have increased or remained stable among immigrant adults and among native youth during this last period (OECD, 2015a). Research has also shown that women from disadvantaged groups fare systematically worse than men, including in the labour market (Kabeer, 2010; World Bank, 2013; OECD, 2015a). In figure III.7, the gap between the share of women and men in skilled, non-manual occupations is larger among indigenous peoples than among the non-indigenous in the Plurinational State of Bolivia (panel A) and among members of scheduled castes, scheduled tribes and other backward classes in India than among the rest of that country's population (panel B). That is, not only do women from disadvantaged minorities in these two countries fare worse than minority men or non-minority women in terms of occupation, but belonging to an indigenous group or a scheduled caste also has a larger negative effect on women than on men. Similarly, research in eight countries of Latin America shows that, at comparable levels of schooling, indigenous women receive lower labour incomes than indigenous men and non-indigenous women (ECLAC, 2015).

Figure III.7

**Share of workers in skilled jobs, by sex and indigenous status or caste-based reservation status, selected countries**

## A. Plurinational State of Bolivia, 2003

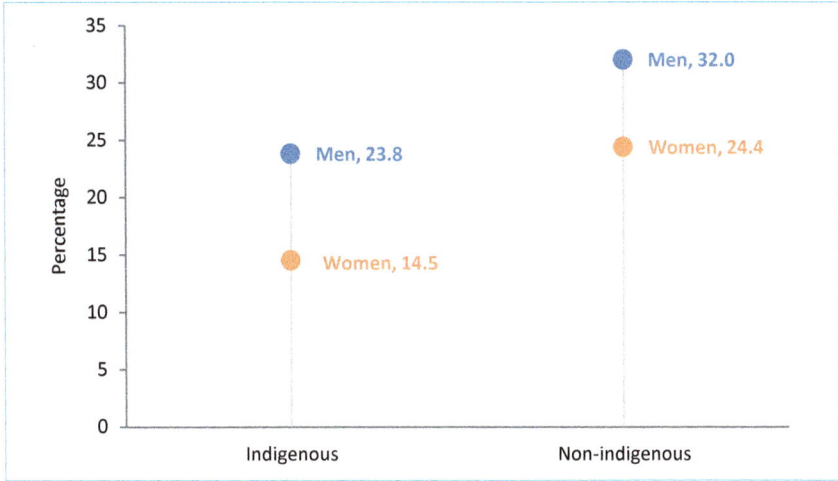

## B. India, 2005-2006

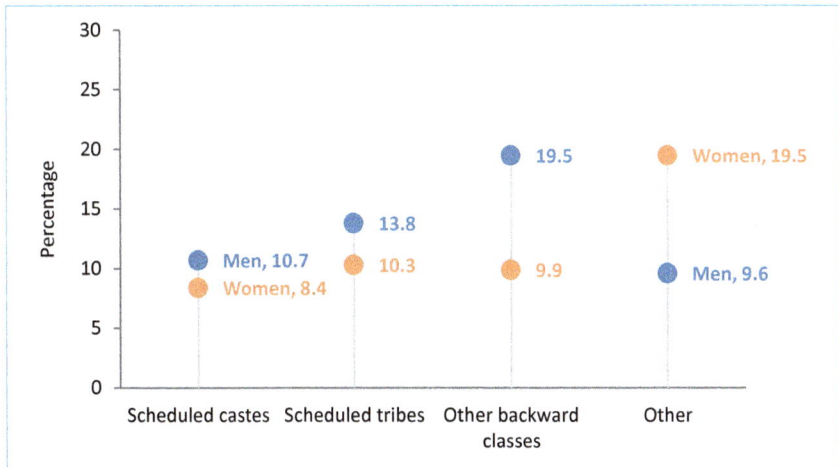

*Source:* Calculations are based on data from Demographic and Health Surveys.

## 2. Poverty outcomes

Despite the overall progress seen in poverty reduction, there are significant disparities in levels of income and in the risk of poverty experienced by different social groups, partly as a result of gaps in access to education, health care, employment and productive assets. Evidence suggests, for instance, that indigenous peoples constitute more than 10 per cent of the world's poor despite accounting for just about 4 per cent of the world's total population (Hall and Patrinos, 2012). In OECD countries, immigrants are twice as likely as the native-born to live in households which fall within the poorest income decile and below the national poverty threshold, even at comparable levels of education (OECD, 2015a). In 11 European countries with significant Roma populations, 87 per cent of the Roma are at risk of poverty – defined by the European Union as living on an income below 60 per cent of the national median – while only 46 per cent of non-Roma individuals living near Roma communities and 17 per cent of the total population of these countries are at risk of poverty (European Union Agency for Fundamental Rights, 2012).

Not only are members of these social groups more likely to live in poverty, but they have lower average incomes and experience deeper poverty than the rest of the population. The illustrative examples shown in figure III.8 indicate that the reported average income of indigenous persons is lower than that of the rest of the population. Additional research indicates that the ethnicity poverty gap – that is, the amount of income that would be needed to lift people to the poverty line – is significant in many countries. In China, ethnic minorities would require twice the amount of income as the majority just to reach the poverty line and thereby escape poverty; in Gabon, indigenous peoples would need three times as much income, while in Viet Nam, it would take seven times as much income for ethnic minorities to reach the poverty line (Hall and Patrinos, 2012). Persons with disabilities also possess fewer assets and endure worse living conditions than persons without disabilities, as illustrated in figure III.9, which is similar to the situation of older persons, partly because of higher health-care expenditures and other disability-related costs (WHO and World Bank, 2011; United Nations, 2013a).

Location – specifically, the fact that these minority groups live in rural areas and in remote locations more often than the majority – plays an important role in the poverty outcomes observed. Estimates of multidimensional destitution or extreme multidimensional poverty, defined as extreme deprivation in 10 non-monetary indicators, indicate that destitution is more prevalent among rural than among urban populations and that the urban-rural gap in destitution is larger than the urban-rural poverty gap in the majority of countries with data (Alkire, Roche and Vaz, 2014).[53]

---

[53] Multidimensional destitution has more extreme deprivation cut-offs in the 10 indicators used than does multidimensional poverty. For instance, households are counted as destitute if two or more children have died (while multidimensional poverty requires only that one child died), if one member

Figure III.8

**Income per capita of indigenous persons, latest available data since 2000**
(As a percentage of income per capita of non-indigenous persons)

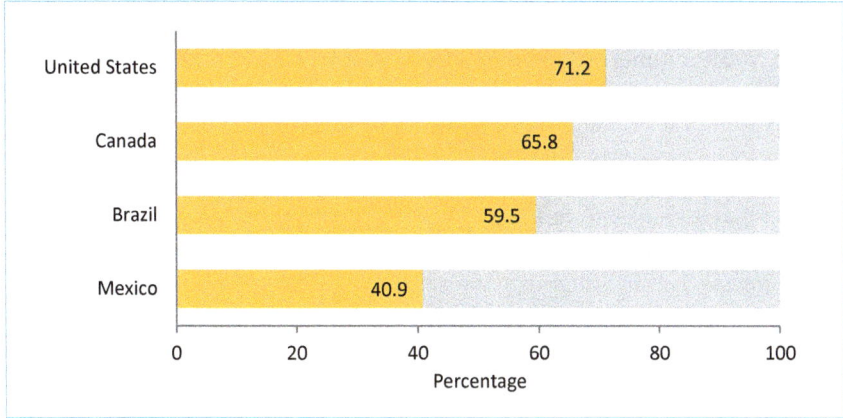

*Source:* Calculations are based on census data from the Minnesota Population Center (2015).
**Note:** Data are from the most recent population census (2000 or 2010 round), containing data by indigenous status and total personal income in the previous month or year as collected by national statistical offices and available from the Minnesota Population Census repository.

Figure III.9

**Income per capita of persons with disabilities, latest available data since 2000**
(As a percentage of income per capita of persons without disabilities)

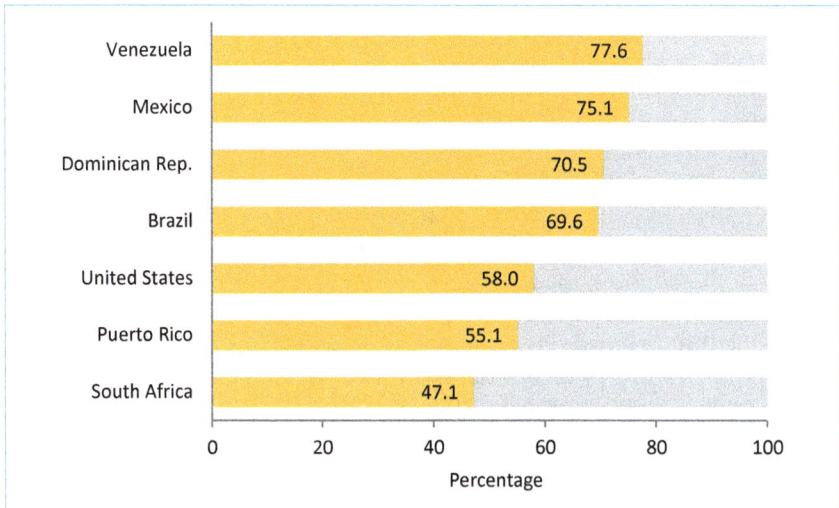

*Source:* Calculations are based on census data from the Minnesota Population Center (2015).

Furthermore, members of these groups are more likely to remain in poverty over the long term. Research on the dynamics of poverty, based on a growing body of longitudinal data, indicate that certain attributes, such as caste, ethnicity, religion and class, heighten the risk of chronic poverty and of transmitting poverty to the next generation (Bird, 2007; Bhide and Mehta, 2004; Sumner, 2013; Reddy, 2015). Reddy (2015) found that not only are intergenerational social mobility and related escapes from poverty lower among men in scheduled tribes and scheduled castes than among other men, but the former also experienced a stronger-than-average decline in mobility, particularly upward mobility, between 1983 and 2012. Research also points to the fact that, in addition to having less education and fewer assets, members of these social groups receive lesser returns on the assets they do possess. Some groups, namely migrants and some ethnic minorities, also face barriers in accessing social protection schemes. They are excluded not only from economic institutions but also from social and political ones, as discussed in the next section, or if not entirely excluded, are included on adverse terms (ODI, 2014).

As observed in section A, whether development is leaving some groups behind depends on context. For example, Alkire, Roche and Vaz (2014) found that the gap between the multidimensional poverty index (MPI) of the poorest and richest ethnic group increased between 2001 and 2006 in Benin while in Kenya the poorest ethnic group enjoyed the largest absolute reduction in poverty during the 2000s (Alkire, Roche and Vaz, 2014, table A.11). As for the spatial dynamics of exclusion, these authors observed that, in 34 developing countries studied during the 2000s, 26 experienced significant reductions in multidimensional poverty in urban areas and 30 recorded reductions in rural areas. Furthermore, in rural areas the MPI headcount ratio was reduced faster than in urban areas − by 1.3 per cent and 1 per cent per year respectively. Likewise, rural reductions in multidimensional destitution were statistically significant in 27 countries, whereas urban reductions were significant in only 20 countries. Analysis by the United Nations (2013a) also showed that, despite persistent rural disadvantages, improvements in education, health and nutrition during the last decade have often been faster in rural than in urban areas of developing countries, even though trends vary significantly across countries. Results are even more mixed at the subnational regional level. In a study of 31 countries, the poorest subnational area made the largest strides in reducing multidimensional poverty in only nine countries (Alkire, Roche and Vaz, 2015). The majority of those countries that saw the fastest declines in multidimensional poverty also succeeded in reducing disparities across regions (Alkire, Roche and Vaz, 2015).

Even though income data on individual household members are

---

is severely malnourished, etc. For a comparison of rural-urban levels of multidimensional destitution and multidimensional poverty, see Alkire, Roche and Vaz (2014), tables A.5 and A.13.

generally lacking, the existing evidence indicates that differences exist also in the intrahousehold distribution of resources within and across social groups. Research on the gender dimension of expenditure allocations shows that resources are often not shared equitably between boys and girls – with boys benefiting disproportionately from investments in health care, private education and childcare – and that women are often excluded from economic decision-making within their households (United Nations, 2015a). Female and male poverty rates are similar overall, but not at all ages or for all household characteristics. Women in developed countries are more likely than men to be poor at older ages, particularly when living alone, while differences by sex among youth aged 18-24 years are noticeable only in a small number of countries. In Latin America and the Caribbean in contrast, women are most likely to be poorer than men in young adulthood, that is, between the ages of 25 and 34 (United Nations, 2015a). Poverty is also more prevalent among female-headed households than among male-headed households, even though poverty reduction has been faster in the former, at least across Africa, since the late 1990s (Milazzo and van de Walle, 2015). There are many characteristics that can affect decision-making and resource allocation within the household beyond sex, namely age and disability, and these vary across cultures and over time. However, there has been little analysis of most of them (Bolt and Bird, 2003).

## 3. Conclusions

There are significant differences in access to the labour market and in employment opportunities among social groups. These differences persist in many of the examples shown once the effects of education, age structure and area of residence are accounted for. Thus employment inequalities are not driven exclusively by differences in human capital and other basic socioeconomic characteristics. Partly as a result of these employment disadvantages, indigenous peoples, ethnic minorities, migrants and persons with disabilities are more likely to live in poverty and experience deeper poverty than the rest of the population.

Discrimination plays a key role in holding back some groups, as discussed in chapter IV. However, the inequalities observed cannot be attributed solely to bias. The characteristics of different social groups and the circumstances in which they live or seek employment may not be comparable even after accounting for the effect of educational attainment, place of residence or age on employment status. For example, education and place of residence affect access to resources that are not adequately measured through a basic quantitative approach, namely social capital and economic opportunities. Even within what national censuses or surveys define as rural areas, the places where each ethnic group resides may differ in terms of land endowments, access to services and other attributes. Alesina, Michalopoulos and Papaioannou (2016) showed, for instance, that contemporary differences in development in ethnic homelands have a significant geographic component and that geographic inequality is highly correlated with inequality among ethnic groups and with overall levels of development. Similarly, even at comparable educational levels, returns to education may be lower among disadvantaged groups because of the inferior quality of the education some receive (Hall and Patrinos, 2012). The root of these inequalities may certainly lie in historical exclusion and discrimination, including the appropriation of the most valuable lands of indigenous peoples and other ethnic minorities by colonizers or other groups. However, these inequalities now have a direct effect on these groups' opportunities and outcomes, regardless of whether discriminatory behaviours in the labour market persist.

## C.  Unequal participation in political, civic and cultural life

The analysis of social inclusion would be incomplete without consideration of the relationships and interactions of individuals and groups, as well as their political participation. Equal opportunity to participate in political life and an equitable distribution of power, voice and agency in a society are key to ensuring that no one is left behind. These can also be considered as elements of a broad definition of "citizenship" beyond legal status[54] that encompasses access to resources (including benefits such as pensions), opportunities, participation, agency and choice, and the right to social mobility.

Examination of political, civic and cultural aspects in the study of social exclusion is important for three other reasons. First, lack of participation in political, civic and cultural processes implies limited power and voice in affecting the attitudes, norms, institutions and policies that drive social exclusion in the first place. Second, participation in these processes generates relationships and networks that can lead to collective action and build social capital, which in turn affects access to employment, income, health and education. Third, since many aspects of political, civic and cultural participation are voluntary in nature, they reveal subjective facets of social inclusion that are not captured by indicators that measure, for instance, access to income, shelter and employment (Bevelander and Pendakur, 2011).

This section contains a summary of findings from the empirical literature and an examination of data from the World Values Survey.[55] In the first

---

[54]   Legal status is used here as synonymous with *nationality*, which typically confers the rights to live and work in a particular nation State and to participate in its politics while being subject to taxation.

[55]   Successive waves of the World Values Surveys include representative national samples of the residents of more than 90 countries throughout the world, covering a period of more than 30 years. Throughout this section, data are shown only for those countries with at least 100 respondents per group and where the differences between groups tested are statistically significant at p<0.01, unless

subsection, disparities in political participation are assessed on the basis of data on self-reported voting in national elections, indicators of political activism, including participation in demonstrations and boycotts, and the representation of different social groups in Government. In the second subsection, there is a discussion of membership in voluntary associations and levels of generalized trust as measures of participation in civic and cultural life. Also covered in this section are issues of access to justice and rule of law, measured by confidence in the police and courts.

## 1. Unequal political participation

### a. Participation in the democratic process

Voting in national and local elections forms the basis of the democratic process. It measures the degree to which individuals take part in decision-making processes on a very broad level and therefore constitutes an important measure of social inclusion (Burchardt, Le Grand and Piachaud, 2002). Conversely, the systematic exclusion of individuals and groups from political participation calls into question the legitimacy of governing institutions.

Many of the models used to predict voter turnout are focused on the effects of demographic and socioeconomic characteristics: higher education, in particular, and higher income lead to stronger political engagement when measured by voting behaviour, particularly in developed countries (Pande, 2011). The relationship between educational attainment and voting behaviour is less direct in developing countries partly due to institutional constraints, such as electoral malpractice in the form of vote buying or intimidation and electoral violence, or due to limited access to information about the political process and politicians' actions (Pande, 2011). Institutional barriers to registering and voting affect participation as well, as do social networks, trust in the political system, attitudinal factors, such as partisanship, political interest and political efficacy, and mobilization by political actors (Ramakrishnan and Espenshade, 2001).

With regard to institutional barriers to registering and voting, very few countries have legal provisions that exclude citizens from voting in all elections on the basis of ascribed characteristics, such as race, ethnicity or sex, which is far from the case a century ago. Yet disparities in voting patterns remain. For instance, although there are no restrictions on voter registration among people with disabilities in the United Kingdom, they are less likely to be registered to vote that people with no disabilities, have lower voter turnout and encounter difficulties in terms of physical access to voting locations, and these are not overcome by absentee voting due to the unclear directions provided (Barnes and Mercer, 2010).

---

otherwise noted.

Differences in self-reported voter turnout by race and ethnicity are significant in about half of countries with data from WVS.[56] In countries where such differences are significant, those who identify with an ethnic majority group report higher voter turnout than those belonging to ethnic minority groups in all but two countries shown in figure III.10: Iraq and South Africa.[57] In Iraq, a higher percentage of Kurdish and Turk than Arab respondents reported having voted in elections. It should be noted that the autonomous Kurdistan Region in northern Iraq holds separate elections, including the one held in 2013, which was the same year as the World Values Survey was last conducted in Iraq. In South Africa, those who identified as white, coloured or Asian more frequently reported voting than those who identified as black, which reflects the historical legacy of apartheid in that country. The largest racial and ethnic gap in voting is seen in the Netherlands – the only European country shown in figure III.10 – despite Government efforts to increase the political participation of ethnic minorities at the local level.[58]

A number of factors can account for why the differences by race and ethnicity are not significant in other countries. One important distinction is that several of the countries where racial and ethnic differences in voting are not significant have compulsory voting laws, including Australia, Brazil, Chile (although such laws were abandoned in that country in 2012), Mexico and Peru; these countries enforce mandatory voting through a number of sanctions, such as fines or disenfranchisement (López Pintor and Gratschew, 2002). Where voting is compulsory, differences in voter turnout between social groups tend to be lower (López Pintor and Gratschew, 2002).

The right to vote in a country is generally determined by legal citizenship, thus excluding non-naturalized immigrants. In this sense, difficulties in the acquisition of citizenship (and in registering to vote once citizenship has been obtained) constitute a barrier to the political participation of migrants. However, evidence suggests that in general those migrants who have become citizens of the country in which they live do not exercise their voting rights as often as native-born citizens. Among OECD countries, for instance, native-born citizens were generally more likely to have voted in the last election than immigrants who had become naturalized citizens (OECD, 2015a). Among

---

[56]   Survey data on self-reported voter turnout generally indicate higher levels of voting than that reflected in national records. However, national records are not strictly comparable with survey data. A question in the World Values Survey, for instance, does not refer to a specific election in question, but instead general voting behaviour: "When elections take place, do you vote always, usually or never?"

[57]   Due to the high percentage of immigrants not eligible to vote among racial and ethnic minorities in some countries, the analysis here excludes non-naturalized immigrants, except in Singapore, where a question on citizenship was not included in the survey.

[58]   Since 1985 foreign residents have been eligible to vote in local elections. By 1998 the four main migrant groups were proportionally represented in the municipal councils of the four largest cities in the Netherlands (Fennema and Tillie, 2001).

Figure III.10

**Percentage of respondents who indicated they always or usually vote in national elections, by race/ethnicity, latest available data since 2010**

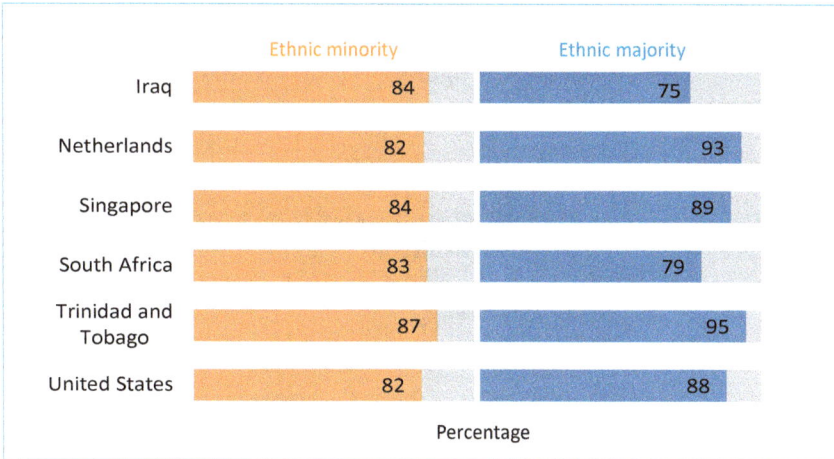

*Source:* World Values Survey, Wave 6 (2010-2014).

**Note:** Data are displayed only for countries with World Values Survey data available, where sample sizes are equal to or greater than 100 for each group and where the difference in the likelihood of voting by ethnicity is significant at the p<0.01 level.

For the countries included in the figure, ethnic minority respondents include those respondents who identified as Kurdish, Turkish or "other" in Iraq; as black, Asian or "other" in the Netherlands; as Malay, South Asian or Arab in Singapore; as white, South Asian, East Asian or coloured in South Africa; as Indo-Trinidadian or "other" in Trinidad and Tobago; and as Hispanic or Latino, non-Hispanic black, non-Hispanic Asian or Pacific islander or two or more races in the United States of America. Racial/ethnic gaps in voter turnout were not statistically significant at this level in Algeria, Australia, Brazil, Chile, Colombia, Kazakhstan, Kyrgyzstan, Mexico, Peru, Uzbekistan and Taiwan Province of China.

If the definition of statistical significance is relaxed to p<0.05, statistically significant differences are exhibited in Belarus and Ghana in favour of members of ethnic minority groups, and in Libya, Malaysia and New Zealand in favour of those respondents identifying with the ethnic majority group.

naturalized citizens, those who have been living in their country of residence for 10 years or longer vote more often than foreign-born citizens who have resided in the country for less than 10 years (OECD, 2015a, figure 11.A1.2). Furthermore, migrants married to native citizens from the host countries or those whose social networks include native citizens and those who participate in voluntary associations have higher voter turnout than those who do not (Togeby, 1999; Fennema and Tillie, 2001; Beverlander and Pendakur, 2011). Evidence from Canada, the Netherlands and the United States suggests also that migrants who originate from countries without a democratic system in place are less likely to vote than those who come from a democratic country (Fennema and Tillie, 2001; National Academies of Sciences, Engineering and Medicine, 2015). Thus, such elements as access to citizenship and voter registration are not the only factors that affect the political exclusion of migrants.

Historically, suffrage has also been denied to women, although currently very few countries have legal provisions that exclude women from voting in all elections. Voter turnout does not differ significantly between men and women in the majority of countries that participated in the latest round of WVS, with some exceptions. Shown in figure III.11 are those countries and areas

Figure III.11

**Percentage of women and men who indicated they always or usually vote in national elections, latest available data since 2010**

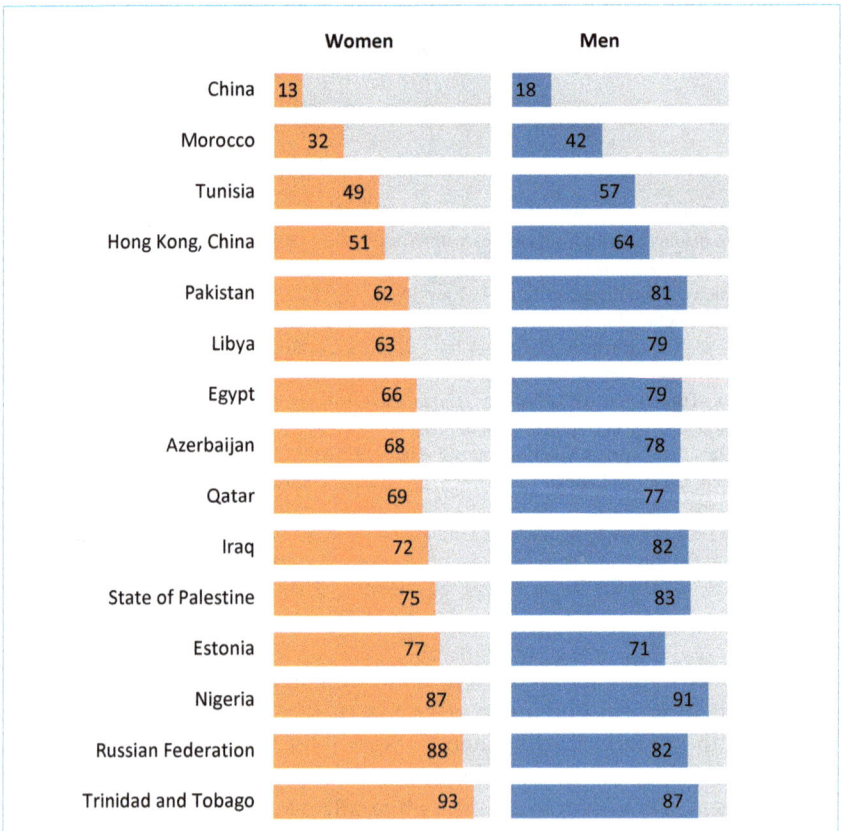

| | Women | Men |
|---|---|---|
| China | 13 | 18 |
| Morocco | 32 | 42 |
| Tunisia | 49 | 57 |
| Hong Kong, China | 51 | 64 |
| Pakistan | 62 | 81 |
| Libya | 63 | 79 |
| Egypt | 66 | 79 |
| Azerbaijan | 68 | 78 |
| Qatar | 69 | 77 |
| Iraq | 72 | 82 |
| State of Palestine | 75 | 83 |
| Estonia | 77 | 71 |
| Nigeria | 87 | 91 |
| Russian Federation | 88 | 82 |
| Trinidad and Tobago | 93 | 87 |

*Source:* World Values Survey, Wave 6 (2010-2014).
**Note:** Data are displayed only for countries with World Values Survey data available, where sample sizes are greater than 100 and where the difference in the likelihood of voting by sex is significant at the p<0.01 level.
If the level of significance is relaxed to p<0.05, women were more likely to report voting often in national elections in Belarus and South Africa, and men were more likely to report voting often in national elections in Kuwait, Lebanon and the Republic of Korea. Significant differences were not found in data for 39 countries and areas with data.

for which gender disparities in self-reported voter turnout were significant, according to WVS data. In Azerbaijan; Egypt; Iraq; Libya; Morocco; Nigeria; Pakistan; Qatar; the State of Palestine; Tunisia; and Hong Kong, China, the percentage of declared voters is higher among men than women. Women, however, declared that they had voted more often than men in Estonia, the Russian Federation and Trinidad and Tobago.

Prevailing norms, attitudes and behaviours about women's role in society can constrain women's access to political processes. Indeed, countries in the Middle East and North Africa have the highest prevalence of views reinforcing traditional gender roles, according to WVS data as measured by the percentage of respondents who believe that education is more important for boys than for girls and that men make better political leaders than women (World Bank, 2013). The socioeconomic disadvantages experienced by women in the form of lower educational attainment, labour force participation and income could result in less interest in politics as well.

Even though trend data to assess political aspects of inclusion are limited, studies indicate that traditional gender differences in voting behaviour declined starting in the 1980s, or even reversed, in many developed countries (López Pintor and Gratschew, 2002). In the United States, for instance, voter turnout of women has exceeded that of men in presidential elections since 1980, with women's participation being higher than men's among voters younger than 35 years of age (López Pintor and Gratschew, 2002). Voting rates for ethnic minorities (persons of African and Hispanic descent), however, have trailed behind whites since the 1970s (File, 2015).

Gender disparities in voter turnout and the barriers to political participation posed by low educational attainment may be partly addressed by improving political knowledge. Evidence from rural Pakistan – where there are strikingly low levels of literacy among women – indicates that information campaigns significantly increased the likelihood of women's voter turnout and reduced the likelihood of a woman voting for the same candidate as her spouse (Gine and Mansuri, 2011). In the same vein, civic workshops that educated voters increased political participation (as measured by increased attendance at rallies and signing of petitions) in post-conflict rural Liberia through improvements in voter information and coordination, thus enabling voters to better express their desires at the ballot box (Mvukiyehe and Samii, 2015). However, it is often difficult to separate the impact of improved access to electoral information from the mobilization impact of these campaigns in experimental research on voter turnout (Pande, 2011).

Regarding age differentials, youth of voting age tend to vote less frequently than older voters, while older persons are generally more likely to vote than both youth and adults (see figure III.12).[59] One of the common explanations

---

[59] The World Values Survey includes representative samples of the adult population 18 years or

for these differences is that lower interest and motivation to engage in political activity and higher mobility depress voter turnout among youth (Harder and Krosnick, 2008). Among older persons, increased free time and lower overall consumption relative to other age groups result in higher political participation despite the fact that overall levels of education and income tend to be lower among older persons (Campbell, 2002; Leighley, 1995). Campbell (2002) suggested that, in the United States, strong reliance on the Government to guarantee income security through the provision of monthly payments under the Social Security System leads to higher political interest and engagement among low-income older persons compared with low-income individuals of other ages. While the age differences in the likelihood of voting are significant in all countries shown in figure III.12, the size of the gap is smallest among those countries with mandatory voting laws, namely Argentina, Brazil and Peru.

### b. Participation in political activism: petition signing, protesting peacefully and boycotting

Voting is only one of many indicators of political participation, which can also be expressed through political or civic activities, such as signing petitions, attending peaceful demonstrations or participating in boycotts. For those excluded from conventional political parties and electoral politics, political activism provides an alternative participatory mechanism. While indicators on signing petitions, or participating in peaceful protests or boycotts derived from WVS do not reflect the depth and extent of political activism, they do serve as markers of at least cursory participation in political activity beyond voting.

Political activism is not restricted by citizenship or age. If the lower propensity to vote among young people or migrants is solely due to legal barriers, it may be expected that there would be no difference in other forms of political activism according to age or migrant status. According to WVS, there are no significant differences by age or migrant status in the frequency of signing petitions and participating in protests in the large majority of countries with data. Where significant age differentials exist, they are generally in favour of youth (figure III.13), including in such countries as Brazil, Chile and Tunisia, which in recent years have witnessed important social movements dominated by young people.

The examples of these countries suggest that young people can leverage informal political engagement through activism on issues of importance to them in order to improve such issues despite low political efficacy or voter disengage

---

older in the majority of countries, which is also the population eligible to vote save in a few cases, such as Japan and Malaysia, where the legal age of voting is set at 20 and 21 years of age respectively. The exception to this rule is South Africa, where 15 years is the legal age to vote, and WVS respondents were aged 15 and older as well. Although young respondents may have been of legal age to vote at the time of the survey, they may have not yet been eligible to vote due to their age if the most recent national election had been held before they came of age.

Figure III.12

**Percentage of respondents who indicated they always or usually vote in national elections, by age group, latest available data since 2005**

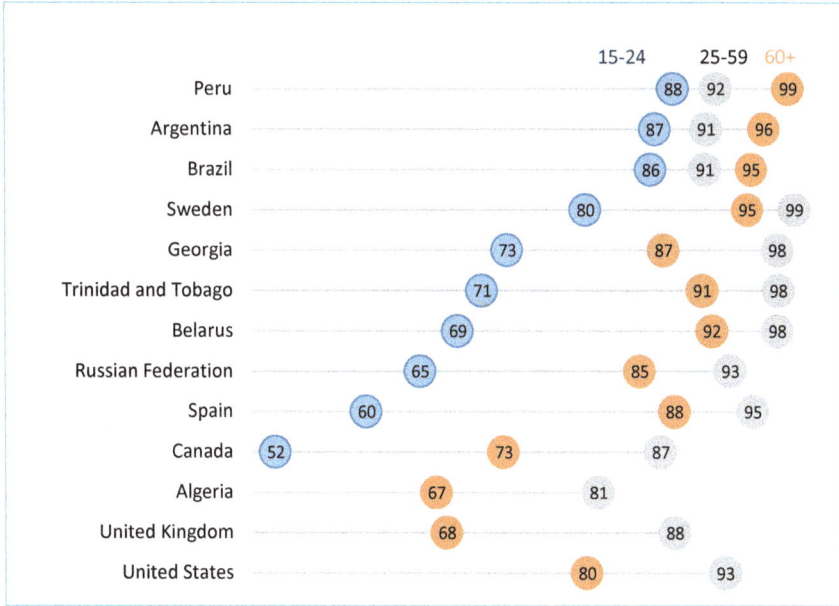

| | 15-24 | 25-59 | 60+ |
|---|---|---|---|
| Peru | | 88 | 92 | 99 |
| Argentina | | 87 | 91 | 96 |
| Brazil | | 86 | 91 | 95 |
| Sweden | | 80 | 95 | 99 |
| Georgia | 73 | 87 | 98 |
| Trinidad and Tobago | 71 | 91 | 98 |
| Belarus | 69 | 92 | 98 |
| Russian Federation | 65 | 85 | 93 |
| Spain | 60 | 88 | 95 |
| Canada | 52 | 73 | 87 |
| Algeria | 67 | 81 | |
| United Kingdom | 68 | 88 | |
| United States | 80 | 93 | |

*Source:* World Values Survey, Waves 5 (2005-2009) and 6 (2010-2014).
**Note:** Calculations include only cases where sample sizes are equal to or greater than 100.
Data are displayed only for countries with World Values Survey data available and where the difference in voter turnout between youth and adults aged 25-59 years and between adults aged 25-59 and older adults is significant at the p<0.01 level.

ment (or inability to vote). While such engagement is used here as a manifestation of inclusion, it may also be a symptom of the exclusion of youth from formal political processes and, more broadly, from economic and social life.

### c. Equal representation in political systems

In inclusive and democratic societies, the composition of political parties and government bodies ideally should reflect that of the country's population. Policy measures and social movements have advocated, sometimes successfully, for measures to encourage more equal representation. Electoral quotas for women, for instance, exist in more than 120 countries.[60] Although women's political representation as measured by the proportion of women in parliament nearly doubled globally from 12 per cent in 1997 to 22 percent in 2015, only a small number of countries have surpassed the parity line of 50

---

[60] For a more detailed global analysis of gender quotas in single or lower houses of parliament, see United Nations (2015a).

Figure III.13

**Proportion of individuals signing petitions, protesting or boycotting in the year preceding the survey, by age group, latest available data since 2006**

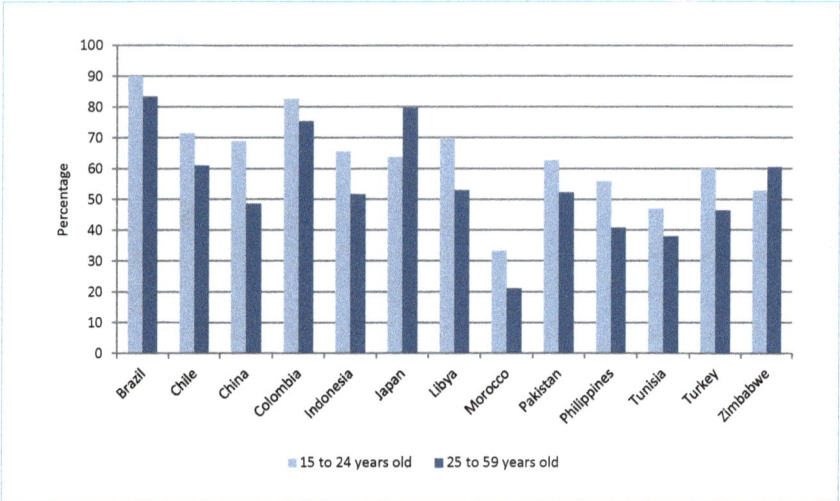

*Source:* World Values Survey, Waves 5 (2005-2009) and 6 (2010-2014).
**Note:** Data are displayed only for countries with World Values Survey data available, where sample sizes are equal to or greater than 100 and where the difference in the likelihood of political action by age is significant at the p<0.02 level.
Significant differences by age were not found in 47 countries and areas with data. If the level of significance is relaxed to p<0.05, youth were more likely to engage in political activism in Moldova; Trinidad and Tobago; and Hong Kong, China, whereas adults 25-59 years old were more likely to engage in political activism than youth in Australia.

per cent (United Nations, 2015a). Women's representation in the executive branches of Government has also increased, although they continue to be grossly underrepresented, especially in high-ranking government positions (United Nations, 2015a). Nordic countries, where the representation of women in national parliaments has been the world's highest for decades, no longer hold the record. Rwanda was ranked number one in 2015 (64 per cent of women) followed by the Plurinational State of Bolivia (53 per cent) (United Nations, 2015a).

Some countries have established reserved seats and quotas for other disadvantaged groups in order to improve their political representation. India, for instance, has seats reserved for scheduled castes, scheduled tribes and other backward classes (Deshpande, 2013). In Nepal, ethnic minority groups were underrepresented in political parties and all three branches of Government until the introduction of a proportionate representation and reservation system in 2007 (Gurung, Tamang and Turin, 2014). Similarly, several countries in Latin America and the Caribbean reserve a small percentage of parliamentary or legislative seats for indigenous people (Htun and Ossa, 2013).

Proportional representation in political bodies has often increased the inclusiveness and responsiveness of Government to the needs and viewpoints of groups traditionally excluded from decision-making processes. In general, women in parliament are more likely than men to prioritize gender and social issues, such as childcare, equal pay, parental leave, pensions, reproductive rights and protection against gender-based violence (Inter-Parliamentary Union, 2008). After a constitutional amendment reserved one third of seats and one third of head positions for women in local councils in India's *panchayat* system, women's participation as eligible voters increased in the councils, which also more often addressed women's concerns than had previously been the case (Chattopadhyay and Duflo, 2004). Similarly, increased political representation of scheduled castes and scheduled tribes increased their influence on policymaking (Pande, 2003).

## 2. Differences in participation in civic and cultural life

Participation in civic and cultural life is closely tied to political and other forms of participation, such that disentangling the impact that interactions among family, friends, colleagues and associational memberships have on individual and community well-being is a complex matter. Frequent social interaction can generate social capital upon which individuals can draw in times of need, including to find employment, and is therefore particularly important for individuals and households with less economic resources. High levels of social capital have also been found to promote collaboration and cooperative action at large and therefore have positive effects on economic development, institutions and governance. Research indicates, for instance, that societies with higher levels of social capital stand a better chance of becoming democratic and stable (Kuzio, 2001). However, social networks do not automatically bestow benefits on individuals and groups. In some cases, such networks may in fact foster exclusion, particularly if they are composed solely of individuals from the same social group, community or socioeconomic stratum (Granovetter, 2005; Lin, Ensel and Vaughn, 1981). In these cases, while social networks may be strong, they frequently lack the power and capital to achieve the groups' desired ends (DeFilippis, 2001).

The evidence reviewed shows that the size of one's social network and the availability of social support provided through networks differ significantly by age, income level and social and cultural context. Several studies have demonstrated, for instance, positive effects of social capital and support on the health and well-being of older persons (Litwin, 2010). Data from the British Household Panel Survey indicate that, among older adults in the United Kingdom, talking to neighbours and meeting with people "most days" was positively associated with the availability of social support, as was participation in sports clubs and religious organizations, and having children[61] (Gray, 2009). Older adults in the Mediterranean countries of France, Greece, Israel, Italy and Spain had larger families and households and received more social support from within the household, but expressed more loneliness, exhibited more depressive symptoms and were more likely to perceive their income as inadequate than their peers in the non-Mediterranean countries of Austria, Belgium, Denmark, the Netherlands, Sweden and Switzerland (Litwin, 2010).[62] Conversely, older adults in non-Mediterranean countries reported lower social support from within the household but greater exchange of support with individuals outside of the household and lower levels of loneliness, depression and income inadequacy (Litwin, 2010). The comparison between these two groups of countries thus highlights the ways in which the relationship between informal ties and social support differs depending on cultural and country-specific factors in the context in question.

Several studies have documented the role of social capital generated by migrant networks in increasing the likelihood of migrating abroad (Massey, 1990). Social capital generated by migrant networks is posited to reduce the costs and risks of migration through the provision of information or assistance at the place of destination by individuals who have migrated previously. Having broader networks with "weaker" ties (extended family and friends) appears to increase the likelihood of migrating abroad as well (Liu, 2013). Research in Thailand indicates that individuals rely more on their friends in the village than on resources provided by household members when deciding whether to migrate within the country (Garip, 2008).

Once arriving in a host country, social networks can help migrants settle or find a job. However, they can also have a negative impact on the socioeconomic situation of migrants and even on the educational and employment prospects of their children. Portes and Rumbaut (2001) found that the socioeconomic achievements of the second generation of migrants in the United States do not depend so much on whether they integrate into the host society but rather into what segment of that society they assimilate. In some cases, the social or ethnic groups to which migrants belong as well as their children's peer groups can have a negative impact on educational and overall socioeconomic achievements. Those authors underlined the importance of social capital within the immigrant community, in addition to parental human capital, family structure and gender relations in determining the process of acculturation and its outcomes among the children of immigrants.

---

[61]   Gray (2009) created an index of social support based on answers to the following five questions: (a) Is there anyone who you can really count on to listen to you when you need to talk?; (b) Is there anyone who you can really count on to help you out in a crisis?; (c) Is there anyone who you can totally be yourself with?; (d) Is there anyone who you feel really appreciates you as a person?; and (e) Is there anyone who you can really count on to comfort you when you are very upset?

[62]   Litwin's own grouping of countries.

These examples point to the important role of one's immediate surrounding or neighbourhood in the formation of social capital. Specifically, homogenous neighbourhoods reinforce the advantages or disadvantages associated with one's social class (Massey, 1996). As explored in section A, the neighorhood effects on children's developmental and schooling outcomes are thought to be largely mediated through peer and adult influences, which have an independent effect beyond household characteristics (Jenks and Meyer, 1990). In part, this situation reflects the collective socialization of children sustained by the levels of social capital within a neighbourhood (as opposed to an individual's cache of social capital). Mutual trust and solidarity among neighbours builds collective efficacy, through which residents act for the common good to supervise children, maintain public order and reduce interpersonal violence.[63]

The empirical literature has also assessed the impact of participation in more formal networks, including through membership in community organizations, volunteering, religious attendance and participation in sports groups.[64] WVS data indicate that membership in voluntary associations is on the decline among respondents of all ages. Such membership has indeed declined for individuals born in 1970 or later in the large majority of countries, as shown in figure III.14. According to this figure, if there was little or no change over time in belonging to a voluntary organization, a country's point would fall on or close to the 45-degree diagonal line. Data reveal, however, that nearly all countries in the figure fall below the 45-degree line, indicating lower levels of associational membership in 2012 than in 1995 among members of the 1970 cohort. Colombia, India and Poland constitute the main exceptions to this general trend as they fall above the diagonal line.

In his study on social capital and civic engagement in the United States, Putnam (2000) maintained that there is a strong relationship between the decline in membership in voluntary associations, overall trust in others as well as in institutions and, more broadly, the functioning of institutions. Yet trends from WVS suggest that there has been little change in overall levels of social trust in countries with data both among young people and among older cohorts between the mid-1990s and the early 2010s (Larsen, 2014). This may be due in part to the fact that social trust tends to be stable over a person's life-course and, consequently, overall levels of trust change slowly, through successive cohorts (Larsen, 2014).

Research on six countries in transition (Kazakhstan, Moldova, Serbia, Tajikistan, the former Yugoslav Republic of Macedonia and Uzbekistan) shows that, although there is frequent social contact with family, relatives and friends, there is very low membership in voluntary organizations and

---

[63]  For the case of Chicago, see Sampson, Raudenbush and Earls (1997).

[64]  For instance, see Moser (2009).

Figure III.14

**Membership in voluntary associations among respondents born in 1970 or later in selected countries, 1995 and 2012**

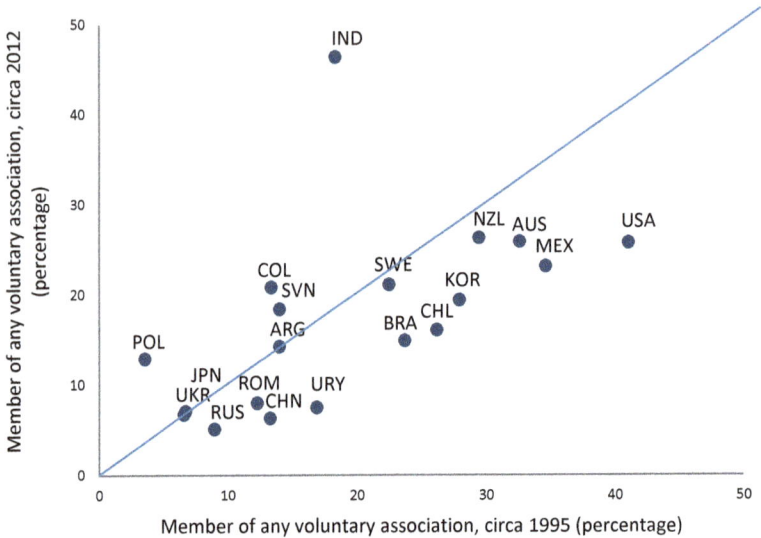

Source: World Values Survey, waves 3 (1995-1998) and 6 (2010-2014).
**Note:** In order to discern trends, analysis is limited to those countries that participated in the last three waves of the World Values Survey with data on voluntary associational membership and with the samples having at least 100 respondents.

low levels of social trust in these countries, similar to what is reflected by WVS data (UNDP, 2011). Furthermore, survey results indicate a high level of trust in acquaintances and people within an individual's social network, but low levels of trust among neighbours as well as a lack of trust in government institutions (UNDP, 2011). Additional research indicates that interpersonal trust and trust in Governments in countries in transition are on the rise, however, with an increasingly positive impact on individuals' life satisfaction (Habibov and Afandi, 2015).

In addition to trust in others, trust and confidence in national institutions, such as the courts, the police and local government, are critical to ensure active citizen participation in political processes, to make public bodies more locally accountable and responsive and to secure public cooperation with the police and compliance with the law (Jackson and Bradford, 2010). Ethnic minorities in several countries with WVS data express significantly lower confidence in the police and the courts (figure III.15). The confidence gap is largest in the United States, where only 54 per cent of ethnic minorities have strong confidence in the police as compared with 79 per cent of individuals belonging to the racial majority. The lower levels of confidence in these institutions among ethnic

Figure III.15

**Percentage of respondents indicating a great deal or quite a lot of confidence in the police and the courts, by race or ethnicity in selected countries, latest available data since 2011**

### A. Confidence in the police

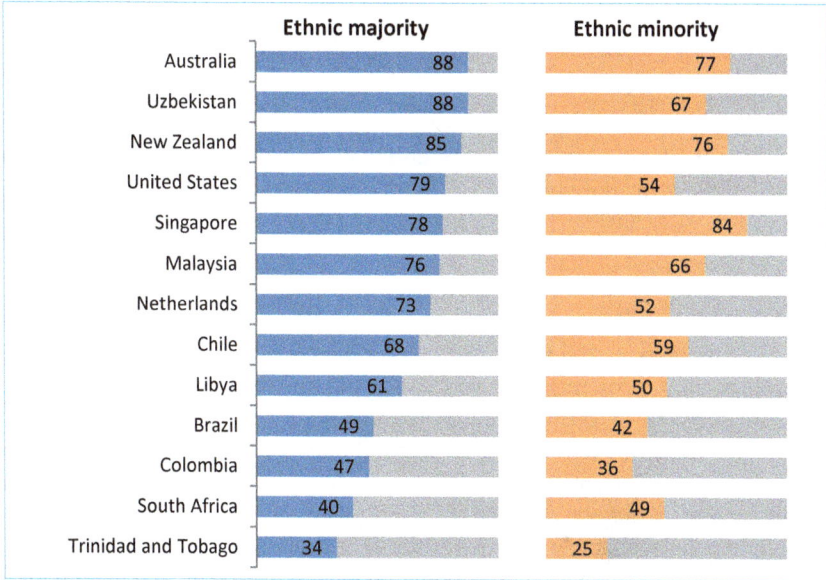

### B. Confidence in the courts

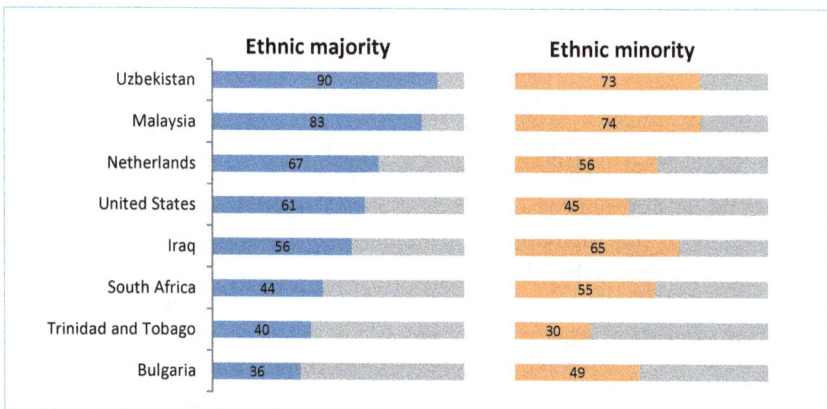

*Source:* World Values Survey, Waves 5 (2005-2009) and 6 (2010-2014).

**Note:** Data are displayed only for countries with World Values Survey data available, where sample sizes are equal to or greater than 100 and where the difference in level of confidence by race and ethnicity is significant at the p<0.01 level.

For the countries included in the figure, ethnic minority respondents include those respondents who identified as Asian, aboriginal or "other" in Australia; as Asian, indigenous, brown or black in Brazil;

as Turkish, Gypsy, Asian or "other" in Bulgaria; as indigenous, Asian, black or "other" in Chile; as Kurdish, Turkish or "other" in Iraq; as black, Asian or "other" in the Netherlands; as Chinese or South Asian in Malaysia; as Malay, South Asian or Arab in Singapore; as black, Asian or coloured in South Africa; as Indo-Trinidadian or "other" in Trinidad and Tobago; as Hispanic or Latino, non-Hispanic black, and non-Hispanic Asian or Pacific islander in the United States; and as Karakalpak, Tatar, or of another Central Asian country in Uzbekistan.

Racial/ethnic gaps in confidence in the police were not statistically significant in 10 countries with data. Racial/ethnic gaps in confidence in the courts were not statistically significant in 21 countries with data.

---

minorities challenge their legitimacy and effectiveness in gaining compliance of the public with the law and cooperation with law enforcement in these countries (Tyler, 2003).

## 3. Conclusions

In many countries, individuals who belong to certain groups – women, racial and ethnic minorities, migrants and young people – vote less frequently and are less likely to be represented in Government by individuals of similar backgrounds, according to WVS data and the literature reviewed. Education is an important determinant of differences in political participation across social groups. However, the section highlights many other factors that affect participation as well, including institutional barriers to registering and voting. In some countries, youth circumvent these barriers by using alternative channels of political activism, namely they are more likely to participate in peaceful demonstrations and sign petitions than older population groups. Notwithstanding these findings, the lack of engagement in political, civic and cultural activities among some individuals and groups is concerning and plays against the foundations of democracy – representation, rule of law and protection of freedom and rights.

Social capital is an important source of support and agency for individuals and groups that face social exclusion. Frequent contact with family, friends and neighbours provides social support that positively affects health and economic well-being. In many cases, members of vulnerable and marginalized groups enjoy dense networks of community group relations; what they lack is power to achieve their ends. Social networks can have a negative influence as well, however; a large body of work has measured the adverse effects of living in neighbourhoods of concentrated disadvantage, particularly on young children.

WVS data demonstrate no discernable trends in levels of social trust among countries and areas participating in the survey. Levels of trust and confidence in the police and the courts, however, vary significantly by race and ethnicity in some countries, challenging the legitimacy of these institutions in protecting the rule of law for all and promoting good governance.

## D.  Implications for monitoring progress in inclusion

A person's chances in life depend significantly on group ascription. Group-based differences in access to education, health care, infrastructure and employment as well as inequalities in political participation are pervasive and symptomatic of the exclusion of members of certain groups. These disadvantages reinforce one another: lower levels of health care and education go hand in hand with higher levels of poverty and unemployment, and often also with less voice in political and civic life. Similarly, the employment situation affects not only a person's income but also his or her participation in social and political life. Thus progress in one domain alone will not be sufficient to end social exclusion.

The inequalities observed are often rooted in historical circumstances but tend to persist after the structural conditions that created them change. The evidence presented in this chapter shows, for instance, that persons of African descent continue to experience significant disadvantages in South Africa and in other countries that no longer impose formal barriers to the participation of racial minorities. While discrimination continues to play a key role in holding back some groups, as the next chapter shows, it is argued that the legacy of past inequalities has a direct effect on these groups' opportunities and outcomes, regardless of whether discriminatory behaviours persist or have been eradicated. Groups that suffered from discrimination in the past start off with less assets, social capital and political power while those who historically had privileged positions tend to accumulate more and obtain greater returns on their assets.

This chapter as well as the literature on social exclusion show many positive trends, from broader representation of disadvantaged groups in political processes to a reduction of inequalities in access to education. However, group-based inequalities vary significantly across countries and by group. Whether development is leaving some people behind – and consequently whether it is promoting social inclusion – depends on context as well as on the indicators used to assess progress. The examples of Ghana, Mali and Peru highlighted in section A show, for instance, that progress in child health is not necessarily echoed in improvements in access to infrastructure and vice versa. Table III.2 further illustrates this point. On average, in the 33 developing countries included in the analysis that underlines the data shown, declines in the proportion of youth without primary education, the prevalence of child mortality and the proportion of children undernourished vary significantly by indicator and depending on the criteria used to classify groups.[65] For instance, child mortality declined faster among rural households in the sample, while there were stronger reductions in malnutrition in urban

---

[65]   It should be noted that the underlying sample is not the same for each of the three indicators: the education indicator (proportion of youth with low education) requires the presence of at least one young person (aged 15-24 years) in the household while the health indicators can be calculated only for households with children born in the last 10 years.

Table III.2

## Annual changes in education, child mortality and undernourishment, by subgroup, 1998-2007

|  | Proportion of youth with less than primary education | Proportion of children who died before age 5 | Proportion of children undernourished |
|---|---|---|---|
| **Place of residence** |  |  |  |
| Urban | -1.8 | -2.7 | -1.1 |
| Rural | -1.8 | -2.8 | -0.6 |
| **DHS wealth quintile** |  |  |  |
| Lowest wealth quintile | -1.3 | -2.8 | -0.7 |
| Highest wealth quintile | -3.1 | -1.7 | -2.0 |
| **Occupation of household head** |  |  |  |
| Skilled, non-manual[a] | -1.9 | -1.5 | -0.1 |
| Unskilled manual | -4.1 | 0.0 | -7.4 |
| **Ethnicity[b]** |  |  |  |
| Ethnic minorities | -2.5 | -3.1 | -0.7 |
| Largest ethnic group | 0.3 | -0.4 | -0.6 |

*Source:* Calculations are based on Sumner (2013), with underlying data from Demographic and Health Surveys.
**Note:** Based on data for 33 developing countries: Armenia, Bangladesh, Benin, Plurinational State of Bolivia, Burkina Faso, Cambodia, Cameroon, Chad, Egypt, Ethiopia, Ghana, Guinea, Haiti, India, Indonesia, Kenya, Madagascar, Malawi, Mali, Morocco, Mozambique, Nepal, Niger, Nigeria, Pakistan, Philippines, Rwanda, Senegal, Tanzania, Uganda, Viet Nam, Zambia and Zimbabwe.
[a]    Managerial, professional, technical and clerical occupations.
[b]    Ethnic minorities are grouped exclusively on the basis of size. It should be noted that the numerically largest ethnic groups are not consistently the better-off groups.

areas during the period. The proportion of youth with little education declined fastest among households where the head of the household was working in an unskilled, manual job, whereas households with children headed by an unskilled, manual worker saw no improvements in childhood mortality. Ethnic minorities benefited from considerably larger declines in childhood mortality than did the largest ethnic group, yet trends in malnutrition were similar for both groups.

These examples highlight the need to monitor progress in different dimensions of social inclusion separately, adapting the choice of indicators to the purpose for which they are to be employed and to the country context. Different indicators highlight different features of social exclusion; while they can help in understanding the phenomenon, they cannot be expected to provide a complete representation of the state of a society (United Nations, 2010).

Given the multiplicity of indicators available, combining them into one single index may hold appeal. However, for the purpose of international comparisons, the diversity of country circumstances puts the usefulness of combining indicators into question. The reduction of a multidimensional phenomenon to a single number can also be questioned on a conceptual basis. Specifically, the importance of each component and therefore the weight assigned to each indicator involve value judgements. Should disparities in labour market participation be given more or less weight than disparities in access to health services or education, for instance? Is political participation more valuable than participation in civic events and are the two forms of participation interchangeable? Not only would very diverse country contexts be ranked similarly on the basis of composite indicators and vice versa, but variations in the weight given to each component would result in significant changes in country rankings (Ravallion, 2010; United Nations, 2010).

Different indicators highlight different aspects of social exclusion and help improve understanding of the phenomenon but, by themselves, they do not provide explanations. Findings in this and the previous chapters suggest that there are multiple mechanisms through which individuals and entire social groups are left behind. Yet discrimination stands out as a universal and pervasive driver of exclusion. In chapter IV, this social ill is examined in more detail, with evidence presented on different types of discrimination and a discussion of its effects on the victims of discrimination.

While concrete strategies to promote social inclusion and empowerment must therefore be context-specific, certain elements are often present when countries are successful in creating the enabling conditions for the meaningful participation of all members of society. Specifically, as is illustrated in chapter V, countries that have adopted an inclusive approach to policy have expanded opportunities by promoting universal access to key good-quality services, such as health care and education; they have actively addressed discrimination and addressed the special needs of those groups that face the greatest challenges in overcoming exclusion; and they have taken action to ensure that social, economic, political and legal institutions are open and inclusive.

## ANNEX

Figure A.III.1

**Share of workers in highly- and semi-skilled non-manual occupations,[a]
by indigenous status in selected countries and areas,
latest available data since 2000**

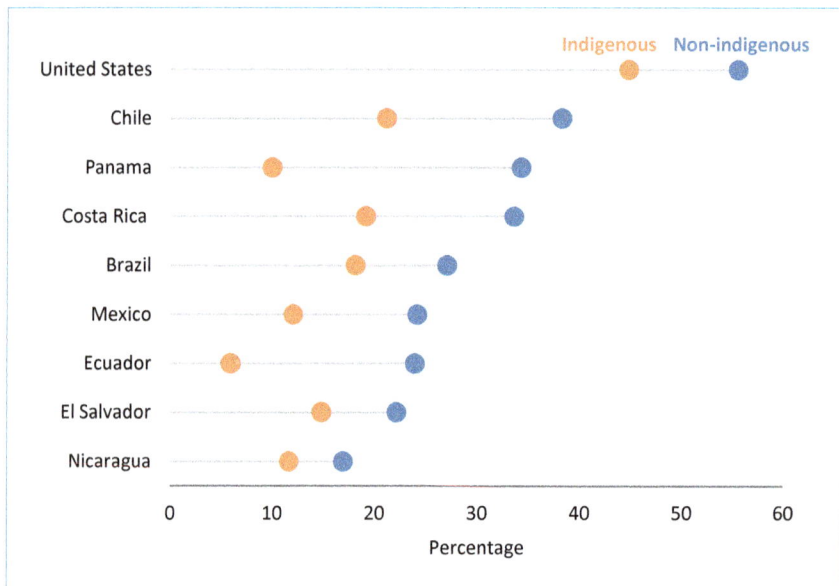

*Source:* Calculations are based on census data from the Minnesota Population Center (2015).
**Note:** Data are from the most recent population census (2000 or 2010 round) containing data by indigenous status and occupation as collected by national statistical offices and available from the Minnesota Population Census repository.

[a] Defined as the share in managerial, professional, technical and clerical occupations (International Standard Classification of Occupations 2008 groups 1, 2, 3 and 4). Clerical occupations include mainly insurance and real estate agents, secretaries and other office employees, clerks, bankers and cashiers. These are non-manual jobs that require some secondary education and training and are frequently performed away from home.

Figure A.III.2

**Share of workers in highly- and semi-skilled non-manual occupations by race[a] in selected countries, latest available data since 2000**

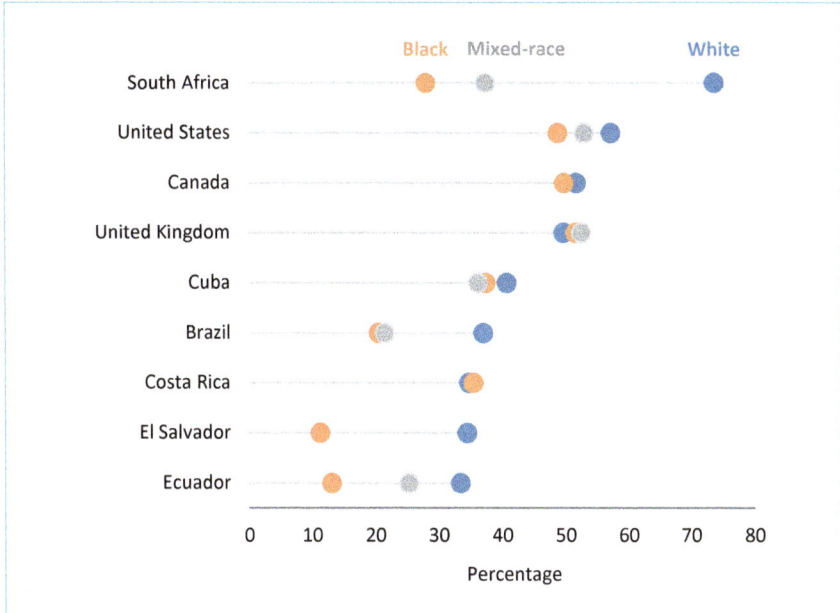

*Source:* Calculations are based on census data from the Minnesota Population Center (2015).

**Note:** Cross-national comparisons must be made with caution because racial classifications have strong social determinants and therefore vary by country. The data shown are based on census questions that specifically referred to "race" or "colour" or physical characteristics.

[a] Some census samples include racial categories other than white, black or African descent and mixed-race. For comparative purposes, these additional categories are not shown here.

Chapter IV

# Prejudice and discrimination: barriers to social inclusion

## Key messages

- *Significant progress has been made in repealing discriminatory policies and laws but formal discrimination persists in many countries.*

- *Prejudice and negative stereotypes are expressed in subtle ways. Measuring their reach empirically is therefore difficult.*

- *The existing evidence suggests that discriminatory practices remain widespread and continue to affect the way people work, the opportunities they have, the quality and nature of the relationships they forge, their health and well-being, as well as their sense of agency.*

The examples presented in chapter III add evidence to the fact that societies continue to make distinctions based on ethnicity, race, sex or gender and other characteristics that should have no bearing on people's achievements or on their well-being. The unjust or prejudicial treatment of people on the basis of their identity or their ascribed characteristics is not the only driver of exclusion, but it is a particularly pervasive one. Discrimination constrains the ability of individuals to participate meaningfully in society. It affects the opportunities that people have, the choices they make and outcomes that define their overall well-being. Assessing the impact of discrimination, which plays out in law, policy and practice, and isolating its effect from that of other factors that affect participation and overall well-being is challenging, as mentioned in chapter III. The present chapter contains an overview of research on discrimination. Although the main aim is to summarize the research findings, the chapter also contains analyses of the strengths and weaknesses of the different sources of data and methodologies used to measure discrimination.

The United Nations addresses discrimination as a human rights concern. The Charter of the United Nations reflects the determination of the signatories to "reaffirm faith in fundamental human rights, [and] in the dignity and worth of the human person", including through practising tolerance. Among the purposes of the United Nations is "to achieve international cooperation... in promoting and encouraging respect for human rights and for fundamental freedoms for all without distinction as to race, sex, language, or religion"

(United Nations, 1945). The Universal Declaration of Human Rights[66] further stipulated the right of all human beings to equality before the law and to equal protection of the law against discrimination or any incitement thereto. It elaborated the prohibited grounds of discrimination by specifying that all persons are entitled to the rights and freedoms that it set forth "without distinction of any kind, such as race, colour, sex, language, religion, political or other opinion, national or social origin, property, birth or other status".[67] The Committee on Economic, Social and Cultural Rights has since elaborated on these points: "The nature of discrimination varies according to context and evolves over time. A flexible approach to the ground of 'other status' is thus needed…".[68] It also laid out a definition of discrimination as constituting "…any distinction, exclusion, restriction or preference or other differential treatment that is directly or indirectly based on the prohibited grounds of discrimination and which has the intention or effect of nullifying or impairing the recognition, enjoyment or exercise, on an equal footing, of Covenant rights".[69]

The principle of non-discrimination applies throughout international human rights law and legally obliges Governments to respect, protect and fulfil human rights. That principle is inherent in all major human rights treaties, and is the primary focus of several conventions, including the International Convention on the Elimination of All Forms of Racial Discrimination,[70] the Convention on the Rights of Persons with Disabilities,[71] the International Convention on the Protection of the Rights of All Migrant Workers and Members of Their Families,[72] and the Convention on the Elimination of All Forms of Discrimination against Women.[73]

## A.  Formal discrimination as a barrier to social inclusion

Historically, many laws and policies have been explicit in singling out specific groups for favourable treatment and limiting or denying rights to others (see example in box IV.1). Additionally, there are laws that are not discriminatory but may be applied in ways that have negative impacts on disadvantaged

---

[66]  General Assembly resolution 217 (A) III.

[67]  Ibid., art. 2.

[68]  E/C.12/GC/20, para. 27.

[69]  Ibid., para. 7. "Covenant" here refers to the International Covenant on Economic, Social and Cultural Rights, which is monitored by the Committee on Economic, Social and Cultural Rights.

[70]  General Assembly resolution 2106 (XX).

[71]  General Assembly resolution 61/106, annex I.

[72]  General Assembly resolution 45/158, annex.

[73]  General Assembly resolution 34/180, annex.

Box IV.1

## Jim Crow laws in the United States

In the United States in the late 1800s, southern state and local governments, resisting federal law, adopted a discriminatory system of laws known as "Jim Crow". These laws mandated the strict separation of persons of African descent and white people in all facets of life, thus resulting in the segregation of schools, restaurants, transport vehicles, marriage, parks, housing and employment, thereby essentially creating a secondary class of citizenship (American RadioWorks, 2016; McKanders, 2010). Furthermore, the imposition of such barriers as literacy tests and poll taxes for all voters disproportionately disenfranchised men of African descent as well as poor white men who could not meet their requirements.

These laws and measures largely went unchallenged by the federal Government. In 1896, the Supreme Court (Plessy vs. Ferguson) institutionalized the principle of "separate but equal". This principle, employed as justification of Jim Crow laws, belied the inferior spaces and services permitted to persons of African descent and their often brutal treatment at the hands of – or overlooked by – the law (McKanders, 2010). It was not until 1954 that the Supreme Court overturned the principle (Brown vs. Board of Education) (Library of Congress, 2011). Yet Jim Crow laws remained in place until 1964 when the final blow against them was delivered with the passage of the Civil Rights Act, which banned discrimination on the grounds of race, colour, religion, sex and national origin in multiple areas, including places of public accommodation and employment. The Voting Rights Act of 1965 was aimed at overcoming any legal barriers at the state and local levels that prevented persons of African descent from exercising their right to vote under the 15th amendment (1870) to the Constitution of the United States.

groups, reinforcing their exclusion. The negative effects of such grievous legal provisions often persist long after they have been rectified.

While in recent decades numerous discriminatory laws and policies have been repealed and protective ones promulgated, formal discrimination has deep roots and persists to this day. With regard to gender inequality, for example, the World Bank (2015) reported that, of 173 countries and areas examined, more than 150 have at least one law that discriminates against women. In 18 countries and areas in the world, women cannot get a job if their husbands feel it would not be in the family's interest to do so. Female surviving spouses in 35 countries or areas do not enjoy the same inheritance rights as male surviving spouses, and in 32 countries married women cannot apply for passports in the same way as married men (World Bank, 2015). Moreover, more than 50 countries have discriminatory nationality or citizenship laws. For example, married women in 48 countries cannot extend their citizenship to foreign spouses on an equal basis with their male counterparts, nor can married mothers in 18 countries pass on citizenship to their children born in the country on par with married fathers. These restrictions can result in denial of social benefits, such as public health care, limited access to jobs and restricted freedom of movement (Equality Now, 2016).

Similarly, many religious and ethnic minorities continue to face formal barriers to citizenship, voting and access to justice. The Minorities at Risk project at the University of Maryland reported that, as of 2006, there were 196 major ethnic or religious minorities in the world facing some form of overt political discrimination – with such discrimination occurring in 108 of the 126 countries and areas considered by the project to be home to substantial ethnic minority groups (University of Maryland, 2015). Likewise, persons with disabilities are formally disadvantaged in employment in some countries where the minimum wage may be lowered or waived for persons in this group (ILO, 2014e).

Discrimination in law according to sexual orientation and gender identity is particularly widespread. The International Lesbian, Gay, Bisexual, Trans and Intersex Association lists 75 countries that have criminal laws against sexual activity by lesbian, homosexual, bisexual, transgender or intersex people, and 8 countries where the death penalty can be imposed for such activity (Carroll and Itaborahy, 2015). Furthermore, 60 per cent of Governments in 2012 reported the existence of laws and policies that present obstacles to effective prevention, treatment, care and support for people living with the human immunodeficiency virus (HIV), and 44 countries still impose restrictions on the entry, stay or residence of people living with HIV (Joint United Nations Programme on HIV/AIDS, 2013).

While the number of overtly discriminatory laws and policies is declining, Governments are increasingly implementing laws and policies designed to prevent discrimination as well as policies to promote the well-being of and give voice to disadvantaged groups. Where protective laws are in place, their enforcement poses challenges and is often inadequate. For example, some countries have legislation that mandates that the physical environment be made accessible to people with disabilities. Yet in France, where all public and private establishments open to the public are required to be physically accessible, just 15 per cent of establishments were accessible to persons with disabilities as of 2012 (United Nations, 2015b). Effective implementation calls for judicial and related institutions to have sufficient administrative, financial and other capacity. This entails thorough knowledge of the law, clear lines of responsibility and appropriate resources and coordination mechanisms, among other things. Moreover, officials must have the will to fully respond to violations and be subject to oversight. At the same time, low awareness among the public of their rights and the legal system governing them is also an impediment to implementation, as many individuals – in particular those who are excluded – do not know that they are legally protected from discrimination or, if they do know, may not be aware of how to report acts of discrimination, which can involve complex, poorly accessible and even costly procedures. Victims may also avoid pursuing legal cases for fear that doing so would subject them to scrutiny, stigma or reprisal. Some people are unable to provide documentation proving their identity, which may be necessary to claim their rights, including to legal services.

Even in countries with non-discriminatory and protective laws in place, prejudice, stereotypes and discriminatory practices prevail. Despite legal protection, some individuals and groups are subject to bias, negative attitudes and stereotyping, including among public officials. For example, the Public Report on Basic Education in India (PROBE Team, 1999) cited cases of teachers banning lower-caste children from enrolling in school, while Hanna and Linden (2012) found that lower-caste children – and males in particular – are more likely than other students to have teachers negatively assess their academic performance. Measuring  prejudicial attitudes and discriminatory behaviours is therefore necessary to provide a fuller picture of the kind of unfair treatment meted out every day to people on the basis of, among other things, their age, race, ethnicity, sexual orientation, gender identity or disability status.

## B.  Measuring interpersonal discrimination

Much like the broader process of social exclusion, the prevalence of discrimination varies depending on the way in which it is measured. In general, research suggests that perceived discrimination is underreported (Kaiser and Major, 2006). Publicly registered incidents of discrimination, such as legal cases brought against employers or public authorities, reported incidents of hate crimes, or complaints registered with non-governmental organizations, are of limited use for cross-country comparisons or to examine trends in the prevalence of discrimination. People's willingness to report such cases depends on the policy environment – whether discrimination is prevented by law – the challenges involved in reporting complaints and the perceived effectiveness of the police and judiciary in addressing and sanctioning such cases. In general, few cases are reported unless policies and institutions are favourable to the pursuit of discrimination claims (European Union Agency for Fundamental Rights, 2009). As policies and institutions vary over time and between countries, official figures must be interpreted with caution. In many cases, incidents of discrimination simply do not enter into official data. For instance, a study of selected regions and cities in nine countries found that only about 10 per cent of women who had been physically abused sought assistance from legal or social services (World Bank, 2011).

Beyond official statistics, research methods employed to measure discrimination include studies of perceptions, attitude surveys, econometric studies, laboratory experiments and field experiments. Perception studies, attitudinal surveys and experimental techniques usually measure prejudicial attitudes, that is, negative and stereotypical views of persons based on their membership in certain groups. Discriminatory acts – behaviours directed against persons because of their membership in a particular group – are frequently measured by field experiments. The following sections provide an overview of these methods and illustrate how each has been used to detect the presence and extent of discrimination.

## 1. Indirect evidence of discrimination through statistical analyses

As shown in chapter III, inequalities across social groups can often be observed even after controlling for the distinct composition of each group, including differences in educational levels and other human capital endowments. These "residual" inequalities are often attributed to the impact of discrimination. In statistical analyses of intergroup differences in intergenerational mobility, race, for instance, remains a significant variable once differences in initial socioeconomic conditions are accounted for.[74] Research on Brazil would suggest, however, that race plays a stronger role in explaining differences in upward social mobility among individuals from lower socioeconomic strata than among the upper classes (Ribeiro, 2006).

In Europe, education alone has not been sufficient to deliver upward mobility for children of migrants, implying that other barriers are blocking the access of this second generation to opportunities in the labour market (Glastra, 1999; Gowricharn, 1989). A growing body of empirical evidence indicates that social mobility is significantly lower among non-European than among European migrants (Altzinger and others, 2015; Attias-Donfut and Wolff, 2009). Beyond discrimination, some of the residual differences in the labour market situation and social mobility of migrants as compared with non-migrants are due to unequal language skills and undervalued educational credentials, including those acquired by migrants in their countries of origin[75] (Rooth and Saarela, 2007; Bengtsson, Lundh and Scott, 2005; Roberts and Campbell, 2006). In order to control for language and other "nation-specific" forms of human capital, Rooth (2002) assessed differences in the probability of being employed between foreign-born individuals adopted as children and natives in Sweden. Holding constant age, sex, education and age at adoption, the study found that differences in the probability of employment between adoptees with visibly non-Nordic looks (darker skin colour, different ethnic groups) and natives were significant, while those between adoptees from Northern Europe and natives were not significant, suggesting the presence of discrimination on the basis of skin colour (Rooth, 2002).

The main limitation of statistical analyses is that prejudice and discriminatory behaviours are not measured directly, but only inferred. Any difference that is not explained by the model used is assumed to be the result of discrimination, yet the results may simply reflect the influence of variables omitted from the analyses, other than discriminatory norms and practices.

---

[74]    For the case of Brazil, see, for instance, Marteleto and Dondero (2016); Hasenbalg and Silva (1988); Caillaux (1994); Telles (2003); and Ribeiro (2010 and 2006).

[75]    The question is also whether lack of recognition of academic degrees and other qualifications earned in the country of origin is a legitimate form of differential treatment or whether it is a form of discrimination. An increasing number of countries have formal pathways to assess and recognize formal qualifications acquired abroad (see, for instance, International Organization for Migration, 2013). However, formal recognition does not necessarily translate into fair assessment by employers.

The inability to account for all possible sources of unmeasured causes limits scholars' ability to make strong causal claims.

## 2. Perceived experiences of discrimination

An alternative approach to measuring discrimination is inquiring about perceptions, including situations in which individuals feel that they have been treated unfairly, either through surveys or qualitative studies. While data on people's perceptions and values are still scarce, they are increasingly being collected in both developed and developing countries.

Based on such studies, members of racial or ethnic minority groups in many countries have been found to perceive that they face discrimination in day-to-day encounters, although perceived discrimination varies greatly depending on context as well as on the source of information used. One of the largest surveys aimed at measuring perceived discrimination and racial victimization was conducted in 2008 by the European Union Agency for Fundamental Rights. In that survey, 23,500 immigrants and members of ethnic minorities in all 27 European Union Member States were interviewed. Among other questions, respondents were asked about perceptions and personal experiences of discrimination on the basis of their ethnicity, immigrant background or on multiple grounds in nine areas of everyday life, including at work, at school and by health-care and social service personnel. The results showed that 1 in 4 respondents reported feeling discriminated against in the previous 12 months on at least 2 of the following grounds: ethnic or immigrant origin, gender, age, disability, sexual orientation, religion or belief or "other" reasons (European Union Agency for Fundamental Rights, 2009). Place of work and job searches emerged as the most frequent areas of discriminatory treatment. Discrimination on the basis of ethnicity or immigrant origin was found to be more significant than discrimination on other grounds, including age and gender. In particular, individuals whose ethnicity or race is more visible vis-à-vis the majority population feel discriminated against more frequently and on a broader range of grounds than other minorities; close to 50 per cent of Roma and more than 40 per cent of persons of African origin reported experiencing discrimination in the previous 12 months, as compared with 10-15 per cent of persons of Eastern European background (European Union Agency for Fundamental Rights, 2009). However, sex, age and socioeconomic disadvantage were still shown to be important factors in experiencing discrimination. An average of 46 per cent of respondents who reported discrimination on different grounds were in the lowest income quartile in their host country (European Union Agency for Fundamental Rights, 2009).

Measures of perceived discrimination have been included in other surveys. In the 2010-2014 round of the World Values Survey, respondents were asked whether they had perceived racist behaviour occurring in their neighbourhood. Figure IV.1 shows the percentage of respondents reporting that racist behaviour occurs "frequently" or "very frequently" in their neighbourhood, by ethnic group – ethnic minorities or members of the majority population – and by region of the world. As should be expected, perceptions of racist behaviour are stronger among ethnic minorities in all regions and particularly in Africa.

Figure IV.1

**Percentage of survey respondents reporting frequent racist behaviour in their neighbourhood by region, 2010-2014**

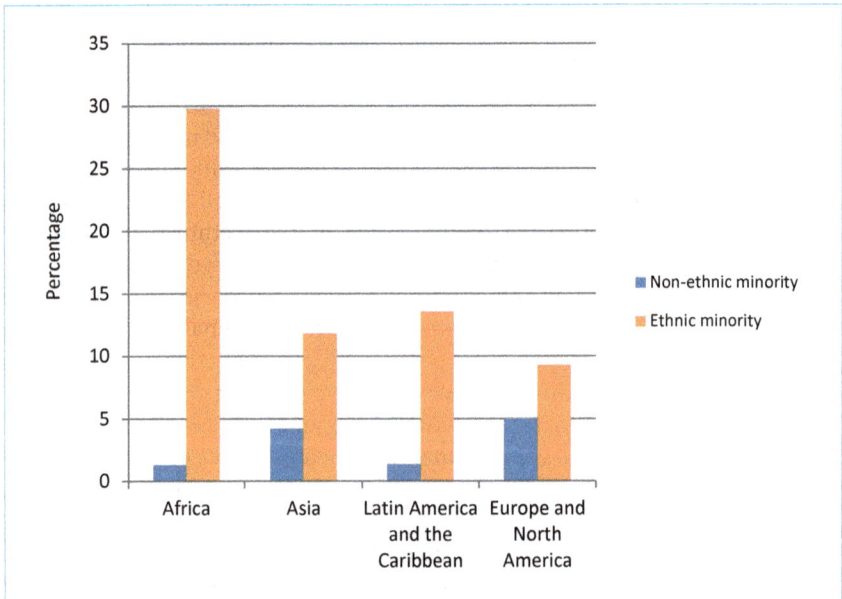

*Source:* World Values Survey Wave 6 (2010-2014).
**Notes:** Regional averages based on data for 12 countries in Africa (Algeria, Egypt, Ghana, Libya, Morocco, Nigeria, Rwanda, South Africa, Tunisia, United Republic of Tanzania, Uganda, Zimbabwe), 31 countries and areas in Asia (Armenia, Azerbaijan, Bahrain, Bangladesh, China, Cyprus, Georgia, Hong Kong Special Administrative Region (SAR) of China, India, Indonesia, Islamic Republic of Iran, Iraq, Japan, Jordan, Kazakhstan, Kuwait, Kyrgyzstan, Lebanon, Malaysia, Pakistan, Philippines, Qatar, Republic of Korea, Saudi Arabia, Singapore, Taiwan SAR of China, Thailand, Turkey, Uzbekistan, Viet Nam, Yemen), 12 countries in Latin America and the Caribbean (Argentina, Brazil, Chile, Colombia, Dominican Republic, Ecuador, El Salvador, Guatemala, Mexico, Peru, Trinidad and Tobago, Uruguay and Venezuela) and 40 countries in Europe, North America and Oceania (Albania, Australia, Austria, Belarus, Belgium, Bosnia and Herzegovina, Bulgaria, Canada, Croatia, Czechia, Denmark, Estonia, Finland, France, Germany, Greece, Hungary, Iceland, Ireland, Italy, Latvia, Luxembourg, Macedonia (The Former Yugoslav Republic of), Malta, Netherlands, New Zealand, Norway, Poland, Portugal, Republic of Moldova, Romania, Russian Federation, Slovakia, Slovenia, Spain, Sweden, Switzerland, Ukraine, United Kingdom, United States of America).

## 3. Attitudinal studies

One of the shortcomings of subjective perception data is that they measure the views of those subject to discrimination and may therefore not be representative of discriminatory intent. While measuring discrimination through lived experiences can be an effective tool for diagnosing perceived marginalization, it is more valid when complemented by measures of prejudicial attitudes among dominant groups.

World Values Surveys assess prejudicial attitudes through a set of questions on whether respondents would object to having certain groups of people as neighbours. As shown in figure IV.2, the majority of respondents in 18 countries with data objected to having as neighbours persons suffering from

Figure IV.2

**Percentage of survey respondents who object to having each of the groups shown as neighbours[1] in selected countries,[2] 1990-1994 and 2010-2014**

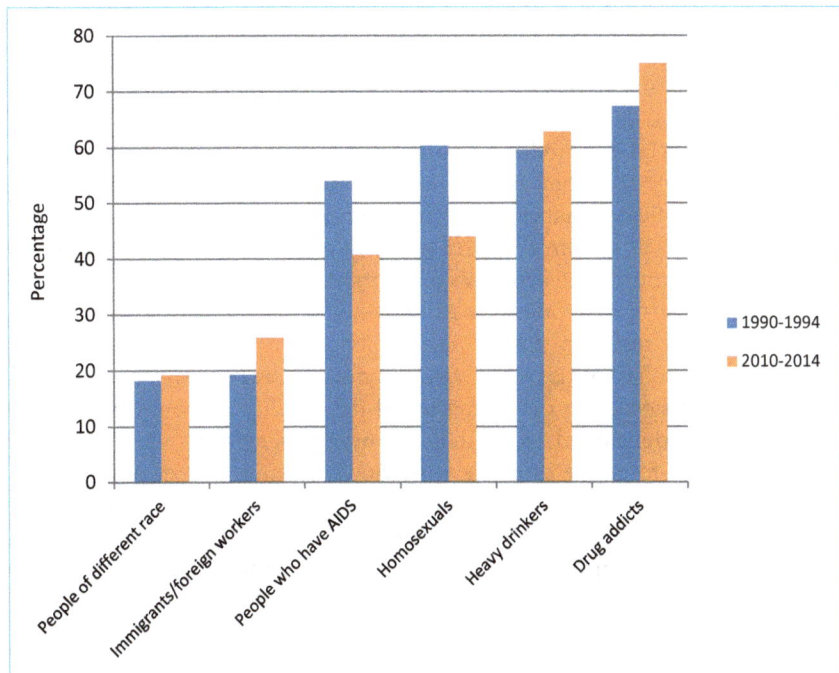

*Source:* World Values Survey, 1990-1994 and 2010-2014 waves.

[1] The figure shows the percentage of respondents who mentioned each of the groups listed in their response to the following question: "On this list are various groups of people. Could you please mention any that you would not like to have as neighbours?"

[2] Average percentage for 18 countries with data: Argentina, Belarus, Brazil, Czech Republic, Chile, China, India, Japan, Mexico, Nigeria, Poland, Russian Federation, Slovakia, South Africa, South Korea, Spain, Switzerland and Turkey.

addictions. According to these data, prejudice against migrants and people of a different race increased from the period 1990-1994 to 2010-2014, while bias against homosexuals and persons living with AIDS declined during the period. Attitudes towards migrants often become more negative in periods of economic insecurity or following large waves of immigration. The perceptions that most often lead to such negative attitudes are that migrants take away jobs from natives; that they commit illegal acts; that they are ungrateful to the host country and do not assimilate, learn the language or adhere to the rules; and that they drain the welfare system (World Bank, 2013, table 5.2, p. 163). Additional research conducted mainly in countries with economies in transition indicates that, while sociodemographic characteristics, such as levels of education, income, employment status and individuals' social capital, have influence on the levels of tolerance towards these groups, country context is the most important determinant of prejudicial attitudes (Lakhani, Sacks and Heltberg, 2014).[76] In other words, a country's institutions, history and overall values matter more for tolerance and respect of others than levels of education or employment in the countries examined.

## 4. Experimental survey techniques

While surveys are useful in detecting how widespread discriminatory attitudes are, one of the limitations of surveying prejudicial beliefs is the prevalence of social desirability response bias, or the pressure on participants to give responses that they believe to be consistent with prevailing social norms, instead of those that reflect their own true beliefs. Differences between countries as well as within the same country over time may be attributable to variation in the social acceptance of prejudicial views, rather than the actual prevalence of such opinions. Moreover, personally held prejudices and stereotypes may result in unintentional bias and more subtle, unconscious discriminatory behaviour of which the individual may be unaware (Hebl and others, 2002). In order to overcome social desirability response bias, social scientists have developed experimental survey techniques which provide the opportunity to gauge differences in views or attitudes towards various social groups without requiring any direct comparisons between groups. In-depth interviews have been shown to be highly effective in eliciting candid discussions about sensitive hiring issues, for instance (Kirschenman and Neckerman, 1991; Moss and Tilly, 1996; Newman, 1999; Wilson, 1997).

In the early work of Schuman and others (1988) in the United States, individuals were asked about the right of a community to prevent families

---

[76]    Findings from this research are based on the second Life in Transition survey, conducted in 2010 by the European Bank for Reconstruction and Development in 29 countries with economies in transition and in 5 other European countries in order to assess people's views and attitudes in the context of political change. For more information about the survey, see www.ebrd.com/what-we-do/economic-research-and-data/data/lits.html.

from moving into their neighbourhood based on their race. While respondents did not show prejudice against persons of African descent or other ethnic groups when asked about the right of a family to move to a particular area, they were more willing to express opposition to government attempts to introduce anti-discrimination laws when reference was made to protecting the right to move of families made up of persons of African descent, relative to other groups. Discriminatory attitudes were influenced by perceived income and social class: opposition to having a neighbour from a minority ethnic group declined if such a neighbour belonged to the middle class (defined in terms of income or occupational category).

Survey experiments have also been used to reveal the prevalence of discriminatory attitudes and behaviours in the social and political life of developing countries. Bhavnani (2013), for instance, presented voters in India with fictional candidates having different names which were designed to reflect upper- or lower-caste backgrounds, and then registered their willingness to vote for that candidate as their representative. He found that potential voters vastly discriminated in favour of upper-caste candidates. Non-scheduled (higher) caste candidates averaged 10.3 per cent of the votes, while scheduled (lower) caste candidates averaged just 1.5 per cent. Such discriminatory responses not only reflect prejudicial attitudes, but are also a consequence of living in a discriminatory society where upper-caste politicians are perceived as having better chances to secure benefits for their constituents (Bhavnani, 2013).

## 5. Field experiments to detect discriminatory practices

Field experiments combine experimental methods with field-based research and help stimulate real-world interactions. For instance, instead of asking respondents to assess the quality of two hypothetical job applications in a laboratory setting, a field experiment would present two equally qualified job applicants to real employers within the scenario of an actual job hunt. Since an open preference for members of a specific social group or prejudice against members of other groups is often both legally and socially undesirable, institutions usually mask their discriminatory actions behind non-racial justifications.

Studies based on experimental methods have most often been used to detect labour market discrimination. Large inter-ethnic differences in callback rates for job applications, for example, were detected by Bertrand and Mullainathan (2004) in the United States during fieldwork regarding employment advertisements in two newspapers. After having randomly assigned résumés of similar quality and postal addresses, it was observed that a name associated with the white population yielded as many more callbacks as did an additional eight years of experience on a résumé. Furthermore, applicants living in higher-income neighbourhoods with a white majority had a higher probability of being asked back for an interview.

In the United States, while the Age Discrimination in Employment Act 1967 makes it unlawful to consider the age of an applicant in hiring and remuneration decisions, experimental studies have found such a bias to exist. Older workers are subject to worse hiring outcomes than their younger counterparts, although it is usually difficult to determine whether the delays in hiring are due to discrimination, higher reservation wages or clustering in "sick" industries (Hirsch, Macpherson and Hardy, 2000). Lahey (2006), however, showed that a younger job seeker needed to file, on average, only 18 applications before landing an interview call, whereas older job seekers needed to file 25.

Similarly, Hebl and others (2002) found discrimination in hiring on the basis of sexual orientation. Applicants entered a shopping mall to apply for the job of storekeeper, with the applicant's sexual preference made evident via statements professionally printed on baseball hats. Interpersonal discrimination was detected through the length of the total time of interaction – with employers engaging less with applicants that they may have assumed to be homosexual, through the level of attention paid to questions asked by the stigmatized test group and through perceived negativity in remarks and attitudes. In addition, those applicants appearing to be homosexual were hired at a rate that was 75 per cent that of the control group (Hebl and others, 2002).

In Sweden, Ahmed and Hammarstedt (2008) found ethnic discrimination in the housing market. Three fictitious tester profiles, one with a typical male Swedish name ("Erik"), one with a typical female Swedish name ("Maria") and one with a typical male Arabic or Muslim name ("Ali"), applied for vacant rental apartments advertised on the Internet. Using the "Maria" profile, 53 per cent of applications led to positive callbacks and 19 per cent to invitations to showings. As for the "Erik" profile applications, 41 per cent received invitations to make further contact, and about 10 per cent led to invitations to showings. By contrast, applications under the "Ali" profile received an 18 per cent response rate, with only 4 per cent leading to invitations to viewings. Similar differences were found with respect to the neighbourhoods where the housing units were located, with the Swedish-sounding profiles having received more responses in wealthier urban areas (Ahmed and Hammarstedt, 2008).

The evidence cited in this section indicates that the use of field experiments, though still in its infancy, provides the best evidence yet of the actual existence and prevalence of discriminatory practices. However, while they demonstrate conclusively that such norms exist, field experiments are still small in size due to their cost.

## C. Internalized stigma and reduced sense of agency

Persistent exposure to discrimination can lead individuals to internalize the prejudice or stigma that is directed against them. Such internalization may be manifested in shame, poor self-esteem, fear and stress, as well as poor mental and physical health (Williams, Neighbors and Jackson, 2003). Beyond these debilitating effects, discrimination may also impede individuals' achievement and their capacity to make decisions and act on them, that is, their agency. In other words, individuals sometimes effectively behave in ways that conform to how others perceive them.

A survey regarding HIV-related stigma and discrimination conducted among people living with HIV in nine countries in the Asia-Pacific region found that a significant percentage of respondents reported feelings of shame (ranging from 54 to 76 per cent) and guilt (from 43 to 76 per cent) as well as low self-esteem (from 22 to 81 per cent) (Global Network of People Living with HIV and others, 2011). Many respondents isolated themselves, avoided accessing needed health-care services and chose to withdraw from work, education or training, or to not apply for a job or promotion. A positive association between shame and poverty has also been well established in the context of discrimination (Chase and Bantebya-Kyomuhendo, 2014).

Discrimination and exclusion are correlated with negative physical and mental health effects as well. Discrimination has, for instance, been associated with self-reported poor health, psychological distress, anxiety and depression, hypertension as well as potential disease risk factors, such as obesity and substance abuse (Pascoe and Smart Richman, 2009). In particular, the perception of discrimination increases the likelihood of participating in unhealthy behaviours, such as smoking and overeating, and reduces participation in behaviours that foster good health, such as disease screening and management (Pascoe and Smart Richman, 2009). A survey in the United Kingdom, for instance, found that lesbian, homosexual and bisexual adults have a higher prevalence of poor mental health and low well-being when compared with heterosexuals (Semlyen and others, 2016). In New Zealand, a study found that both deprivation and perceived discrimination contribute to health inequalities between Māori and persons of European descent, with the Māori disproportionately reporting poor or fair self-rated health, low physical functioning, low mental health and cardiovascular disease (Harris and others, 2006). That mental illness is itself subject to stigma creates the potential for additional discrimination.

Internalized discrimination can be further manifested in other ways, too. Studies have shown that women often ask for less money than do men in seeking jobs and are more likely to accept initial wage offers without negotiation (Babcock and Laschever, 2003; Moreno and others, 2004). A related effect of discrimination can be triggered when an individual's identity is cued or emphasized in a context that has relevance to a stereotype of that identity, such as intellectual ability. This phenomenon, termed "stereotype threat", is defined as "being at risk of confirming, as self-characteristic, a negative stereotype about one's group" (Steele and Aronson, 1995). Such stereotypes and their impacts take hold at a young age. In recent experiments in India, low-status and high-status groups of children and youth were asked to solve mazes; monetary incentives were provided. In control treatments, Indian boys in both high-caste and low-caste groups solved mazes equally well when their caste was not publicly revealed. However, when social identity was made public in mixed group sessions, low-caste participants performed significantly worse (Hoff and Pandey, 2006). An experiment focused on children aged 5-13 years in the United States addressed two stereotypes simultaneously: that Asian students perform better than other ethnic groups, and that women perform worse than men. Asian girls as young as five years old performed better on a test when their ethnic identity was "activated" – through a pre-test questionnaire that emphasized ethnicity – and worse when their gender identity was activated (Ambady and others, 2001). The fact that negative stereotypes and feelings of powerlessness negatively affect performance helps to explain why historical inequalities often persist once progressive reforms have been implemented.

Although agency is also difficult to measure (see box IV.2), qualitative research suggests that lack of agency is central to the perceived ill-being of women and of people living in poverty. As thoroughly illustrated in the three publications produced by the World Bank, entitled *Voices of the Poor*, feelings of impotence and powerlessness are expressed persistently in explaining poverty; "you know good but you cannot do good", as described by a study participant in Ghana (Narayan and others, 2000, p. 32). Much of the sense of powerlessness is attributed to experiences with employers, landlords, bankers and public officials and institutions that, in the view of people living in poverty, undermine and exclude them (Narayan and others, 2000). For women, discriminatory social norms affect key decisions that shape agency. Specifically, the inequitable allocation of household resources between boys and girls has often resulted in less education and nutrition for girls, as described in chapter III of the present report. Gender norms that attribute submissive qualities to women and that assign domestic and breadwinning roles to female and male identities, respectively, continue to influence people's sense of agency and their willingness to exercise it. Although values evolve, findings from a field study in 20 countries would suggest that gender norms have not changed drastically over time or across cohorts, but tend to evolve slowly (Muñoz Boudet and others, 2013). The softening of gender norms often comes with increases in education and in women's participation in the labour market, which have also strengthened women's collective agency and contribute to further relaxing of gender roles.

Research on agency also shows that the ability to make choices varies across groups in a range of spheres: a woman may have control over income

Box IV.2

## The challenges of measuring agency

Agency, which is often defined as the ability to envisage and act upon one's goals or to make meaningful choices, is a crucial component of social inclusion. However, measuring levels of individual agency and comparing these across groups, places and times is particularly challenging. Agency is a relative concept, as the range of meaningful choices available to one person within a reference group, such as a country or community, is usually defined relatively according to the range of choices available to another person within that group. Typically, measures of female agency in a community are devised considering the range of choices available to men within that community; the sense of agency among ethnic minorities is measured relative to ethnic majorities and that of people with disabilities relative to those without disabilities. It is also a subjective and context-specific phenomenon – in practice meaning different things to different people.

Often, attempts at measuring agency have been focused on observable actions in concrete domains, such as one's freedom of movement, or control over financial resources (Ibrahim and Alkire, 2007). The importance of each domain varies by context. As Mahmud, Shah and Becker (2012) pointed out in their study on women's empowerment in Bangladesh, an indicator of freedom of mobility is more relevant in a patriarchal context, where women are traditionally confined to the home, than in a Western context. Even within the same community, agency may be experienced and exercised in different ways depending on an individual's wealth and age, which would also affect the relative weight put on specific indicators. Moreover, a person's sense of agency is influenced by cognitive processes of reflection and analysis, and attitudes to or rejection of subordination, which are even more difficult to measure objectively (Kishor and Gupta, 2004). Kabeer (1999), for instance, argued that many women's internal acceptance of their own subordinate status within a household makes the exercise of agency much more difficult in claims on household resources and reproductive decisions. Similarly, recent research has shown the psychological pathways through which a life in poverty and the associated feelings of shame and inadequacy can limit agency, for example preventing some people living in poverty from accessing services (Lakhani, Sacks and Heltberg, 2014).

The concept of agency therefore has significance within a concrete community or country. While cross-country opinion polls and surveys, including the Gallup World Poll and the World Values Survey, contain questions aimed at assessing the perceived sense of agency among respondents, context-dependent measures should complement general, internationally comparable ones (Ibrahim and Alkire, 2007).

or decisions in her household but may be hesitant to participate in political meetings or engage in collective action because of her sex, her ethnicity or social status, and may be excluded from the labour market due to these or other attributes (Alkire, 2005). The exercise of agency is therefore most often assessed in concrete domains or through multiple indicators, even though the majority of studies highlight the links among different domains (Ibrahim and Alkire, 2007; World Bank, 2011). In other words, participation in the labour market broadens networks and sources of information and can therefore give political voice to members of ethnic minorities, persons with disabilities or women. Such participation has also been found to promote women's agency within the household (World Bank, 2011).

## D. Conclusions

In recent decades, much has been done to end legally imposed discrimination against individuals and groups and policies that sustain unfair treatment in economic, social, cultural and political spheres of life. However, while formal institutions may have become fairer, formal discrimination nonetheless persists. What is more, based on the ample anecdotal and comparatively limited empirical evidence that exists, discriminatory norms and interpersonal instances of discrimination remain widespread and continue to structure group-based differences in societal outcomes. Yet while formal institutional barriers faced by marginalized groups are easy to detect, informal barriers are frequently more subtle, and authors of studies on discrimination have long grappled with the challenge of empirical measurement.

Studies of perceptions, attitude surveys, statistical analyses and field experiments have shown that discriminatory behaviours can be quantified across countries and over time. Multiple indicators and sources of evidence demonstrate the persistence of both prejudicial attitudes and norms in societies. In other words, discrimination remains a fundamental problem in the world today. National institutions, both formal and informal, play a large role in attitudes towards specific social groups and on overall levels of tolerance. The literature reviewed is testimony to the tangible as well as the intangible impact that discriminatory behaviours and prejudicial attitudes have on the way people work, the opportunities they have, the quality and nature of the relationships they forge, their health and well-being and the decisions they make. Field experiments make the effects of prejudiced decision-making clear in terms of the social exclusion of marginalized groups. They also show that prejudice is deeply entrenched and can limit the impact of laws, services and income for those groups that suffer from discrimination.

While discrimination is decried around the globe and legal obligations and guidelines exist to fight it, much work remains to be done to achieve the goal of a world free of discrimination and prejudice. Continued efforts to capture the extent of discrimination and better understand its effects are a necessary step towards realizing this goal. As the next chapter shows, ending discrimination and removing other obstacles that hinder the capacity of disadvantaged groups to participate in society and to engage in decision-making is a long-term process. It requires several processes: reforming institutions, investing in human capital and influencing certain norms and behaviours that often have historical roots. However, failure to create the conditions for the empowerment and participation of those who are socially, economically or politically excluded comes with high costs.

Chapter V

# Policy imperatives for leaving no one behind

## Key messages

- *In order to leave no one behind, Governments must promote social inclusion as well as tackle the barriers that create and sustain exclusion. A universal approach to social policy, complemented with special or targeted measures, is key to addressing the underlying causes of exclusion and social injustice.*

- *Leaving no one behind calls for institutional change as well. Ensuring that institutions are inclusive can contribute to levelling the playing field and providing all citizens with opportunities to participate in public life on equal terms.*

- *Changing the social, cultural and political norms that underpin or perpetuate unequal power relations and the disadvantages experienced by some social groups is often a long-term process, dependent on national and local circumstances, but with political will Governments can influence and help transform them.*

In committing to the full implementation of the 2030 Agenda, Member States recognized that the dignity of the human person is fundamental. They are also endeavouring to reach first those that are furthest behind. The fact remains that today, some human beings are condemned to endure short or miserable lives as a result of their origin, race, ethnicity, religious affiliation, economic status or because they have a disability. Overcoming the biases associated with these circumstances requires a policy approach that puts human beings at the centre of development, as agreed at the World Summit for Social Development in Copenhagen more than 20 years ago. What is needed is an approach that expands the opportunities to improve people's quality of life – now and in the future – and protect their rights. An approach which considers economic growth as a means to leave no one behind, rather than an end in itself.

Policy approaches to address exclusion and leave no one behind have often been centred on the promotion of the rights and capabilities of disadvantaged social groups. There is nonetheless growing recognition that action to promote social inclusion must go beyond group-specific approaches. It is contended in the present report that, while breaking the cycle of poverty and exclusion does require policies and strategies which actively seek and facilitate the participation of those individuals and social groups that face the greatest challenges in overcoming such ills, measures are also called for that would address the underlying social, economic and political causes of inequality and social injustice.

As noted in the previous chapters, the process of social inclusion is shaped by national and local circumstances – from economic, social and political institutions to norms, behaviours and social relations. Therefore, no single set of policies or strategies is applicable across all countries and in all contexts. Instead, successful examples point to several imperatives to address the structural causes of exclusion and social injustice. The first imperative is to establish a universal approach to social policy, complemented by special or targeted measures to address the distinct obstacles faced by disadvantaged, marginalized or otherwise excluded social groups. The second imperative is to overcome the misalignment often observed between social development goals and macroeconomic policy frameworks. The third broad imperative is to promote inclusive institutions.

The universal provision of social protection as well as good-quality health and education services can address a range of exclusionary barriers. Access to good-quality education in particular empowers individuals economically by enhancing their human capital, but it also entitles them socially and politically. Further, such education can build confidence among groups facing systemic disadvantages by enabling them to participate more meaningfully in public and civic life.

Analysis throughout the report has highlighted the role that economic, social, political, legal and cultural institutions play in either perpetuating exclusion or, alternately, promoting inclusion. Ensuring that institutions are inclusive can contribute to levelling the playing field, providing all people with opportunities to participate in public life on equal terms. Institutions can also foster positive change in attitudes and behaviour. In this chapter, therefore, there is an examination of how Governments as well as the international community can encourage institutional environments in which policies for inclusion are more likely to be adopted, take hold and flourish. Such norms and values evolve slowly and are affected by context, culture and history, but – as the examples presented in the next sections indicate – Governments can influence and help to transform them. Institutional change is often a long-term process, dependent on national and local circumstances. However, with concerted effort and political motivation, it is possible to change institutions.

## A. Addressing exclusion: forward-looking strategies for social development

### 1. The importance of a universal approach to social policy for promoting inclusion

Inclusive societies are those that have ensured equal access to opportunities and guaranteed fairness in the distribution of outcomes. Evidence shows that a lack of social protection or inadequate coverage is linked to entrenched poverty and insecurity, rising inequality and underinvestment in human capital (ILO, 2014c; UNRISD, 2010). In high-income countries, recent fiscal consolidation programmes following the global financial and economic crisis that began in 2008 have contributed to worsened poverty and social exclusion, including among older persons, women with young children and persons with disabilities. In the European Union, 123 million people were at risk of poverty or social exclusion in 2012 compared with 116 million in 2008, with 800,000 more children living in poverty than in 2008 (ILO, 2014c; UNRISD, 2010).

The universal provision of services in such key areas as health care and education, coupled with social protection for all members of society, contributes to social inclusion in a number of important ways. By ensuring that access to good-quality public goods and services is extended to all members of society, regardless of status, ethnicity, sex or age, the State acknowledges that all individuals, households and communities are worthy of consideration and should benefit from the basic entitlements that come with such consideration (UNRISD, 2010). Identifying and legally recognizing all individuals and groups, ensuring that they are counted, as well as engaging with potential beneficiaries and understanding their needs, and making certain that they count, are key to any attempt at ensuring the universal provision of social services.

A universal approach to social policy also contributes significantly to realizing the normative human rights commitments that underpin social inclusion. Through that approach, the responsibility and duty of the State is realized in terms of guaranteeing the protection of social rights for all in such areas as education, health care and housing, without discrimination. These rights, as laid out in the "International Bill of Human Rights"[77] and other universal human rights instruments, are of intrinsic value as well as important means for promoting the well-being of all. Governments around the world have grounded the extension of free primary education, for example, in the universal right to basic education. In recent times, such Latin

---

[77]   The Universal Declaration of Human Rights, which was adopted by General Assembly resolution 217 A (III), forms the first part of the International Bill; the second and third parts consist of two covenants: the International Covenant on Economic, Social and Cultural Rights and the International Covenant on Civil and Political Rights and its two Optional Protocols, which were adopted by General Assembly resolution 2200A (XXI).

American countries as Brazil have increasingly emphasized social justice and citizenship rights as part of social policy reforms (UNRISD, 2010). Jamaica has been able to create a normative framework that obligates the Government to continually seek solutions to housing challenges that its citizens face by recognizing the human right to shelter through laws, policies and international treaties (UNRISD, 2010). Similarly in India, the National Rural Employment Guarantee Act passed in 2005 is aimed at realizing the right to work for all Indian citizens, while experiments with a basic income guarantee programme have been conducted in the Indian state of Madhya Pradesh under the justification of the right to a basic minimum income (Davala and others, 2015).

Critically, a rights-based approach to promoting social inclusion – with emphasis on social justice, fairness and solidarity – directly challenges the values, social norms and attitudes that give rise to exclusionary behaviour and practices within communities. This aspect is important as policies aimed at fostering equal opportunities can easily be undermined if they do not tackle discriminatory beliefs and practices (Lakhani, Sacks and Heltberg, 2014).

Clearly, universal approaches to social policy will be realized in different forms in various country contexts. Common to all approaches, however, is the recognition of the duties and responsibilities of the State towards all members of society. Under the Social Protection Floor Initiative of the United Nations system, for instance, a nationally defined set of minimum guarantees is proposed for all citizens without discrimination.[78] It is therefore illustrative of a policy approach with a universal vision and scope that can be implemented in different ways at the national level based on county-specific institutional and administrative structures, fiscal space and social policy needs, objectives and priorities. The European Union's "Europe 2020" strategy for growth, combined with the eradication of poverty and social exclusion, is an example of an overarching regional policy framework which has inspired consistent national plans while still reflecting specific political, social and economic priorities. At the national level, the national development plan of Rwanda, Vision 2020, is grounded in social inclusion and calls for equity-oriented national policies. A health system for all citizens is central to the plan and has helped to sharply reduce premature mortality rates and increase life expectancy (Binagwaho and others, 2014).

The case for a universal approach to social policy inevitably raises concerns about its affordability. When it comes to social protection, ILO has estimated that the cost of providing a universal social protection floor is affordable, even for least developed countries. For a selected set of low- and low-middle-income countries in sub-Saharan Africa and Asia, a basic package of social protection, including old-age and disability pensions and family allowances, but excluding health care, was estimated to cost between 2.2 per cent and 5.7 per cent of GDP (ILO, 2008).

---

[78]    E/2009/114, para. 26.

Delivering comprehensive universal health-care coverage is generally more expensive than providing basic social protection. OECD countries spent 8.9 per cent of GDP on health care in 2013 (OECD, 2015c). Thailand has been able to implement a comprehensive universal coverage scheme with an expenditure of 6 per cent of GDP (WHO, 2016). Yet a growing number of developing countries are rolling out universal health-care coverage programmes. In most cases, countries are moving slowly towards the universal provision of services, with the aim of gradually improving benefits, quality and financial protection by focusing initially on the needs of people living in poverty and other disadvantaged groups who most often are not covered by programmes in place (Cotlear and others, 2015; Cecchini and others, 2015). Universal access to primary and secondary education is less costly, with OECD countries spending an average of 3.7 per cent of their GDP on such services (OECD, 2015d). Recent estimates suggest that, for low- and lower-middle-income countries to meet some of their targets of delivering universal pre-primary, primary and secondary education under Sustainable Development Goal 4, Governments will need to increase spending from 3.5 per cent to 6.3 per cent of their GDP between 2012 and 2030 (UNESCO, 2015c).

Social protection programmes currently are strongly dependent on international aid, especially in low-income countries of sub-Saharan Africa. The challenge for many poor countries is to raise additional revenues domestically and through development assistance. Some developing countries have seen a rise in public revenues during the last decade. This rise has been partly on account of both indirect and direct taxes, but equally important have been the increase in non-tax income in commodity-exporting countries, the rise in official development assistance, particularly in countries recovering from conflict, and a reduction in the interest burden of public debt.

Policy-oriented research indicates that there is scope for further mobilizing domestic resources and therefore expanding fiscal space in developing countries (Hujo, 2011). There is also potential for increasing the redistributive impact of taxation and social transfers in both developed and developing countries, for example, through higher tax rates on top earners and dividends on property, as well as strengthening tax collection systems that broaden the domestic tax base. The mobilization of domestic resources through modernized, progressive tax systems, improved tax policy and more efficient tax collection is a key action area that was agreed by Heads of State and Government in Addis Ababa.[79] The Addis Ababa Action Agenda of the Third International Conference on Financing for Development also includes a commitment to combat tax evasion and corruption through strengthened national regulation and increased international cooperation, and to reduce opportunities for tax avoidance.[80] These are not quick or easy processes but,

---

[79]   General Assembly resolution 69/313, para. 22.

[80]   Ibid., para. 23.

while systems will need to adapt to local circumstances, mobilizing domestic resources constitutes the most effective way of raising public revenues sustainably in the long tem. Taxation revenue is generally deemed superior to other sources because of its stability and its potential for financing programmes offering universal coverage. Prioritizing a broad and progressive revenue base can itself promote social inclusion not only by bolstering national fiscal space, but also by contributing to the kind of social solidarity and public "buy in" discussed previously.

## 2. Complementing a universal approach with special measures

Even under a policy framework grounded in universalism, certain segments of the population face greater challenges than others in overcoming social exclusion, as illustrated in chapter 3. In general, certain groups and geographical areas benefit disproportionately from publicly provided goods and services as well as resource rents. For example, the quality of education is often better in urban areas than in rural ones, even under a framework designed to ensure universal access. Its provision in urban areas tends to be less costly and more efficient, and the recruitment and retention of the most talented teachers is usually easier, as is administrative monitoring and oversight (UNESCO, 2015a). However, within urban areas, significant variations may also exist in the quality of schools and other public services between poor and rich neighbourhoods (UNESCO, 2015a). Other inequalities based on individual or group characteristics, such as sex, disability status, or ethnicity, can also prevent certain people from accessing services, or affect the quality of the services that they are able to access (United Nations, 2013b). Complementary special efforts are therefore needed, even if temporarily, to overcome these barriers and make universal provision more effective in promoting social inclusion.

Special or targeted measures include affirmative action policies, targeted monetary transfers and preferential access to credit for people living in poverty and extreme poverty, transport vouchers for persons with disabilities, as well as policies which recognize and protect languages, including interpretation services for indigenous language speakers. Affirmative action policies are aimed at redressing discrimination suffered by certain social groups. Reservation of seats for women in national and local government bodies in India and Rwanda have been shown to improve political participation for females (Powley, 2006; Chattopadhyay and Duflo, 2004). Preferences in university admission have helped students from low-income families and minority backgrounds to access higher education in Brazil (Gacitúa-Marió and Woolcock, 2008) and the United States (Kahlenburg, 2012). However, the full potential of such measures to improve social inclusion is strongly dependent on context. While better-connected or wealthier women may find more opportunities in politics as a result of female quotas, poorer women may see little change in their prospects for participation. Equally, preferential access to universities assists only the relatively small number of students from historically excluded groups who have completed secondary education. Additional research is needed to assess the overall impacts of these policies on other key inclusive outcomes, such as the reduction of poverty or income inequality (Marcus, Mdee and Page, 2016).

Targeting suffers from other problems: the high levels of administrative capacity required for means-testing, high transaction costs, the risk of political capture by the elites or the richest regions and its potential impact on social segmentation have been widely documented (United Nations, 2009). In recent decades, targeting has often been suggested by multilateral financial institutions and donors as a way to achieve social objectives without a significant rise in social spending (United Nations, 2009). In practice, however, social policies are rarely based on purely universal or purely targeted approaches; some measures are universal while others are targeted towards groups that need particular support and are difficult to reach through universal measures. Both types of spending may be justified depending on each country's situation. Criticism levelled at targeted or special measures for disadvantaged groups has been most acute when such measures have been used to replace universal ones rather than to complement them (ECLAC, 2015).

Often, special measures may be grounded in national and international legal instruments, including constitutions, conventions and declarations, aimed at protecting the rights of such groups. In Canada, constitutional reform in 1982 was designed to protect the rights of aboriginal citizens. Similarly, the United States in 1990 passed the Americans with Disabilities Act to prohibit discrimination based on persons' disability status and to impose accessibility requirements on public and private entities. At the global level, one of the purposes of the United Nations Convention on the Rights of Persons with Disabilities and its Optional Protocol is to change attitudes and approaches towards persons with disabilities by viewing such persons as "subjects" with rights who are capable of claiming those rights, making informed decisions on their lives and, overall, being active members of society. The Convention has been ratified by 160 States.[81]

Empirical literature on the link between such instruments and practical impacts for rights holders is, however, mixed. DeLeire (2000), for instance, found that in the 10 years following the adoption of Americans with Disabilities Act, persons with disabilities in the United States were less likely to be employed than persons without disabilities, as employers wanted to avoid the associated costs of ensuring accessibility. However, other authors have found positive relationships between constitutionally protected rights and improved outcomes for rights holders (Heymann, Raub and Cassola, 2014). Moreover, there is strong qualitative evidence to suggest that such

---

[81]   https://treaties.un.org/Pages/ViewDetails.aspx?src=TREATY, accessed on 25 October 2016.

legal codification of the rights of historically excluded groups can promote an attitudinal shift, both in society at large in terms of recognition and acceptance and among individuals in the excluded group in terms of a sense of entitlement, belonging and pride (Mattlin, 2015).

Nonetheless, if special or targeted measures are to genuinely promote inclusion, Governments must design them in ways that minimize chances of stigmatization. Affirmative action policies, for instance, need to be implemented within a broad framework of improved access to services for all, to ensure that they do not cement negative attitudes and a perception that members of groups targeted by such policies have not "earned" the advantages provided.

Measures targeting the empowerment of women must avoid features that perpetuate gender stereotypes or social stigmas, such as conditions that increase women's unpaid caregiving and domestic work (UN Women, 2015). Instead, social transfer schemes can provide incentives for men to take on childcare or other social care responsibilities. Labour market policies that require the provision of paid family leave, particularly paternity leave, have immense potential to contribute to women's participation in the labour market, including women's advancement in their jobs or careers (Pew Research Center, 2015). The private sector can lead in promoting more inclusive business practices, correcting gender imbalances in the workforce by confronting taboos against hiring women, eradicating gender pay gaps, investing in knowledge and skills of female employees as well as providing flexible working arrangements for all staff. Governments can also build the capacity of health and social services to eliminate gender-based violence, or work with civil society to enable women and girls to effectively enjoy their rights to health care and reproductive health services and sanitation. These measures can include building adequate sanitation facilities in schools, or conducting awareness-raising campaigns on the responsibilities of men to tackle sexism and gender-biased attitudes, such as taboos concerning menstruation (UN Women, 2015).

Governments must also recognize the need to integrate temporary special measures and social safety nets into broader social protection systems. While some groups, such as persons with disabilities, may always require specific efforts to ensure their inclusion, the ultimate goal of this approach should be to bring everyone up to the same starting line – to leave no one behind. Enhancing equality of opportunity and voice for all, coupled with social programmes that build human capital, help households manage risks and cope with shocks, will in the long run reduce the continued reliance on such special measures. Moreover, while targeted interventions help in addressing some dimensions of social exclusion for specific groups, without a broad-based universal approach grounded in social justice that is aimed at directly combating inequalities and generating solidarity around development objectives, such progress may not be sustainable.

## 3.  Coherent policies for inclusive development

Universal access to social protection and to social services is necessary to shield all individuals and groups from economic shocks and other contingencies and promote their inclusion. However, social policies alone will not bring about the structural transformations that are necessary to promote inclusive development. By bringing them together, complementary social and economic policies can be used to foster social inclusion. They can help create employment and decent work and therefore provide opportunities for wealth creation for all segments of society. Indeed, aligning macroeconomic, social and environmental policies will enhance prospects for the achievement and sustainability of inclusive and equitable development.

Several economic and social policies can "work together" to boost demand in a sustainable manner through the creation of measures to increase decent work and universal social protection, rather than through speculation in credit and asset markets. This policy shift will require improved policy coherence, namely by aligning macroeconomic policy frameworks with social goals. It will mean paying greater attention to income distribution and to the creation of full employment and decent work for all − not only to keeping inflation low and controlling budget deficits. Maintaining levels of public expenditure and accepting budget deficits during economic downturns may be one important consequence of such a shift in attention.

In order for growth to be sustained and inclusive, economic policies must be concerned with the ability of growth to create full employment and decent work for all (OECD, 2014). As discussed in chapter II, labour market and employment policies, including collective bargaining and unionization, wage-setting mechanisms and minimum wage laws, are also essential to support inclusive growth. Environmentally sustainable growth which protects, rather than erodes, natural assets is crucial to ensuring that the effects of climate change do not continue to limit the ability of people living in poverty, or disadvantaged and marginalized groups to participate in society on improved terms (United Nations, 2016a). Similarly, for vulnerable urban populations, including slum dwellers, policies that support sustainable urbanization, including investments in green technologies and infrastructure, will be a crucial part of an inclusive development strategy. Sustainable urbanization should promote and protect communities and livelihoods, rather than disrupt them, as well as invest in public spaces and facilities that are accessible to all and encourage social interaction and civic participation.

Inclusive economic and social policies are mutually reinforcing. While macroeconomic policies can and should pursue social welfare and justice, well-designed social policies can enhance macroeconomic growth and post-crisis recovery through investments in human resources development and redistributive measures that increase productivity and aggregate demand. They can also build political stability, a robust determinant of long-term economic growth (Alesina and others, 1996). A number of countries have recognized the importance of social protection to promote inclusive and sustainable growth. China and Thailand, for instance, have expanded and strengthened national social protection mechanisms while pursuing complementary economic and employment policies that emphasize broad-based and sustainable improvements in living standards, especially among low-income earners and the middle class (ILO, 2014c). In other countries, recent emphasis on balancing public budgets has increased volatility in the real economy and the labour market, resulting in declines in public investments in infrastructure, technologies and human capital, which are critical for stimulating aggregate demand and economic activity during times of crisis. Approaches that embed social policies in a wider range of coordinated macroeconomic, employment, labour market and fiscal policies are therefore crucial to creating inclusive societies.

## B.  The importance of inclusive institutions

As the structures, rules and practices that shape the way in which people behave, institutions play a key role in either perpetuating exclusion or alternately, promoting and achieving inclusion. They are the framework within which decisions on social, economic and environmental issues are made, policies are designed and all forms of social interaction are structured. Institutions and norms that promote open and inclusive processes create the conditions needed for the reduction of poverty and inequality, as do accountable and responsive Governments that encourage the participation of individuals and communities in social, economic and political life. Supportive institutional environments can make policies that promote inclusion more likely to be to be adopted, take hold and flourish.

This section explores whether and how institutions can be transformed so as to promote equity, voice, participation and empowerment, and an exami-nation of the role that Governments can play in encouraging institutional change.  Although some institutions can change quickly, namely political institutions following national elections, institutional change is often a slow and gradual process. Once inclusive and participatory political institutions are in place, however, they create checks and balances that prevent the abuse of power and tend to support the creation of inclusive economic and social institutions.

### 1.  Institutions for equity

Levels of public spending and regulation over markets and property rights have distributional effects and can either support or undermine social inclusion. The institutionalized racial segregation of the system of apartheid in South Africa, for instance, limited access to resources and opportunities among non-whites and therefore created social exclusion, as did the legacy of so-called Jim Crow laws in the United States, as discussed in chapter IV.

Changes in institutional arrangements regarding the ownership and use of land, the rights of workers and entrepreneurs, all have shown potential to promote inclusion. Institutional acknowledgement of the customary rights of indigenous peoples over land in a growing number of countries, for example, has helped support entrepreneurship, economic security and development among these historically excluded groups. Similarly, a range of gender-sensitive reforms in land titling and inheritance laws across Latin America and the Caribbean, including ending formal gender discrimination in land ownership and inheritance as well as preferential treatment for women in titling, contributed to a significant increase in the percentage of women registered as landowners (Deere and León de Leal, 2001). Legislative frameworks that encourage collective action and bargaining rights can also help empower workers and small-scale producers. In rural settings, cooperatives and other producer organizations and self-help groups have been effective at increasing incomes of members as well as building confidence for participation in community and political life.

Improving access to legal institutions and ensuring equality before the law is also key to promoting inclusion. People living in poverty generally have limited awareness of their rights and lack legal literacy. Pursuing justice also comes at a high cost, both monetary and in terms of lost working time. Therefore, such strategies as programmes and campaigns to enhance legal awareness and literacy, low-cost legal services, alternative dispute resolution mechanisms and reform of traditional or customary justice systems that disadvantage certain social groups have the potential to tackle social exclusion through multiple channels. In Indonesia, for example, the Government implemented reforms of religious courts nationwide, introducing court fee waivers and increasing the availability of legal information at the village level. These steps resulted in a fourteenfold increase in the number of clients living in poverty who became able to access such courts and a fourfold increase in the number accessing circuit courts in remote areas (World Bank, 2013).

Corruption is a major institutional barrier to inclusion and equity. It erodes trust between Governments and citizens as well as among citizens, who may feel that certain individuals or groups receive favourable treatment as a result of corrupt practices. Combating corruption, changing incentive structures and mindsets, fighting entrenched corrupt norms, including in the management of resource rents, and combating illicit financial transfers have all had varying degrees of success in this regard (Fosu, 2013). Successful anti-corruption efforts have also often been initiated from the bottom up, challenging behaviours that generate corruption and creating an increased sense of responsibility to fight it (Panth, 2011; van der Gaag and Rowlands, 2009).

## 2. Institutions for participation and voice

Barriers to participation, including discrimination, make it much more difficult for excluded and marginalized groups to express their concerns and have their voices heard and translated into meaningful action (Silver, 2012). Promoting inclusive institutions therefore involves the identification and elimination of such barriers as well as active efforts to create enabling conditions for all individuals and social groups to participate and express their voice. When those who are most at risk of exclusion are able to participate in such processes, institutions are more likely to address their needs.

Participatory processes are also necessary to avoid violent expressions of social discontent that exclusionary and unjust institutions can provoke. Social movements and local associations have traditionally been important in this regard. They have given people living in poverty and those who belong to other excluded groups a voice and greater agency to articulate their interests. Often informal and uncoordinated, these forms of collective action are an essential countervailing force to the excessive concentration and use of power. Historically, social mobilization efforts have raised and advanced issues that have subsequently become important priorities for the State, including issues such as environmental degradation and women's rights (Mulgan, 2007). They have helped discourage people from joining violent conflicts and have opened space for the exercise of civic and political rights. They have challenged stereotypes of poverty or those based on group identity. They have also played a role in building self-esteem and shared identities among, for instance, workers in the informal sector, and have brought recognition to their work. As discussed in chapter III, social capital – the gains that come from cooperation between individuals and groups and the creation of social networks – is as important to empowerment as is human capital. By investing in social capital through supporting social mobilization, helping build collective associations and strengthening community action, Governments are enabling individuals and groups to become agents of change and development. Governments can create an enabling environment for such grass-roots movements by building capacity, opening spaces for consultation and forming alliances between social movements and political institutions, including parliamentary committees and political parties. Changes in legislation may also be necessary to legitimize such movements and strengthen them.

The Internet, social media networks and mobile technologies can also be used to enhance public participation and service delivery and support social mobilization. Online civil society platforms, such as *Por Mi Barrio* in Uruguay and *I Change My City* in India, connect to existing government complaint systems, enabling urban residents to report public service problems (World Bank, 2016). However, recent evidence also suggests that such initiatives can reinforce rather than replace existing accountability mechanisms, relying on offline mobilization for sufficient uptake and generating the most success when addressing fairly straightforward information and monitoring problems (World Bank, 2016).

Legislation and regulation that guarantees the rights of citizens to information and to engagement with public institutions is essential, and building institutional capacity in information-sharing and the organization of public consultation forums needs to be developed. Access to accurate and relevant information on such issues as basic human rights and entitlements, the availability of basic services and work opportunities is required for effective participation in governance and other decision-making processes as well as to hold Governments accountable. Transparency initiatives, when complemented by accountability mechanisms, such as auditing and oversight, help to ensure that public institutions are responsive and policies are effectively implemented. For example, in the Philippines public financial management reforms in 2010 were focused on improving public access to information on the allocation, disbursement and status of programmes, official invitation of civil society participation throughout the national budget cycle and a commitment to the international Open Budget Initiative;[82] these measures have resulted in a vastly increased involvement by civil society actors within decision-making processes (Dressel, 2012).

At the State level, no single ministry alone can promote participation. The principle of leaving no one behind should cut across all ministries and agencies. However, institutional arrangements alone may not determine success. In all potential avenues for change, leadership and reform-minded individuals within government who have experience in other spheres, such as civil society and academia, can be crucial in mediating between citizen interests and competing interests and pressures. Similarly, openness from policymakers to seek collective solutions, as well as patience from citizens to allow reforms to emerge slowly through a process of trial and error rather than to expect an immediate quick fix, can also be important ingredients for bringing about inclusive institutional change (Booth, 2012).

## 3. Institutions for recognition

Institutional environments that ensure recognition and respect for equality as well as diversity are also essential for promoting social inclusion. Fostering respect for diversity requires strengthening formal mechanisms that officially acknowledge excluded groups as well as challenging values, attitudes and behaviours that discriminate and exclude.

Official recognition requires strengthening systems of civil registration and legal identification. Making sure that groups that have often been "invisible"

---

[82] For further information, see www.internationalbudget.org/opening-budgets/open-budget-initiative/.

in official statistics, including ethnic minorities, persons with disabilities, foreigners, homeless persons and persons in institutions, are recognized and counted in these systems can be a powerful tool to promote inclusion. Basic civil registration, particularly of births, establishes legal identity. It lays the foundation for citizens to claim their rights and facilitates the interaction between citizens and their Governments on rights and obligations. Without civil registration, children of excluded groups are much less likely to enrol in school, for example, limiting the potential of such services to act as a vehicle for inclusion. Civil registration systems equip Governments with the necessary information for their endeavours to meet the needs of their citizens and invest in their future through resource allocation, institutional arrangements and design, and the provision of public services. The decision of India in 2010 to launch the Aadhaar[83] programme to enrol the biometric identifying data of all its 1.2 billion citizens, for example, was a critical step in enabling fairer access of the people to government benefits and services. Programmes such as Aadhaar have tremendous potential to foster inclusion by giving all people, including the poorest and most marginalized, an official identity. Fair and robust systems of legal identity and birth registration are recognized in the new 2030 Agenda for Sustainable Development as an important foundation for promoting inclusive societies.

Respect for difference and diversity involves challenging social and cultural norms, values, attitudes and behaviours, such as racism, xenophobia, sexism and homophobia, that perpetuate structural injustice, discrimination and exclusion. Such exclusionary attitudes can permeate all facets of a society; inclusive institutional change has often involved addressing them through a range of channels. Formal guidance and training to tackle discriminatory beliefs and change the mindsets of power-holding individuals, such as government officials, police officers and members of the judiciary, can be a particularly important tool to promote such change. Similarly, public media and communications campaigns as well as civic education focused on tolerance and respect (such as the example described in box V.1), combined with campaigns for legal reform or better enforcement of existing laws and regulations, have been used to confront discrimination. In Thailand, the trade union movement, along with disabled persons' organizations and campaigns to promote positive images of people with disabilities in the media, played an important role in supporting international norms enshrined in the United Nations Convention on the Rights of Persons with Disabilities, which was ratified by the Government of Thailand in 2008 (ILO, 2011b).

---

[83]     Aadhaar is a transliterated word meaning "foundation" or "base" in Hindi. For further information about the programme, see https://uidai.gov.in/beta/your-aadhaar/about-aadhaar.html.

## Box V.1

### Promoting social inclusion through human rights education

Human rights education is a powerful tool for removing barriers to participation and facilitating social inclusion of disadvantaged individuals and groups. Refugees often face limitations on the enjoyment of economic, social and political rights due to their particular status. Their voices may not be heard, or they might be unaware of their rights. When exclusion and lack of awareness of rights reinforce each other, human rights education in schools presents a special opportunity to break this cycle. Moreover, promoting attitudes of inclusion, tolerance, peaceful resolution of conflict and respect for diversity among children and youth, helps embed these values more broadly.

The United Nations Relief and Works Agency for Palestine Refugees in the Near East (UNRWA) has pioneered a unique policy on human rights, conflict resolution and tolerance in its education programme in Jordan, Lebanon, the Occupied Palestinian Territory, which comprises the West Bank, including East Jerusalem, and the Gaza Strip, and the Syrian Arab Republic. It integrates child and youth-friendly activities and human rights-based teaching methodologies into all subjects and classes that UNRWA provides for 500,000 Palestine refugee students enrolled in UNRWA primary and preparatory schools and, in Lebanon, in secondary schools also.

In a region laden with risks to education, including widespread conflict, and in which Palestine refugees experience profound vulnerability, UNRWA promotes safe learning environments where students explore the many aspects of human rights and tolerance, not only through study but also by participating in purpose-designed activities. Role-playing and group games, for example, help students to learn about and critically reflect on sensitive social issues, such as gender roles and discrimination in all its forms. In so doing, they learn that concrete actions can be taken to help strengthen social inclusion, which is all the more important in contexts where the refugee community faces exclusion. Empathy and critical thinking are key to the process, in which students are encouraged to understand the importance of social inclusion as well as the repercussions of attitudes, values and actions that contribute to exclusion – such as discrimination and racism. Implemented in an increasingly challenging environment, where many Palestine refugee children may experience exclusion, discrimination and other human rights violations, the programme also teaches children and youth to resolve conflicts through dialogue rather than violence. The human rights programme of UNRWA has an impact beyond school walls as students, supported by faculty, try to reach the entire refugee community through public events and advocacy, including via media. An UNRWA evaluation found that 98 per cent of participants in the UNRWA Human Rights Day 2015 commemorations in schools said that they had a "greater appreciation for diversity among different people" (UNRWA, 2016).

To strengthen the application of human rights concepts, UNRWA has also established school parliaments in all of its 691 schools across the five fields where it operates. On any given day, the elected school parliamentarians are actively promoting the inclusion and empowerment of young people, by mediating grievances between faculty and students, or forming support groups for peers at risk of dropping out of school or succumbing to early marriage. School parliaments have also resulted in greater participation in community life of people with disabilities; they are nurturing the civic spirit of inclusion and participation of children in decision-making both in school and in their community.

Internal evaluations show that students who are exposed to human rights education tend to support gender equality, value diversity and take action to end bullying and violence inside and outside of school. Heba abu Laban, a 13-year-old member of her school parliament in Gaza, commented: "I have learned a lot about diversity and human rights. Now I know that people have different religions or colours, but while we all have the right to be different, we need to be treated equally" (UNRWA, 2015). In explaining the impact of the programme on her students, UNRWA teacher Maison Askar said: "There is less intolerance among students in the school; they are more respectful with each other and towards each other's opinions. They consciously listen to each other" (UNRWA, 2015).

## 4. The role of Governments in promoting inclusive institutions

Changing institutions requires challenging norms and values that evolve slowly and are deeply affected by context, culture and history. Those who benefit economically or politically from existing power imbalances often resist such change, as it threatens their vested interests.[84] Even when there is political commitment to promote inclusion and participation, complex and at times conflicting group and individual interests create resistance to rapid change. Any move towards more inclusive institutions necessarily requires a challenge to the existing incentives and constraints that Governments face from powerful sections of their constituencies.

Institutions and norms that promote inclusion and empowerment are influenced by actions taken by many stakeholders, including States as well as members of civil society, social movements, trade unions and associations of self-employed workers, the private sector, the media and, most importantly, individuals and groups who live in poverty or are otherwise socially excluded. In practice, it is often the formation of broad coalitions of various stakeholders, rather than action by the State or civil society alone that leads to the formation of pluralistic, inclusive institutions. However, the role of Governments remains key to creating the institutional conditions for social inclusion. Governments are best positioned to remove the formal and informal institutional barriers that prevent some individuals and groups from taking action to improve their well-being and expand their choices. Only Governments can establish inclusive and secure legal, administrative and regulatory environments at the national and local levels; they possess the mandate and resources to provide services and infrastructure on the scale needed. Action by Governments is also crucial in curtailing the excessive concentration of power and influence that ultimately results in exclusion.

While the private sector has at times been a driver of exclusion through exploitative, unfair and unsafe practices in employment and in the provision of essential services, it can also be a crucial partner for Governments in encouraging inclusive institutions. Voluntary standards and corporate social responsibility initiatives, encompassing decent labour conditions, fair remuneration and contracting, occupational health and safety, more environmentally sound production patterns as well as sustained and sustainable investments in the long-term welfare of society, can support the efforts of Governments towards inclusive institutions.

There is no one-size-fits-all template for how Governments or other stakeholders can initiate the process of institutional change, but with concerted effort and political motivation, they can influence it. Encouragingly, even limited institutional changes initiated by key individuals or power-holders can

---

[84]    Acemoglu and Robinson (2012) provided numerous historical examples of elites sustaining exclusive or inefficient institutions that benefit themselves.

gradually grow in significance over the course of time. Research suggests that inclusive political institutions tend to support inclusive economic and social institutions by creating checks and balances that prevent the concentration of wealth. Similarly, more inclusive economic institutions create incentives for further breaking down exclusionary political and social barriers (Acemoglu and Robinson, 2012).

Taking initial steps – however modest – towards a more inclusive approach, can slowly encourage different interest groups to come together and push for further change. For example, policymaking or problem-solving mechanisms that promote broader participation, even if limited at first, create new pathways for the participation of individuals and groups previously excluded from decision-making processes. These new voices can help to create momentum for further change and for those institutions to look beyond the needs of their current beneficiaries. Participatory mechanisms can also affect long-standing institutional cultures and the mindsets and behaviour of those individuals involved in making decisions. While the success of such efforts depends greatly on national and local circumstances, as well as on the actions of other stakeholders, including the private sector, it is clear that Governments must lead the way.

## C. Conclusions

The evidence presented in the report illustrates that a person's chances in life depend significantly on group ascription. Group-based differences in access to education, health care, infrastructure and employment as well as inequalities in political participation are pervasive and symptomatic of the exclusion of members of certain groups. These disadvantages reinforce one another. In particular, lower levels of health and education go hand in hand with higher levels of poverty and unemployment, as well as with less voice in political and civic life. Thus, progress in one domain alone will not be sufficient to end social exclusion.

The analysis underscores the inextricable linkages among the overarching objectives of poverty eradication, full employment and decent work for all and social inclusion – core commitments made at the 1995 Summit for Social Development and now integral parts of the 2030 Agenda. The analysis also calls attention to the Summit's broad vision of social development as a process that involves a fairer distribution of opportunities and resources to foster social justice, equality and the participation of all people in social, economic and political processes. The report further highlights the Summit's people-centred approach to development and the emphasis placed on integrated policy frameworks to tackle inequalities, also reaffirmed in the 2030 Agenda.

Beyond the foundational role of inclusion and the moral imperative to promote it, there are also instrumental reasons to ensure that no one is left behind. There is indeed growing recognition of the importance of reducing inequalities and promoting inclusion to strengthen not only the social but also the economic and environmental dimensions of sustainable development. Member States have agreed that no Sustainable Development Goal – be it on climate change, infrastructure or economic growth – should be considered achieved if the targets are not met for all members of society. Exclusion has economic costs, and the inequitable distribution of income reduces the impact of economic growth on poverty reduction, which itself is both a cause and a consequence of social exclusion. Exclusion has political costs as well, as illustrated in the previous chapters.

However, this awareness has not yet translated into the level of political commitment or the necessary normative shifts that it is argued in this report are imperative for inclusive development. Instead, overreliance on market mechanisms, retrenchment of the redistributive role of the State and growing inequalities have contributed to social exclusion and have even put the social contract under threat in many countries in the last few decades. Often, social policy has become merely a corrective means to temporarily cushion the effects of crises or other shocks. Where identity-based disadvantages have been deliberately supported by the dominant majority, Governments may not have been urged to tackle them. Correcting asymmetries in power, voice and influence is not only the right thing to do, but also the necessary thing to do in order to strengthen the social contract both at the national and global levels.

Meeting the vision of the 2030 Agenda requires a reconsideration of the policy priorities that have prevailed over the last two decades. The experience of countries and regions that have succeeded in reducing inequalities and promoting inclusion has shown that States can affect market forces so as to promote social justice without altering economic competitiveness. Global agreement on the need to enhance policy coherence (targets 17.3 and 17.4 of the Sustainable Development Goals) itself comes from the realization that macroeconomic and social policies have at times had opposing effects on social and economic inclusion. Countries that have benefited from complementary social and economic policies have been able to stimulate inclusive economic growth and create decent work opportunities for all in a sustainable manner. Achieving policy coherence and policy integration in practice still requires evidence-gathering and analysis of good practices, including better understanding of the context of effective policymaking and implementation. Such a learning-from-experience approach is critical for the successful implementation of the 2030 Agenda.

The commitment to leave no one behind and thus ensure that every individual participates with equal rights and enjoys the full range of opportunities expressed in the Sustainable Development Goals is an important step towards reconsidering policy priorities. One year into its implementation, the 2030 Agenda has already succeeded in driving the attention of the international community towards social exclusion and inequality, including through the 2016 session of the high-level political forum on sustainable development under the theme "Ensuring that no one is left behind".[85] However, the extent of inclusion that the 2030 Agenda will help to achieve will depend on how it is implemented. Framing goals in universal terms alone does not ensure universality. Despite aiming for universal primary education, for instance, the Millennium Development Goals failed to promote the action necessary to reach the children furthest behind first, as shown in the present report. At the same time, focusing on extreme states of exclusion and poverty will do little to affect the wider societal, economic and political processes that drive social exclusion in the first place. It is contended in this report that social inclusion cannot be pursued as a sectoral initiative or in a piecemeal fashion. It requires an orientation of policy objectives and priorities towards the well-being of all.

In terms of monitoring, identifying individuals and groups that are left behind and addressing the challenges they face will require better household- and individual-level data, increased availability of microdata and strengthened capacity of national statistical agencies. For instance, to date, few of the current Sustainable Development Goal indicators can be disaggregated by migrant, disability and indigenous status. In addition, as discussed throughout the report, social groups that are omitted from household surveys and censuses are often those at the highest risk of being left behind. A global effort to improve data availability for all population groups, including through improvements in the integration of data sources, has already begun. Further work is needed to enhance the coverage, quality and frequency of data to ensure that the most vulnerable and marginalized people are the first to be reached.

However, improved data alone, where available, have not driven all countries or organizations to address the barriers that disadvantaged groups face. In contrast, some countries have effectively addressed such barriers with imperfect information. In essence, ensuring that all individuals are afforded the same rights and opportunities demands political will and commitment.

Concrete proposals have been put forth for the establishment of mechanisms to ensure that implementation will be targeted first at the individuals and groups that are furthest behind. One proposal calls for setting "stepping stone" equity targets for interim points between 2015 and 2030 in order to identify and highlight gaps in progress across groups (Save the Children, 2014). Another envisions conducting needs assessments at the national level, identifying the groups and communities left furthest behind from achieving each goal in each country and then identifying common challenges, exchanging lessons learned and agreeing on how such challenges will be tackled (ODI, 2016). These and other proposals, including of mechanisms to foster participatory implementation and monitoring

---

[85] For further information, see https://sustainabledevelopment.un.org/HLPF/2016.

processes, illustrate the feasibility and flexibility of translating into action the political commitment to leave no one behind.

# Bibliography

Acemoglu, Daron, and James Robinson (2012). *Why Nations Fail: The Origins of Power, Prosperity, and Poverty.* New York: Crown Publishers.

Addison, Tony, David Hulme, and Ravi Kanbur, eds. (2009). *Poverty Dynamics: Interdisciplinary Perspectives.* Oxford: Oxford University Press.

Ahmed, Ali M., and Mats Hammarstedt (2008). Discrimination in the rental housing market: a field experiment on the Internet. *Journal of Urban Economics*, vol. 64, No. 2, pp. 362-372.

Alesina, Alberto, and others (1996). Political instability and economic growth. *Journal of Economic Growth*, vol. 1, No. 2, pp. 189-212.

_____, Stelios Michalopoulos and Elias Papaioannou (2016). Ethnic inequality. *Journal of Political Economy*, vol. 124, No. 2, pp. 428-488.

Alkire, Sabina (2005). Subjective quantitative studies of human agency. *Social Indicators Research*, vol. 74, No. 1, pp. 217-260.

_____ and James Foster (2011). Counting and multidimensional poverty measurement. *Journal of Public Economics*, vol. 95, Nos. 7–8, pp. 476–487.

_____, José Manuel Roche, and Ana Vaz (2014). Multidimensional poverty dynamics: methodology and results for 34 countries. OPHI Research in Progress Series, No. 41a. Available from www.ophi.org.uk/wp-content/uploads/RP41a_full.pdf?0a8fd7.

_____ (2015). Changes over time in multi-dimensional poverty: methodology and results for 34 countries. OPHI Working Paper, No. 76 (July). Available from www.ophi.org.uk/wp-content/uploads/OPHIWP076.pdf.

_____, and others (2016). Multidimensional Poverty Index 2016: Brief methodological note and results. OPHI Briefing 42. Oxford: University of Oxford.

Altindag, Duha Tore, and Naci H. Mocan (2010). Joblessness and perceptions about the effectiveness of democracy. *Journal of Labor Research*, vol. 31, No. 2, pp. 99-123.

Altzinger, Wilfried, and others (2015). Education and social mobility in Europe: levelling the playing field for Europe's children and fuelling its economy. WWWforEurope Working Paper, No. 80. Available from http://epub.wu.ac.at/4720/1/WWWforEurope_WPS_no080_MS19.pdf.

Alvaredo, Facundo, and Thomas Piketty (2014). Measuring top incomes and inequality in the Middle East: data limitations and illustration with the case of Egypt. Economic Research Forum Working Paper, No. 832. Available from http://piketty.pse.ens.fr/files/AlvaredoPiketty2014ERF.pdf.

Ambady, Nalini, and others (2001). Stereotype susceptibility in children: effects of identity activation on quantitative performance. *Psychological Science*, vol. 12, No. 5, pp. 385-390.

American RadioWorks (2016). Jim Crow laws. Available from http://americanradioworks.publicradio.org/features/remembering/laws.html.

Andrews, George Reid (2004). *Afro-Latin America, 1800-2000.* Oxford: Oxford University Press.

Arnold, Margaret, and Sergio de Cosmo (2015). *Building Social Resilience: Protecting and Empowering Those Most at Risk*. Washington, D.C.: World Bank. Available from www.gfdrr.org/sites/gfdrr/files/publication/Building-Social-Resilience-Protecting-and-Empowering-Those-Most-at-Risk.pdf.

Attias-Donfut, Claudine, and François-Charles Wolff (2009). *Le Destin des Enfants d'Immigrés: Un Désenchaînement des Générations*. Paris: Éditions Stock.

Azeng, Therese F., and Thierry U. Yogo (2015). Youth unemployment, education and political instability: evidence from selected developing countries 1991-2009. Households in Conflict Network Working Paper, No. 200. Brighton, United Kingdom: Institute of Development Studies, University of Sussex. Available from www.hicn. org/wordpress/wp-content/uploads/2012/06/HiCN-WP-200.pdf.

Babcock, Linda, and Sara Laschever (2003). *Women Don't Ask: Negotiation and the Gender Divide*. Princeton, New Jersey, and Oxford: Princeton University Press.

Balbus, John M., and Catherine Malina (2009). Identifying vulnerable subpopulations for climate change health effects in the United States. *Journal of Occupational and Environmental Medicine*, vol. 51, No. 1, pp. 33-37.

Barnes, Colin, and Geof Mercer (2010). *Exploring Disability,* 2nd ed. Cambridge, United Kingdom: Polity Press.

Bell, David N.F., and David G. Blanchflower (2011). Young people and the great recession. IZA Discussion Paper, No. 5674. Bonn: Institute for the Study of Labour (IZA).

Bengtsson, Tommy, Christer Lundh, and Kirk Scott (2005). From Boom to Bust: The Economic Integration of Immigrants in Postwar Sweden. In *European Migration: What Do We Know?*, Kalus F. Zimmermann, ed. Oxford: Oxford University Press.

Benton, Meghan, and others (2014). *Aiming Higher: Policies to get immigrants into middle-skilled work in Europe*. Washington, D.C.: Migration Policy Institute and International Labour Organization.

Bertaux, Daniel, and Paul Thompson (1997). *Pathways to Social Class: A Qualitative Approach to Social Mobility*. Oxford: Oxford University Press.

Bertrand, Marianne, and Sendhil Mullainathan (2004). Are Emily and Greg more employable than Lakisha and Jamal? A field experiment on labor market discrimination. *American Ecomonic Review*, vol. 94, No. 4, pp. 991-1013.

Bevelander, Peter, and Ravi Pendakur (2011). Voting and social inclusion in Sweden. *International Migration*, vol. 49, No. 4, pp. 67-92.

Bhavnani, Rikhil R. (2013). A primer on voter discrimination against India's lower caste politicians: evidence from natural and survey experiments. A working paper available from http://users.polisci.wisc.edu/behavior/Papers/Bhavnani2013.pdf.

Bhide, Shashanka, and Aasha Kapur Mehta (2004). Chronic poverty in rural India: issues and findings from panel data. *Journal of Human Development and Capabilities*, vol. 5, No. 2, pp. 195-209.

Binagwaho, Agnes, and others (2014). Rwanda 20 years on: investing in life. *The Lancet*, vol. 384, No. 9940, pp. 371–375.

Bird, Kate (2007). The intergenerational transmission of poverty: an overview. ODI Working Paper, No. 286, London: Overseas Development Institute and Chronic Poverty Research Centre.

Birdsall, Nancy, Nora Lustig, and Christian J. Meyer (2013). The strugglers: the new poor in Latin America? Center for Global Development Working Paper, No. 337. Washington, D.C.: Center for Global Development.

Blanchflower, David G., and Andrew J. Oswald (2004). Well-being over time in Britain and the USA. *Journal of Public Economics*, vol. 88, pp. 1359-1386.

Blunch, Niels-Hugo, and Dorte Verner (2004). Asymmetries in the union wage premium in Ghana. *World Bank Economic Review*, vol. 18, No. 2, pp. 237-251.

Bolt, Vincent J., and Kate Bird (2003).The intrahousehold disadvantages framework: a framework for the analysis of intra-household difference and inequality. CPRC Working Paper, No. 32, Chronic Poverty Research Centre. Available from www. chronicpoverty.org/uploads/publication_files/WP32_Bolt_Bird.pdf.

Booth, David (2012). *Development as a Collective Action Problem: Addressing the Real Challenges of African Governance*. London: Overseas Development Institute.

Brand, Jennie E., and Sarah A. Burgard (2008). Job displacement and social participation over the lifecourse: findings for a cohort of joiners. *Social Forces*, vol. 87, No. 1, pp. 211-242.

Brännström, Lars (2008). Making their mark: the effects of neighbourhood and upper secondary school on educational achievement. *European Sociological Review*, vol. 24, No. 4, pp. 463-478.

Brass, Paul R. (2003). *The Production of Hindu-Muslim Violence in Contemporary India*. Seattle, Washington: University of Washington Press.

Brubaker, Rogers (2002). *Ethnicity without Groups*. Archives Européennes de Sociologie, XLIII, No. 2, pp. 163-189.

Buckup, Sebastian (2009). The price of exclusion: the economic consequences of excluding people with disabilities from the world of work. Employment Working Paper, No. 43. Geneva: ILO Employment Sector, Skills and Employability Department.

Burchardt, Tania (2000). *Enduring Economic Exclusion: Disabled People, Income and Work.* Layerthorpe, United Kingdom: Joseph Rowntree Foundation.

_____, Julian Le Grand, and David Piachaud (2002). Degrees of exclusion: developing a dynamic, multidimensional measure. In *Understanding Social Exclusion*, John Hills, Julian Le Grand and David Piachaud, eds. Oxford: Oxford University Press, pp. 30-43.

Caillaux, Elisa L. (1994). Cor e mobilidade social no Brasil. *Estudos Afro-Asiáticos*, vol. 26, pp. 53-66.

Campbell, Andrea Louise (2002). Self-interest, social security, and the distinctive participation patterns of senior citizens. *American Political Science Review*, vol. 96, No. 3, pp. 565-574.

Carr-Hill, Roy (2013). Missing millions and measuring development progress. *World Development*, vol. 46 (June), pp. 30-44.

Carroll, Aengus, and Lucas Paoli Itaborahy (2015). *State-sponsored Homophobia: A World Survey of Laws − criminalisation, protection and recognition of same-sex love*. Geneva: International Lesbian, Gay, Bisexual, Trans and Intersex Association. Available from http://old.ilga.org/Statehomophobia/ILGA_State_Sponsored_Homophobia_2015.pdf.

Cecchini, Simone, and others, eds. (2015). *Towards Universal Social Protection: Latin American Pathways and Policy Tools*. United Nations publication, Sales No. E.15. II.G.11.

Chase, Elaine, and Grace Bantebya-Kyomuhendo, eds. (2014). *Poverty and Shame: Global Experiences*. Oxford: Oxford University Press.

Chattopadhyay, Raghabendra, and Esther Duflo (2004). Women as policy makers: evidence from a randomized policy experiment in India. *Econometrica*, vol. 72, No. 5, pp. 1409-1443.

Chen, Martha A., Joann Vanek and Marilyn Carr (2004). *Mainstreaming Informal Employment and Gender in Poverty Reduction: A Handbook for Policy-Makers and other Stakeholders*. London: Commonwealth Secretariat, International Development Research Centre.

Chen, Shaohua, and Martin Ravallion (2012). More relatively-poor people in a less absolutely-poor world. World Bank Policy Research Working Paper, No. 6114. Washington, D.C.: World Bank.

Chetty, Raj, Nathaniel Hendren, and Lawrence F. Katz (2016). The effects of exposure to better neighborhoods on children: new evidence from the moving to opportunity experiment. *American Economic Review*, vol. 106, No. 4, pp. 855-902.

Chetty, Raj, and others (2016). The association between income and life expectancy in the United States, 2001-2014. *Journal of the American Medical Association*, vol. 315, No. 16, pp. 1750-1766

Clark, Andrew E. (2003). Unemployment as a social norm: psychological evidence from panel data. *Journal of Labor Economics*, vol. 21, No. 2, pp. 323-351.

Commission of the European Communities (2003). Joint report on social inclusion summarising the results of the examination of the National Action Plans for Social Inclusion (2003-2005). Available from http://eur-lex.europa.eu/legal-content/EN/TXT/?uri=celex:52003DC0773.

Cotlear, Daniel, and others (2015). *Going Universal: How 24 Developing Countries are Implementing Universal Health Coverage Reforms from the Bottom Up*. Washington, D.C.: World Bank.

Crimmins, Eileen M., and Aaron Hagedorn (2010). The socioeconomic gradient in healthy life expectancy. *Annual Review of Gerontology and Geriatrics*, vol. 30, No. 1, pp. 305-321.

Davala, Sarath, and others (2015). *Basic Income: A Transformative Policy for India*. London: Bloomsbury Publishing.

Deaton, Angus (2008). Income, health, and well-being around the world: evidence from the Gallup World Poll. *Journal of Economic Perspectives*, vol. 22, No. 2, pp. 53-72.

Deeming, Christopher, and Bina Gubhaju (2015). The mis-measurement of extreme global poverty: a case study in the Pacific islands. *Journal of Sociology*, vol. 51, No. 3, pp. 689-706.

Deere, Carmen Diana, and Magdalena León De Leal (2001). *Empowering Women: Land and Property Rights in Latin America*. Pittsburgh, Pennsylvania: University of Pittsburgh Press.

DeFilippis, James (2001). The myth of social capital in community development. *Housing Policy Debate*, vol. 12, No. 4, pp. 781-806.

de Haan, Arjan (2015). Social inclusion and structural transformation: concepts, measurements and trade-offs. UNU-Merit Working Paper, No. 2015-045. Available from www.merit.unu.edu/publications/working-papers/abstract/?id=5882.

DeLeire, Thomas (2000). The wage and employment effects of the Americans with Disabilities Act. *Journal of Human Resources*, vol. 35, No. 4, pp. 693-715.

Deshpande, Ashwini (2013). *Affirmative Action in India.* Oxford: Oxford University Press.

Dickerson, Niki T. (2007). Black employment, segregation, and the spatial organization of metropolitan labor markets. *Economic Geography*, vol. 83, No. 3, July 2007, pp. 283-307.

Dressel, Björn (2012). Targeting the public purse: advocacy coalitions and public finance in the Philippines. *Administration and Society*, vol. 44, No. 6, pp. 65S-84S.

Dudwick, Nora (2012). The relationship between jobs and social cohesion: some examples from ethnography. Background Paper for the *World Development Report 2013*. Washington, D.C.: World Bank. Available from http://siteresources.worldbank.org/EXTNWDR2013/Resources/8258024-1320950747192/8260293-1320956712276/8261091-1348683883703/WDR2013_bp_Relationship_Between_Jobs_and_Social_Cohesion.pdf.

Duryea, Suzanne and others (2006). For better or for worse? Job and earnings mobility in nine middle- and low-income countries. In Susan M. Collins and Carol Graham, eds., *Brookings Trade Forum 2006: Global Labor Markets.* Washington, D.C.: Brookings Institution Press.

Easterly, William (2006). *Social Cohesion, Institutions and growth.* Working paper No. 94. Washington, D.C.: Center for Global Development.

Economic Commission for Africa (2015). *The Africa Social Development Index: Measuring Human Exclusion for Structural Transformation – North Africa* report. United Nations, ECA, Addis Abba.

Economic Commission for Latin America and the Caribbean (2014). *Social Panorama of Latin America 2014.* United Nations, ECLAC, Santiago de Chile, Sales No.: E.15. II.G.6.

_____ (2015). *Inclusive Social Development: The Next Generation of Policies for Overcoming Poverty and Reducing Inequality in Latin America and the Caribbean.* United Nations, ECLAC. S.16-00098. Available from http://repositorio.cepal.org/bitstream/handle/11362/39101/4/S1600098_en.pdf.

Elbers, Chris, and others (2005). Re-interpreting sub-group inequality decompositions. World Bank Policy Research Working Paper, No. 3687. Washington, D.C.: World Bank.

Equality Now (2016). *The State We're In: Ending Sexism in Nationality Laws.* Available from www.equalitynow.org/sites/default/files/NationalityReport_EN.pdf.

European Commission (2014). Taking stock of the Europe 2020 strategy for smart, sustainable and inclusive growth. Brussels: European Commission. COM(2014) 130 final/2.

European Foundation for the Improvement of Living and Working Conditions (2007). *Part-time Work in European Companies: Establishment Survey on Working Time 2004-2005*. Luxembourg: Office for Official Publications of the European Communities. European Foundation for the Improvement of Living and Working Conditions.

European Union Agency for Fundamental Rights (2009). *EU-MIDIS: European Union Minorities and Discrimination Survey – main results report*. Available from http://fra.europa.eu/sites/default/files/fra_uploads/663-FRA-2011_EU_MIDIS_EN.pdf.

_____ (2012). *The Situation of Roma in 11 EU Member States: Survey Results at a Glance*. Luxembourg: Publications Office of the European Union.

Falck, Oliver, Alexandra Heimisch, and Simon Wiederhold (2015). Returns to ICT skills. Paper presented at the American Economic Association 2016 Annual Meeting. Available from www.aeaweb.org/conference/2016/retrieve.php?pdfid=643. Accessed 10 March 2016.

Fennema, Meindert, and Jean N. Tillie (2001). Civic community, political participation and political trust of ethnic groups. *Connections*, vol. 24, No. 1, pp. 26-41.

File, Thom (2015). Who votes? Congressional elections and the American electorate: 1978-2014. Population Characteristics, United States Census Bureau. Available from www.census.gov/content/dam/Census/library/publications/2015/demo/p20-577.pdf.

Filmer, Deon (2008). Disability, poverty, and schooling in developing countries: results from 14 household surveys. *World Bank Economic Review*, vol. 22, No. 1, pp. 141-163.

Fine, Janice (2005). Community unions and the revival of the American labor movement. *Politics and Society*, vol. 33, No.1, pp. 153-199.

Fosu, Augustin Kwasi (2013). Institutions and African economies: an overview. *Journal of African Economies*, vol. 22, No. 4, pp. 491-498.

Fox, Louise, and others (2013). Africa's got work to do: employment prospects in the new century. IMF Working Paper, No. WP/13/201. Available from www.imf.org/external/pubs/ft/wp/2013/wp13201.pdf.

Freeman, Richard B. (2009). Labor regulations, unions, and social protection in developing countries: market distortions or efficient institutions? NBER Working Paper, No. 14789. Cambridge, Massachusetts: National Bureau of Economic Research.

Gacitúa-Marió, Estanislao, and Michael Woolcock, eds. (2008). *Social Exclusion and Mobility in Brazil*. Washington, D.C.: World Bank.

Galster, George C., and Sean P. Killen (1998). The geography of metropolitan opportunity: a reconnaissance and conceptual framework. *Housing Policy Debate*, vol. 6, No. 1, pp. 7-43.

Garip, Filiz (2008). Social capital and migration: how do similar resources lead to divergent outcomes? *Demography*, vol. 45, No. 3, pp. 591-617.

Gatti, Roberta, and others (2014). *Striving for Better Jobs. The Challenge of Informality in the Middle East and North Africa*. Washington, D.C.: World Bank.

Ghesquiere, Francis, and others (2012). *The Sendai Report: Managing Disaster Risks for a Resilient Future*. Washington, D.C.: World Bank. Available from www-wds.worldbank.org/external/default/WDSContentServer/WDSP/IB/2013/08/26/000333037_20

130826105551/Rendered/PDF/806080WP0Senda00Box379809B00PUBLIC0.pdf.

Gine, Xavier, and Ghazala Mansuri (2011). Together we will: experimental evidence on female voting behavior in Pakistan. World Bank Policy Research Working Paper Series, No. 5692. Washington, D.C.: World Bank.

Glastra, Folke (1999). *Organisaties en Diversiteit: Naar een Contextuele Benadering van Intercultureel Management*. Utrecht, Netherlands: Lemma.

Global Network of People Living with HIV, and others (2011). *People Living with HIV Stigma Index: Asia Pacific Regional Analysis 2011*. Geneva: Joint United Nations Programme on HIV/AIDS. Available from www.unaids.org/sites/default/files/media_asset/20110829_PLHIVStigmaIndex_en_0.pdf.

Gowricharn, R. (1989). *Verschillen in Werkloosheid en Etnische Afkomst*. Rotterdam, Netherlands: Onderzoeksrapport Gemeentelijke Sociale Dienst.

Granovetter, Mark (2005). The impact of social structure on economic outcomes. *Journal of Economic Perspectives*, vol. 19, No. 1, pp. 33-50.

Gray, Anne (2009). The social capital of older people. *Ageing and Society*, vol. 29, No. 1, pp. 5-31.

Gurung, Om, Makta S. Tamang, and Mark Turin, eds. (2014). *Perspectives on Social Inclusion and Exclusion in Nepal*. Kathmandu: Tribhuvan University.

Grusky, David B., and Ravi Kanbur, eds. (2006). *Poverty and Inequality*. Redwood City, California: Stanford University Press.

Habibov, Nazim, and Elvin Afandi (2015). Pre-and post-crisis life-satisfaction and social trust in transitional countries: an initial assessment. *Social Indicators Research*, vol. 121, No. 2, pp. 503-524.

Hall, Gillete H., and Harry A. Patrinos, eds. (2012). *Indigenous Peoples, Poverty, and Development*. Cambridge, United Kingdom: Cambridge University Press.

Hanna, Rema N., and Leigh L. Linden (2012). Discrimination in grading. *American Economic Journal: Economic Policy*, vol. 4, No. 4, pp. 146-168.

Harder, Joshua, and Jon A. Krosnick (2008). Why do people vote? A psychological analysis of the causes of voter turnout. *Journal of Social Issues*, vol. 64, No. 3, pp. 525-549.

Hardgrave, Robert L. (1993). India: the dilemmas of diversity. *Journal of Democracy*, vol. 4, No. 4, pp. 54-68.

Harris, Ricci, and others (2006). Effects of self-reported racial discrimination and deprivation on Māori health and inequalities in New Zealand: cross sectional study. *The Lancet*, vol. 367, pp. 2005-2009. Available from www.who.int/social_determinants/resources/articles/lancet_harris.pdf.

Hasenbalg, Carlos Alfredo, and Nelson do Valle Silva, eds. (1988). *Estrutura Social, Mobilidade e Raça*, vol. 7, Rio de Janeiro: Instituto Universitário de Pesquisas do Rio de Janeiro.

Hebl, Michelle R., and others (2002). Formal and interpersonal discrimination: a field study of bias toward homosexual applicants. *Personality and Social Psychology Bulletin*, vol. 28, No. 6, pp. 815-825.

Heymann, Jody, Amy Raub, and Adèle Cassola (2014). Constitutional rights to education and their relationship to national policy and school enrolment. *International Journal of Educational Development*, vol. 39 (November), pp. 121-131.

Hickey, Sam, and Andries du Toit (2007). Adverse incorporation, social exclusion and chronic poverty. Chronic Poverty Research Centre Working Paper, No. 81. Available from http://r4d.dfid.gov.uk/PDF/Outputs/chronicpoverty_rc/81hickey_dutoit.pdf.

Hirsch, Barry T., David A. Macpherson, and Melissa A. Hardy (2000). Occupational age structure and access for older workers. *ILR Review*, vol. 53, No. 3, pp. 401-418.

Hoff, Karla, and Priyanka Pandey (2008). Economic consequences of social identity: discrimination, social identity, and durable inequalities. American Economic Review, vol. 96, No. 2, pp. 206-2011.Htun, Mala, and Juan Pablo Ossa (2013). Political inclusion of marginalized groups: indigenous reservations and gender parity in Bolivia. *Politics, Groups, and Identities*, vol. 1, No. 1, pp. 4-25.

Huicho, Luis, and others (2016). Child health and nutrition in Peru within an antipoverty political agenda: a countdown to 2015 country case study. *The Lancet Global Health,* vol. 4, No. 6, pp. e414-e426.

Hujo, Katja (2011). Financing social and labour market policies in times of crisis and beyond, delivered to UNDESA/ILO EGM on June 23-24, 2011 in Geneva, Switzerland. Available from www.ilo.org/wcmsp5/groups/public/---ed_emp/---emp_policy/documents/meetingdocument/wcms_162929.pdf.

Hulse, Kath, and Wendy Stone (2007). Social cohesion, social capital and social exclusion: a cross cultural comparison. *Policy Studies*, vol. 28, No. 2, pp. 109-128.

Ibrahim, Solava, and Sabina Alkire (2007). Agency and empowerment: a proposal for internationally comparable indicators. *Oxford Development Studies*, vol. 35, No. 4, pp. 379-403.

Iceland, John (2014). *Residential Segregation. A Transatlantic Analysis*. Washington, D.C.: Migration Policy Institute.

Inter-American Development Bank (2008). *Outsiders? The Changing Patterns of Exclusion in Latin America and the Caribbean*. Washington, D.C.: Inter-American Development Bank.

Independent Expert Advisory Group on a Data Revolution for Sustainable Development (2014). *A World that Counts. Mobilizing the Data Revolution for Sustainable Development*. Available from www.undatarevolution.org/wp-content/uploads/2014/12/A-World-That-Counts2.pdf.

Institut national de la statistique et des études économiques (2013). L'hébergement des sans-domicile en 2012. Insee Premiere, No. 1455. Available from www.insee.fr/fr/ffc/ipweb/ip1455/ip1455.pdf. Accessed in January 2016.

Intergovernmental Panel on Climate Change (2012). Summary for policymakers. In *Managing the Risks of Extreme Events and Disasters to Advance Climate Change Adaptation*, Christopher B. Field and others, eds. Cambridge, United Kingdom, and New York: Cambridge University Press, pp. 1-19.

International Labour Organization (2008). Can low-income countries afford basic social security? Social Security Policy Briefings, No. 3. Geneva.

_____ (2011a). Social and solidarity economy: our common road towards decent work. Geneva. Available from www.ilo.org/wcmsp5/groups/public/---ed_emp/---emp_ent/---coop/documents/instructionalmaterial/wcms_166301.pdf.

_____ (2011b). Moving towards disability inclusion. Brochure. Geneva.

_____ (2013a). *World of Work Report 2013. Repairing the Economic and Social Fabric*. Geneva.

_____ (2013b). *Women and Men in the Informal Economy: A Statistical Picture*, 2nd ed. Geneva.

_____ (2013c). *Trabajo Decente y Juventud en América Latina: Políticas para la Acción*. Lima: ILO Regional Office for Latin America and the Caribbean.

_____ (2014a). *Global Employment Trends 2014: The Risk of a Jobless Recovery*. Geneva.

_____ (2014b). *Transitioning from the Informal to the Formal Economy, International Labour Conference, 103rd session, 2014, Report V (1)*. Geneva.

_____ (2014c). *World Social Protection Report 2014/15: Building Economic Recovery, Inclusive Development and Social Justice*. Geneva

_____ (2014d). *World of Work Report 2014. Developing with Jobs*. Geneva.

_____ (2014e). Minimum wage systems: general survey of the reports on the Minimum Wage Fixing Convention, 1970 (No. 131), and the Minimum Wage Fixing Recommendation, 1970 (No. 135). Report III (Part 1B). Paper prepared for the International Labour Conference, 103rd session, organized by the International Labour Organization. Available from www.ilo.org/public/libdoc/ilo/P/09661/09661(2014-103-1B).pdf.

_____ (2015a). *Global Employment Trends for Youth 2015: Scaling up Investments in Decent Jobs for Youth*. Geneva.

_____ (2015b). *World Employment and Social Outlook 2015: The Changing Nature of Jobs*. Geneva.

_____ (2015c). Trends in collective bargaining coverage: stability, erosion or decline? Issue Brief, No. 1, Labour Relations and Collective Bargaining, ILO, October 2015. Available from www.ilo.org/wcmsp5/groups/public/---ed_protect/---protrav/---travail/documents/publication/wcms_409422.pdf.

_____ (2016a). *World Employment and Social Outlook 2016: Transforming Jobs to End Poverty*. Geneva.

_____ (2016b). *World Employment and Social Outlook: Trends 2016*. Geneva: ILO.

_____ (2016c). *World Employment and Social Outlook for Youth 2016*. Geneva. Available from www.ilo.org/global/research/global-reports/youth/2016/lang--en/index.htm.

International Organization for Migration (2013). *Recognition of Qualifications and Competences of Migrants*. Brussels: IOM Regional Office for EU, EEA and NATO.

Inter-Parliamentary Union (2008). *Equality in Politics: A Survey of Women and Men in Parliaments*. Geneva.

Jackson, Jonathan, and Ben Bradford (2010). What is trust and confidence in the police? *Policing*, vol. 4, No. 3, pp. 241-248.

Jencks, Christopher, and Susan E. Mayer (1990). The social consequences of growing up in a poor neighborhood. In *Inner-city Poverty in the United States,* Laurence E. Lynn, Jr. and Michael G.H. McGeary, eds. Washington, D.C.: National Academy of Sciences.

Joint United Nations Programme on HIV/AIDS (2013). *Global Report: UNAIDS Report on the Global AIDS Epidemic 2013.* Available from www.unaids.org/sites/default/files/en/media/unaids/contentassets/documents/epidemiology/2013/gr2013/UN-AIDS_Global_Report_2013_en.pdf.

Jones, Melanie K. (2008). Disability and the labour market: a review of the empirical evidence. *Journal of Economic Studies*, vol. 35, No. 5, pp. 405-424.

Justino, Patricia (2015). Civil unrest and government transfers in India. Evidence Report, No. 108: Addressing and Mitigating Violence. Brighton: Institute of Development Studies.

Kabeer, Naila (1999). Resources, agency, achievements: reflections on the measurement of women's empowerment. *Development and Change*, vol. 30, No. 3, pp. 435-464.

_____ (2006). Social exclusion and the MDGs: the challenge of 'durable inequalities' in the Asian context. Paper prepared for the Asia 2015 Conference: Promoting Growth, Ending Poverty, London, 6-7 March. Available from www.eldis.org/vfile/upload/1/document/0708/DOC21178.pdf.

_____ (2010). Can the MDGs provide a pathway to social justice? The challenges of intersecting inequalities. Brighton: Institute of Development Studies. Available from www.ids.ac.uk/files/dmfile/MDGreportwebsiteu2WC.pdf.

_____ and Ariful Haq Kabir (2009). Citizenship narratives in the absence of good governance: voices of the working poor in Bangladesh. IDS Working Paper, No. 331 (July). Brighton, United Kingdom: Institute of Development Studies.

Kabeer, Naila, Kirsty Milward, and Ratna Sudarshan (2013). Organising women workers in the informal economy. *Gender and Development*, vol. 21, No. 2, pp. 249-263.

Kahlenberg, Richard D. (2012). A new kind of affirmative action can ensure diversity. *Chronicle of Higher Education* (3 October). Available from www.chronicle.com/article/A-New-Kind-of-Affirmative/134840/.

Kaiser, Cheryl R., and Brenda Major (2006). A social psychological perspective on perceiving and reporting discrimination. *Law and Social Inquiry*, vol. 31, No. 4, pp. 801-830.

Kanbur, Ravi (2007). Poverty and conflict: the inequality link. Coping with Crisis Working Paper Series. June. New York: International Peace Academy.

_____ and Anthony J. Venables, eds. (2005). Spatial inequality and development: overview of UNU-WIDER Project, WIDER Project on Spatial Disparities in Human Development. New York: Columbia University. Available from www.arts.cornell.edu/poverty/kanbur/widerprojectoverview.pdf.

Kaneda, Toshiko, Zachary Zimmer, and Zhe Tang (2005). Socioeconomic status differentials in life and active life expectancy among older adults in Beijing. *Disability and Rehabilitation* vol. 27, No. 5, pp. 241-251.

Kapsos, Steven, and Evangelina Bourmpoula (2013). Employment and economic class in the developing world. ILO Research Paper, No. 6 (June).

Kauppinen, Timo M. (2007). Neighborhood effects in a European city: secondary education of young people in Helsinki. *Social Science Research*, vol. 36, No. 1, pp. 421-444.

Kaztman, Ruben, and Alejandro Retamoso (2007). Efectos de la segregación urbana sobre la educación en Montevideo. *Revista de la Cepal*, No. 91. Santiago: United Nations, Economic Commission for Latin America and the Caribbean.

King, Desmond, and David Rueda (2008). Cheap labor: the new politics of "bread and roses" in industrial democracies. *Perspectives on Politics*, vol. 6, No. 2, pp. 279-297.

Kirschenman, Joleen, and Kathryn M. Neckerman (1991). "We'd love to hire them, but...": the meaning of race for employers. *The Urban Underclass*, vol. 203, pp. 203-232.

Kishor, Sunita, and Kamla Gupta (2004). Women's empowerment in India and its states: evidence from the NFHS. *Economic and Political Weekly*, vol. 39, No. 7, pp. 694-712.

Kitschelt, Herbert, and others (1999), *Continuity and Change in Contemporary Capitalism*. Cambridge: Cambridge University Press.

Klinthäll, Martin, and Susanne Urban (2016). The strength of ethnic ties: routes into the labour market in spaces of segregation, *Urban Studies*, vol. 53, No. 1, pp. 3-16

Kunze, Lars, and Nicolai Suppa (2014). Bowling alone or bowling at all? The effect of unemployment on social participation. Ruhr Economic Papers, No. 510. Dortmund, Germany: Technische Universitat Dortmund.

Kuzio, Taras (2001). Transition in post-Communist States: triple or quadruple? *Politics*, vol. 21, No. 3, pp. 168-177.

Labonté, Ronald N., Abdullahel Hadi, and Xavier E. Kauffmann (2011). Indicators of social exclusion and inclusion: a critical and comparative analysis of the literature. É/Exchange Working Paper Series, vol. 2, No. 8. Population Health Improvement Research Network, University of Ottawa, Canada.

Lahey, Joanna (2006). State age protection laws and the Age Discrimination in Employment Act. NBER Working Paper, No. 12048. Cambridge, Massachusetts: National Bureau of Economic Research.

Lakhani, Sadaf, Audrey Sacks, and Rasmus Heltberg (2014). "They are not like us": understanding social exclusion. Policy Research Working Paper, No. 6784. Washington, D.C.: World Bank.

Landmann Szwarcwald, Célia, and others (2010). Health inequalities in Rio de Janeiro, Brazil: lower healthy life expectancy in socioeconomically disadvantaged areas. *American Journal of Public Health*, vol. 101, No. 3, pp. 517-523.

Larsen, Christian Albrekt (2014). Social cohesion: definition, measurement and developments. Paper prepared for the Department of Economic and Social Affairs of the United Nations Secretariat. Available from: http://www.un.org/esa/socdev/egms/docs/2014/LarsenDevelopmentinsocialcohesion.pdf.

Leighley, Jan E. (1995). Attitudes, opportunities and incentives: a field essay on political participation. *Political Research Quarterly*, vol. 48, No. 1, pp. 181–209.

Lenhardt, Amanda, and Emma Samman (2015). In quest of inclusive progress: exploring intersecting inequalities in human development. Development Progress Research Report, No. 4. London: Overseas Development Institute.

Lenoir, René (1974). *Les Exclus: Un Français sur Dix.* Paris: Seuil.

Levitas, Ruth, and others (2007). The multi-dimensional analysis of social exclusion. Department of Sociology and School for Social Policy, Townsend Centre for the International Study of Poverty, and Bristol Institute for Public Affairs, Bristol, United Kingdom: University of Bristol. Available from www.bris.ac.uk/poverty/downloads/socialexclusion/multidimensional.pdf.

Library of Congress (2011). Brown v. Board of Education: a chronological listing of related materials from the Library of Congress. Available from www.loc.gov/rr/program/bib/afam/afam-brown.html. Accessed 17 March 2016.

Liebbrandt, Murray and others (2010). Trends in South African income distribution and poverty since the end of the apartheid. OECD Social, Employment and Migration Working Paper no. 101, 28 May 2010. Available from http://www.oecd-ilibrary.org/social-issues-migration-health/trends-in-south-african-income-distribution-and-poverty-since-the-fall-of-apartheid_5kmms0t7p1ms-en.

Lin, Nan, Walter M. Ensel, and John C. Vaughn (1981). Social resources and strength of ties: structural factors in occupational status attainment. *American Sociological Review*, vol. 46, No. 4, pp. 393-405.

Litwin, Howard (2010). Social networks and well-being: a comparison of older people in Mediterranean and non-Mediterranean countries. *Journals of Gerontology, Series B: Psychological Sciences and Social Sciences*, vol. 65B, No. 5, pp. 599-608.

Liu, Mao-Mei (2013). Migrant networks and international migration: testing weak ties. *Demography*, vol. 50, No. 4, pp. 1243-1277.

López Pintor, Rafael, and Maria Gratschew (2002). *Voter Turnout Since 1945. A Global Report.* Stockholm, Sweden: International IDEA.

Mahmud, Simeen, Nirali M. Shah, and Stan Becker (2012). Measurement of women's empowerment in rural Bangladesh. *World Development*, vol. 40, No. 3, pp. 610-619.

Mamdani, Mahmood (2001). Beyond settler and native as political identities: overcoming the political legacy of colonialism. *Comparative Studies in Society and History*, vol. 43, No. 4, pp. 651-664.

Marcus, Rachel, Anna Mdee, and Ella Page (2016). Anti-discrimination policies and programmes in low- and middle-income countries: experiences in political participation, education and labour markets. Chronic Poverty Advisory Network: Getting to Zero, London: Overseas Development Institute.

Marteleto, Leticia J., and Molly Dondero (2016). Racial inequality in education in Brazil: a twins fixed-effects approach. *Demography*, vol. 53, No. 4, pp. 1185-1205.

Massey, Douglas S. (1990). Social structure, household strategies, and the cumulative causation of migration. *Population Index*, vol. 56, No. 1, pp. 3-26.

_____ (1996). The age of extremes: concentrated affluence and poverty in the twenty-first century. *Demography*, vol. 33, No. 4, pp. 395-412.

Mather, Mark, and Beth Jarosz (2014). The demography of inequality in the United States. *Population Bulletin*, vol. 69, No. 2.

Mattlin, Ben (2015). An act that enabled acceptance, *New York Times,* 25 July. Available from www.nytimes.com/2015/07/26/opinion/sunday/an-act-that-enabled-acceptance.html?_r=1.

McKanders, Karla Mari (2010). Sustaining tiered personhood: Jim Crow and anti-immigrant laws. *Harvard Journal of Racial and Ethnic Justice*, vol. 26, pp. 163. University of Tennessee Legal Studies Research Paper, No. 111. Available from http://ssrn. com/abstract=1648810.

McKinley, Terry (2010). Inclusive growth criteria and indicators: an inclusive growth index for diagnosis of country progress. ADB Sustainable Development Working Paper Series, No. 14 (June). Manila: Asian Development Bank.

Menezes-Filho, Naercio Aquino, and others (2005). Unions and the economic performance of Brazilian establishments. In *What Difference Do Unions Make? Their Impact on Productivity and Wages in Latin America*, Peter Kuhn and Gustavo Márquez, eds. Washington, D.C.: Inter-American Development Bank.

Michalopoulos, Stelios, and Elias Papaioannou (2011). The long-run effects of the scramble for Africa. NBER Working Paper, No. 17620. Cambridge, Massachusetts: National Bureau of Economic Research.

Milanovic, Branko (2012). Global income inequality by the numbers: in history and now − an overview. Policy Research Working Paper Series, No. 6259. Washington, D.C.: World Bank.

Milazzo, Annamaria, and Dominique Van de Walle (2015). Women left behind? Poverty and hardship in Africa. Policy Research Working Paper, No. 7331. Washington, D.C.: World Bank Group.

Ministerio de Energía y Minas, República del Perú (2011). Plan Nacional de Electrificación Rural (PNER) Periodo 2012-2021. Available from http://dger.minem.gob.pe/ ArchivosDger/PNER_2012-2021/PNER-2012-2021%20Texto.pdf.

Minnesota Population Center (2015). Integrated Public Use Microdata Series, International: Version 6.4 [Machine-readable database]. Minneapolis: University of Minnesota.

Montgomery, Mark R., and Paul C. Hewett (2005). Urban poverty and health in developing countries: household and neighborhood effects. *Demography*, vol. 42, No. 3, pp. 397-425.

Moreno, Martin, and others (2004). Gender and racial discrimination in hiring: a pseudo audit study for three selected occupations in metropolitan Lima. Discussion Paper, No. 979. Bonn: Institute for the Study of Labor. January. Available from http://ftp. iza.org/dp979.pdf.

Moser, Caroline O.N. (2009). *Ordinary Families, Extraordinary Lives: Assets and Poverty Reduction in Guayaquil, 1978-2004*. Washington, D.C.: Brookings Institution Press.

Moss, Philip, and Chris Tilly (1996). "Soft" skills and race: an investigation of black men's employment problems. *Work and Occupations*, vol. 23, No. 3, pp. 252-276.

Mulgan, Geoff (2007). *Good and Bad Power: The Ideals and Betrayals of Government*. London: Penguin.

Muñoz Boudet, Ana María, and others (2013). *On Norms and Agency: Conversations about Gender Equality with Women and Men in 20 Countries*. Directions in Development. Washington, D.C.: World Bank.

Mvukiyehe, Eric, and Cyrus Dara Samii (2015). Promoting democracy in fragile States:

insights from a field experiment in Liberia. Policy Research Working Paper, No. 7370. Washington, D.C.: World Bank.

National Academies of Sciences, Engineering, and Medicine (2015). The Integration of Immigrants into American Society. Washington, D.C.: The National Academies Press.

Narayan, Deepa, and others (2000). *Voices of the Poor: Crying out for Change.* New York: Oxford University Press for the World Bank.

Narayan, Deepa, and Patti L. Petesch, eds. (2002). *Voices of the Poor: From Many Lands.* Washington, D.C.: World Bank and Oxford University Press.

Narayan, Ambar, and Sandeep Mahajan (2013). The state of opportunities in South Africa: inequality among children and in the labour market. *Inequality in Focus*, vol. 2, No.1, April, World Bank.

Nathan, Dev, and Virginius Xaxa, eds. (2012). *Social Exclusion and Adverse Inclusion: Development and Deprivation of Adivasis in India.* Oxford: Oxford University Press.

Ncube, Mthuli, and John C. Anyanwu (2012). Inequality and Arab Spring revolutions in North Africa and the Middle East. African Development Bank. *Africa Economic Brief*, vol. 3, No. 7.

Newman, Katherine S. (1999). *No Shame in My Game: The Working Poor in the Inner City.* New York: Random House and Russell Sage Foundation.

Norton, Andrew, and Arjan de Haan (2012). Social cohesion: theoretical debates and practical applications with respect to jobs. Background Paper for the World Development Report 2013. Washington, D.C.: World Bank. Available from http://siteresources.worldbank.org/EXTNWDR2013/Resources192/8260293-1320956712276/8261091-1348683883703/WDR2013_bp_Social_Cohesion_Norton.pdf.

O'Neill, Marie S., Antonella Zanobetti, and Joel Schwartz (2005). Disparities by race in heat-related mortality in four US cities: the role of air conditioning prevalence. *Journal of Urban Health*, vol. 82, No. 2, pp. 191-197. Available from www.ncbi.nlm.nih.gov/pmc/articles/PMC3456567/pdf/11524_2006_Article_375.pdf.

Olsson, Lennart, and others (2014). Livelihoods and poverty. In *Climate Change 2014: Impacts, Adaptation, and Vulnerability. Part A: Global and Sectoral Aspects. Contribution of Working Group II to the Fifth Assessment Report of the Intergovernmental Panel on Climate Change*, C.B. Field, and others, eds. Cambridge and New York: Cambridge University Press, pp. 793-832.

Organisation for Economic Co-operation and Development (OECD) (2010). The High Cost of Low Educational Performance: The Long-Run Economic Impact of Improving PISA Outcomes. Paris: OECD Publishing.

_____ (2011a). *Perspectives on Global Development 2012: Social Cohesion in a Shifting World.* Paris: OECD Publishing.

_____ (2011b). *Divided We Stand: Why Inequality Keeps Rising.* Paris: OECD Publishing.

_____ (2013a). *OECD Skills Outlook 2013: First Results from the Survey of Adult Skills.* Paris: OECD Publishing.

_____ (2013b). How do early childhood education and care (ECEC) policies, systems and quality vary across OECD countries? Education Indicators in Focus, No. 2013/02. Paris: OECD Publishing.

_____ (2013c). *PISA 2012 Results: Excellence Through Equity, Giving Every Student the Chance to Succeed,* Vol. II. Paris: OECD Publishing.

_____ (2014). *All on Board: Making Inclusive Growth Happen.* Paris: OECD Publishing.

_____ (2015a). *Indicators of Immigrant Integration 2015: Settling in.* Paris: OECD Publishing.

_____ (2015b). *OECD Employment Outlook 2015.* Paris: OECD Publishing.

_____ (2015c). *Health at a Glance 2015: OECD Indicators,* Paris: OECD Publishing.

_____ (2015d). *Education at a Glance 2015: OECD Indicators.* Paris: OECD Publishing.

Overseas Development Institute (2013). Working out of chronic poverty: a policy guide. Employment Policy Guide, No. 4. Chronic Poverty Advisory Network. London.

_____ (2014). *The Chronic Poverty Report 2014-2015: The Road to Zero Extreme Poverty.* London: Chronic Poverty Advisory Network.

_____ (2015). Financing the Future: How International Public Finance Should Fund a Global Social Compact to Eradicate Poverty. London.

_____ (2016). *Leaving No One Behind. A Critical Path for the First 1,000 Days of the Sustainable Development Goals.* London.

Pan Ké Shon, Jean-Louis (2011). Residential segregation of immigrants in France: an overview. *Population and Societies*, No. 477, p. 1-4.

Pande, Rohini (2003). Can mandated political representation increase policy influence for disadvantaged minorities? Theory and evidence from India. *American Economic Review*, vol. 93, No. 4, pp. 1132-1151.

_____ (2011). Can informed voters enforce better governance? Experiments in low-income democracies. *Annual Review of Economics*, vol. 3, No. 1, pp. 215-237.

Panth, Sabina (2011). Changing norms is key to fighting everyday corruption. Working Paper, No. 89849. Washington, D.C.: World Bank.

Parks, Virginia (2005). *Geography of Immigrant Labour Markets: Space, Networks and Gender.* El Paso, Texas: LFB Scholarly Publishing LLC.

Pascoe, Elizabeth A., and Laura Smart Richman (2009). Perceived discrimination and health: a meta-analytic review. *Psychological Bulletin*, vol. 135, No. 4, pp. 531-554. Available from www.ncbi.nlm.nih.gov/pmc/articles/PMC2747726/.

Perry, Guillermo E., and others (2007). *Informality: Exit and Exclusion.* Washington, D.C.: World Bank.

Pew Research Center (2015). Raising kids and running a household: how working parents share the load – in close to half of two-parent families, both mom and dad work full time. Available from www.pewsocialtrends.org/files/2015/11/2015-11-04_working-parents_FINAL.pdf.

Popay, Jennie, and others (2008). *Understanding and Tackling Social Exclusion: Final*

*Report to the WHO Commission on Social Determinants of Health from the Social Exclusion Knowledge Network.* Geneva: World Health Organization. Available from www.who.int/social_determinants/knowledge_networks/final_reports/sekn_final%20report_042008.pdf?ua=1.

Portes, Alejandro, and Rubén G. Rumbaut (2001). *Legacies: The Story of the Immigrant Second Generation.* Berkeley and Los Angeles, California: University of California Press.

_____ (2006). *Immigrant America, A Portrait*, 3rd ed. Berkeley, California: University of California Press.

Powley, Elizabeth (2006). Rwanda: the impact of women legislators on policy outcomes affecting children and families. Background Paper for *The State of the World's Children 2007.* New York: UNICEF.

PROBE Team (1999). *Public Report on Basic Education in India.* New Delhi: Oxford University Press.

Putnam, Robert D. (2000). *Bowling Alone: The Collapse and Revival of American Community.* New York: Simon and Schuster.

Ramakrishnan, S. Karthick, and Thomas J. Espenshade (2001). Immigrant incorporation and political participation in the United States. *International Migration Review*, vol. 35, No. 3, pp. 870-909.

Ramos, Raquel Almeida, Rafael Ranieri, and Jan-Willem Lammens (2013). Mapping inclusive growth. IPC-IG Working Paper, No. 105. Brasilia: International Policy Centre for Inclusive Growth. Available from www.ipc-undp.org/pub/IPCWorkingPaper105.pdf.

Rauniyar, Ganesh and Ravi Kanbur (2010). Inclusive development: two papers on conceptualization, application, and the ADB perspective. Manila: Asian Development Bank.

Ravallion, Martin (2010). Mashup indices of development. Policy Research Working Paper, No. 5432 (September). Washington, D.C.: World Bank.

_____ (2014). Are the world's poorest being left behind? NBER Working Paper, No. 20791 (December). Cambridge, Massachusetts: National Bureau of Economic Research.

_____ and Shaohua Chen (2011). Weakly relative poverty. *Review of Economics and Statistics*, vol. 93, No. 4, pp. 1251-1261.

Reddy, A. Bheemeshwar (2015). Changes in intergenerational occupational mobility in India: evidence from national sample surveys 1983-2012. *World Development*, vol. 76, December, pp. 329-343.

Ribeiro, Carlos Antonio Costa (2006). Classe, raça e mobilidade social no Brasil. *Dados*, vol. 49, No. 4, pp. 833-873.

_____ (2010). Class, race, and social mobility in Brazil. In *Discrimination in an Unequal World*, Miguel Angel Centeno and Katherine S. Newman, eds. New York: Oxford University Press.

Ribot, Jesse C. (2010). Vulnerability does not just fall from the sky: toward multi-scale pro-poor climate policy. In *Social Dimensions of Climate Change: Equity and Vulnerability in a Warming World*, Robin Mearns and Andrew Norton, eds. Washington,

D.C.: International Bank for Reconstruction and Development and World Bank, pp. 47-74.

Roberts, Celia and Sarah Campbell (2006). Talk on Trial: Job interviews, language and ethnicity. Department for Work and Pensions Research Report No. 344. Available from https://www.researchonline.org.uk/sds/search/download.do;jsessionid=D9F825 98BB2DE41EB0AE57F1A18AE7C3?ref=B1568.

Roncolato, Leanne, and David Kucera (2014). Structural drivers of productivity and employment growth: a decomposition analysis for 81 countries. *Cambridge Journal of Economics*, vol. 38, No, 2, pp. 399-424.

Rooth, Dan-Olof (2002). Adopted children in the labour market: discrimination or unob-served characteristics? *International Migration*, vol. 40, No. 1, pp. 71-98.

Rooth, Dan-Olof, and Jan Saarela (2007). Selection in migration and return migration: Evidence from micro data. *Economics letters* vol. 94, No. 1, pp. 90-95.

Rueda, David (2005). Insider-outsider politics in industrialized democracies: the chal-lenge to social democratic parties. *American Political Science Review*, vol. 99, No. 1, pp. 61-74.

_____ (2006). Social democracy and active labour-market policies: insiders, outsiders and the politics of employment promotion. *British Journal of Political Sci-ence*, vol. 36, No. 3, pp. 385-406.

Ryder, Guy (2013). Opening remarks to the UNRISD Conference on Social and Solidar-ity Economy. Available from www.ilo.org/global/about-the-ilo/who-we-are/ilo-director-general/statements-and-speeches/WCMS_212653/lang--en/index.htm.

Sabatés, Ricardo, and others (2010). School drop out: patterns, causes, changes and poli-cies. Background paper prepared for the Education for All Global Monitoring Report 2011, No. 2011/ED/EFA/MRT/PI/08. Available from www.unesco.org/new/en/edu-cation/themes/leading-the-international-agenda/efareport/background-papers/2011/.

Saith, Ruhi (2001).Social exclusion: the concept and application to developing countries. QEH Working Paper Series no. 72, University of Oxford. Available from http://www3.qeh.ox.ac.uk/RePEc/qeh/qehwps/qehwps72.pdf.

Sampson, Robert J., Stephen W. Raudenbush, and Felton Earls (1997). Neighborhoods and violent crime: a multilevel study of collective efficacy. *Science*, vol. 277, No. 5328, pp. 918-924.

Save the Children (2014). Leaving no one behind: embedding equity in the post-2015 framework through stepping stone targets. Available from www.savethechildren.org.uk/sites/default/files/images/Leaving_No_One_Behind.pdf.

Sen, Amartya K. (1999). *Development as Freedom*. New York: Oxford University Press.

_____ (2000). Social exclusion: concept, application, and scrutiny. Social Develop-ment Paper, No. 1 (June). Manila: Office of Environment and Social Development, Asian Development Bank.

Scarpa, Simone (2015) The spatial manifestation of inequality: residential segregation in Sweden and its causes. Linnaeus University Dissertations, No. 201/2015. Växjö, Sweden: Linnaeus University Press.

Schneider, Friedrich (2015). Size and development of the shadow economy of 31 Euro-pean and 5 other OECD countries from 2003 to 2015: different developments. Linz,

Austria: Johannes Kepler University. Available from www.econ.jku.at/members/Schneider/files/publications/2015/ShadEcEurope31.pdf.

Schuman, Howard, and others (1988). *Racial Attitudes in America: Trends and Interpretations*, revised ed. Cambridge, Massachusetts: Harvard University Press.

Semlyen, Joanna, and others (2016). Sexual orientation and symptoms of common mental disorder or low wellbeing: combined meta-analysis of 12 UK population health surveys. *BMC Psychiatry*, vol. 16, No. 67.

Servan-Mori, Edson, and others (2014). An explanatory analysis of economic and health inequality changes among Mexican indigenous people, 2000-2010. *International Journal for Equity in Health*, vol. 13, No. 21. Available from www.ncbi.nlm.nih.gov/pmc/articles/PMC3996059/.

Silver, Hilary (2012). Framing social inclusion policies. Draft Background Paper for Inclusion Matters: The Foundation for Shared Prosperity. Washington, D.C.: World Bank.

Solt, Frederick (2014). The Standardized World Income Inequality Database. A working paper. Available from http://myweb.uiowa.edu/fsolt/papers/Solt2014.pdf.

Statistics New Zealand (2014). Disability and the labour market: findings from the 2013 Disability Survey. Wellington. Available from www.stats.govt.nz/~/media/Statistics/browse-categories/health/disabilities/disability-and-labour-market/disability-and-labour-market.pdf.

Steele, Claude M., and Joshua Aronson (1995). Stereotype threat and the intellectual test performance of African Americans. *Journal of Personality and Social Psychology*, vol. 69, No. 5, pp. 797-811.

Stewart, Frances (2002). Root causes of violent conflict in developing countries, *British Medical Journal*, vol. 324, No. 7333, pp. 342-345.

_____ (2004). The relationship between horizontal inequalities, vertical inequality and social exclusion. *CRISE Newsletter No. 1* (Winter), p. 2.

_____, Graham Brown, and Luca Mancini (2005). Why horizontal inequalities matter: some implications for measurement. CRISE Working Paper, No. 19 (June). Center for Research on Inequality, Human Security and Ethnicity (CRISE), University of Oxford.

Strachan, Anna Louise, and Huma Haider (2015). *Gender and Conflict: Topic Guide*. Birmingham, United Kingdom: GSDRC, University of Birmingham.

Sumner, Andy (2013). Who are the poor? New regional estimates of the composition of education and health 'poverty' by spatial and social inequalities. ODI Working Paper, No. 378 (April), Overseas Development Institute.

Székely, Miguel, and Jonathan Karver (2015). Youth out of school and out of work in Latin America: a cohort approach. Policy Research Working Paper, No. 7421 (September). Washington, D.C.: World Bank.

Telles, Edward E. (2003). *Racismo à Brasileira: Uma Nova Perspectiva Sociológica*. Rio de Janeiro: Relume-Dumará.

Togeby, Lise (1999). Migrants at the polls: an analysis of immigrant and refugee participation in Danish local elections. *Journal of Ethnic and Migration Studies*, vol. 25, No. 4, pp. 665-684.

Townsend, Peter (1979). *Poverty in the United Kingdom: A Survey of Household Resources and Standards of Living*. Harmondsworth, United Kingdom: Penguin Books.

Tyler, Tom R. (2003). Procedural justice, legitimacy, and the effective rule of law. *Crime and Justice*, vol. 3, pp. 283-357.

United Kingdom Office of the Deputy Prime Minister (2004). *The Social Exclusion Unit*. London. Available from http://webarchive.nationalarchives.gov.uk/+/http:/www.cabinetoffice.gov.uk/media/cabinetoffice/social_exclusion_task_force/assets/publications_1997_to_2006/seu_leaflet.pdf.

United Nations (1945). *Charter of the United Nations*. 24 October.

_____ (2005) *Report on the World Social Situation 2007: The Inequality Predicament*. Sales No. E.05.IV.5.

_____ (2007). *Report on the World Social Situation 2007: The Employment Imperative*. Sales No. E.07.IV.9.

_____ (2009). *Report on the World Social Situation 2010: Rethinking Poverty*. Sales No. E.09.IV.10.

_____ (2010). *Analysing and Measuring Social Inclusion in a Global Context*. Sales No. E.09.IV.16.

_____ (2013a). *Report on the World Social Situation 2013: Inequality Matters*. Sales No. 13.IV.2.

_____ (2013b). A New Global Partnership: Eradicate Poverty and Transform Economies through Sustainable Development – the report of the High-Level Panel of Eminent Persons on the Post-2015 Development Agenda. Available from https://sustainabledevelopment.un.org/content/documents/8932013-05%20-%20HLP%20Report%20-%20A%20New%20Global%20Partnership.pdf.

_____ (2013c). Implementation of United Nations recommendations for population census topics in the 2010 round. Document prepared for the United Nations Expert Group Meeting on Revising the Principles and Recommendations for Population and Housing Censuses, New York, 29 October to 1 November 2013. Available from http://unstats.un.org/unsd/demographic/meetings/egm/NewYork/2013/UNSD_Population_topics.pdf.

_____ (2015a). *The World's Women 2015: Trends and Statistics*. Sales No. E.15. XVII.8.

_____ (2015b). *Global Status Report on Disability and Development, Prototype 2015* (unedited version). Available from www.un.org/esa/socdev/documents/disability/2016/GlobalStatusReportonDisabilityandDevelopment.pdf.

_____ (2016a). *World Economic and Social Survey 2016: Building Resilience to Climate Change – an opportunity for addressing inequalities*. Sales No. E.16.II.C1.

_____ (2016b). *The Sustainable Development Goals Report 2016*. Sales No. E.16.I.10.

United Nations Children's Fund (2014). Realizing the rights of Roma children and women in Bosnia and Herzegovina, the former Yugoslav Republic of Macedonia, and Serbia. Summary analysis of key findings from MICS surveys in Roma settlements in the three countries. *Insights: Child Rights in Central and Eastern Europe and Central Asia*, Issue 2. Available from www.unicef.org/serbia/Realizing_the_

rights_of_Roma_Children_and_women.pdf.

_____ (2016). *State of the World's Children 2016: A Fair Chance for Every Child.* New York. Available from www.unicef.org/publications/index_91711.html.

United Nations Development Programme (1990). *The Human Development Report.* New York: Oxford University Press for the United Nations Development Programme.

_____ (2011). *Beyond Transition: Towards Inclusive Societies.* Bratislava: United Nations Development Programme Regional Bureau for Europe and the Commonwealth of Independent States.

_____ (2014). *Human Development Report 2014: Sustaining Human Progress – reducing vulnerabilities and building resilience.* New York.

United Nations Educational, Scientific and Cultural Organization (2015a). *EFA Global Monitoring Report 2015: Education For All 2000-2015 – achievements and challenges.* Paris: UNESCO Publishing.

_____ (2015b). A growing number of children and adolescents are out of school as aid fails to meet the mark. Policy Paper, No. 22/Fact Sheet 31. Available from www.uis.unesco.org/Education/Documents/fs-31-out-of-school-children-en.pdf.

_____ (2015c). Pricing the right to education: the cost of reaching new targets by 2030. Education for All Global Monitoring Policy Paper, No. 18, July 2015 update.

_____ (2016). If you don't understand, how can you learn? Policy Paper, No. 24. Paris.

United Nations Entity for Gender Equality and the Empowerment of Women (2015). *Progress of the World's Women 2015-2016: Transforming Economies, Realizing Rights.* New York.

United Nations Office for Disaster Risk Reduction (2011*). Global Assessment Report on Disaster Risk Reduction 2011: Revealing Risk, Redefning Development.* Geneva.

United Nations Relief and Works Agency for Palestine Refugees in the Near East (2015). UNRWA Promotes Diversity and Tolerance on Human Rights Day. Available from www.unrwa.org/newsroom/features/unrwa-promotes-diversity-and-tolerance-human-rights-day.

_____ (2016). Embedding a Culture of Human Rights, non-Violent Conflict Resolution and Tolerance in UNRWA Schools (Phase 3) Progress Report, Reporting Period: 1 October 2015 – 30 March 2016, Project code: PQ15E59.

United Nations Research Institute for Social Development (2010). *Combating Poverty and Inequality: Structural Change, Social Policy and Politics.* Sales No. E.10. III.Y.1.

United States Department of Housing and Urban Development (2014). *The 2014 Annual Homeless Assessment Report (AHAR) to Congress: Part 1 – point-in-time estimates of homelessness. October 2014.* Available from www.hudexchange.info/resources/documents/2014-AHAR-Part1.pdf. Accessed January 2016.

University of Maryland (2015). The Minorities at Risk Project. College Park, Maryland: Center for International Development and Conflict. Available from http://www.mar.umd.edu/.

Urdal, Henrik (2012). A clash of generations? Youth bulges and political violence. Expert Paper, No. 2012/1, United Nations, Department of Economic and Social Affairs,

New York. Available from www.un.org/esa/population/publications/expertpapers/Urdal_Expert%20Paper.pdf

Utting, Peter (2013). Social and solidarity economy: a pathway to socially sustainable development? United Nations Research Institute for Social Development (UNRISD). Available from www.unrisd.org/unrisd/website/newsview.nsf/%28httpNews%29/AB920B156339500AC1257B5C002C1E96?OpenDocument.

Valerio, Alexandria, and others (2014). Measuring skills for employment and productivity: What does it mean to be a well-educated worker in the modern economy? STEP Skills Measurement Program: Snapshot 2014. Washington, D.C.: World Bank. Available from www.worldbank.org/content/dam/Worldbank/Feature%20Story/Education/STEP%20Snapshot%202014_Revised_June%2020%202014%20(final).pdf.

van der Gaag, Nikki, and Jo Rowlands, eds. (2009). *Speaking Out: Case Studies on How Poor People Influence Decision-making*. Oxford, United Kingdom: Oxfam, Practical Action Publishing.

Van Tubergen, Frank (2006). *Immigrant Integration: A Cross-National Study.* El Paso, Texas: LFB Scholarly Publishing LLC.

Vegas, Emiliana, and Lucrecia Santibáñez (2010*). The Promise of Early Childhood Development in Latin America and the Caribbean.* Washington, D.C.: World Bank.

Victora, Cesar G., and others (2008). Maternal and child undernutrition: consequences for adult health and human capital. *The Lancet*, vol. 371, No. 9609, pp. 340-357.

Visser, Jelle (2015). ICTWSS: Database on Institutional Characteristics of Trade Unions, Wage Setting, State Intervention and Social Pacts in 51 countries between 1960 and 2014. Version 5.0. Amsterdam: Amsterdam Institute for Advanced Labour Studies, University of Amsterdam.

Wietzke, Frank-Borge, and Catriona McLeod (2013). Jobs, wellbeing, and social cohesion: evidence from value and perception surveys. Policy Research Working Paper, No. 6447. Washington, D.C.: World Bank.

Wilkinson, Steven I. (2004). *Votes and Violence: Electoral Competition and Ethnic Riots in India*, Cambridge: Cambridge University Press.

_____ ed. (2005). *Religious Politics and Communal Violence*, New Delhi: Oxford University Press.

Williams, David R., Harold W. Neighbors, and James S. Jackson (2003). Racial/ethnic discrimination and health: findings from community studies. *American Journal of Public Health*, vol. 93, No. 2, pp. 200-208. Available from http://ajph.aphapublications.org/doi/full/10.2105/AJPH.93.2.200.

Wilson, William Julius (1997). *When Work Disappears: The World of the New Urban Poor*. New York: Vintage Books.

World Bank (2005). *World Development Report 2006: Equity and Development*. Washington, D.C.: World Bank and Oxford University Press.

_____ (2010). *World Development Report 2010: Development and Climate Change.* Washington, D.C.

_____ (2011). *World Development Report 2012: Gender Equality and Development*. Washington, D.C.

_____ (2012). *World Development Report 2013: Jobs*. Washington, D.C.

_____ (2013). *Inclusion Matters: The Foundation for Shared Prosperity.* Washington, D.C.

_____ (2015). *Women, Business and the Law 2016.* Washington, D.C.

_____ (2016). *World Development Report 2016: Digital Dividends.* Washington, D.C. Available from www-wds.worldbank.org/external/default/WDSContentServer/WDSP/IB/2016/01/13/090224b08405ea05/2_0/Rendered/PDF/World0developm-0000digital0dividends.pdf.

World Health Organization (WHO) (2014). Gender, climate change and health. Discussion paper. Available from www.who.int/globalchange/GenderClimateChange-Healthfinal.pdf?ua=1.

_____ (2016). Global Health Expenditure Database. Available from http://apps.who.int/nha/database/Home/Index/en . Accessed 12 July 2016.

_____ and World Bank (2011). *World Report on Disability.* Geneva: World Health Organization.

World Meteorological Organization (2014). *Atlas of Mortality and Economic Losses from Weather, Climate and Water Extremes (1970-2012).* Geneva.

www.ingramcontent.com/pod-product-compliance
Lightning Source LLC
Chambersburg PA
CBHW071126280326
41935CB00010B/1124